A Rockhound's Guide
to Oregon & Washington

Alison Jean Cole

MOUNTAINEERS
BOOKS

To the good people of the Mount Hood Rock Club,
to whom I owe everything

MOUNTAINEERS BOOKS is dedicated to the exploration, preservation, and enjoyment of outdoor and wilderness areas.

1001 SW Klickitat Way, Suite 201, Seattle, WA 98134
800-553-4453, www.mountaineersbooks.org

Printed in China

First edition, 2025

Design and layout: Melissa McFeeters
Cartographer: Lohnes & Wright
All photographs by the author unless credited otherwise
Photographs, front cover: *Beulah Reservoir on the North Fork Malheur River,* Oregon; back cover: *A carbon distillation of a fossil leaf in diatomite*; frontispiece: *A rainbow of silicate rocks from the Yolla Bolly terrane await you in the Chetco River*; page 10: *A cobble of ancient sediments, metamorphosed over a journey of 250 million years*; page 308: *Colorful volcanic stones dominate the gravel bars in the Cispus River.*

 Produced with support from the Port of Seattle Tourism Marketing Support Program

Library of Congress Cataloging-in-Publication Data
The LC record is available at https://lccn.loc.gov/2024045605. The LC ebook record is available at https://lccn.loc.gov/2024045606

Mountaineers Books titles may be purchased for corporate, educational, or other promotional sales, and our authors are available for a wide range of events. For information on special discounts or booking an author, contact our customer service at 800-553-4453 or mbooks@mountaineersbooks.org.

Printed on FSC-certified materials

ISBN (paperback): 978-1-68051-699-9
ISBN (ebook): 978-1-68051-700-2

An independent nonprofit publisher since 1960

Contents

Site Locator

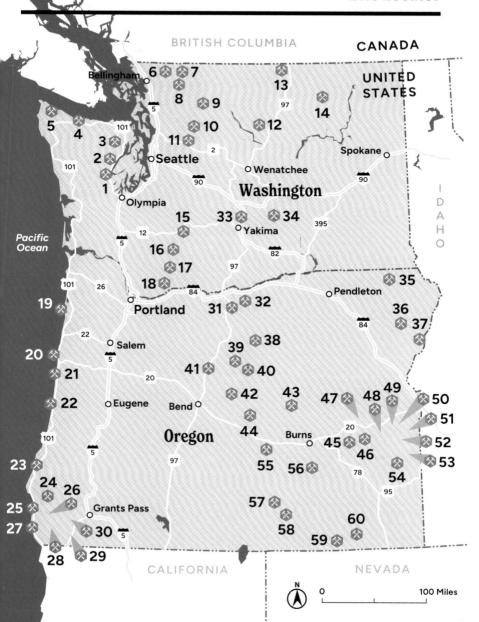

BRITISH COLUMBIA · CANADA

UNITED STATES

Bellingham

6 7
13
8 9
14
10 12
97
5 4
101
3 11
Seattle
2
1 Olympia
Spokane

2
Wenatchee
90
90
I D A H O

Washington

Pacific Ocean

15 33 34
Yakima
12 395
16 82
17 97
18 84
Portland
35
31 32
Pendleton
36
84
37

22 39 38
Salem
5
41 40
20
20 42 43 47 48 49 50
22 Eugene Bend
51
44 45 46
52
Oregon
Burns
53
23 55 56 78 54
95
24 26
25 Grants Pass 57
27 30 5 58 59 60
28 29

CALIFORNIA · NEVADA

N
0 100 Miles

Geology Maps

(See Appendix 2, Geologic Time Scale for more information)

Sedimentary Rocks

- Cenozoic–Pleistocene
- Cenozoic–Neogene
- Cenozoic–Paleogene
- Mesozoic
- Paleozoic and older

Volcanic Rocks

- Cenozoic–Pleistocene and younger
- Cenozoic–Neogene
- Cenozoic–Paleogene
- Mesozoic
- Paleozoic and older

Washington

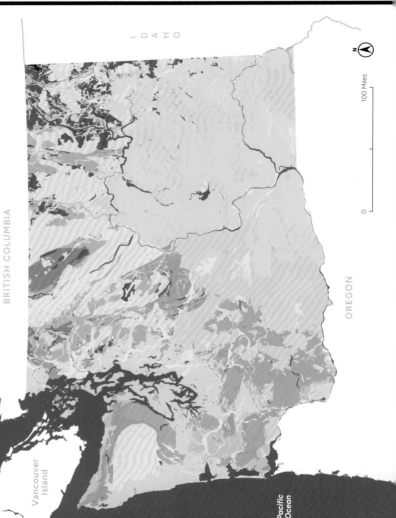

IDAHO

BRITISH COLUMBIA

OREGON

Vancouver Island

Pacific Ocean

N

100 Miles

0

Intrusive Igneous Rocks

- Cenozoic
- Mesozoic
- Paleozoic and older

Metamorphic Rocks

- Cenozoic
- Mesozoic
- Paleozoic
- Amphibolite & Serpentinite
- Carbonates (Marble)

Unconsolidated Deposits

- Holocene (present day)
- Pleistocene

- water

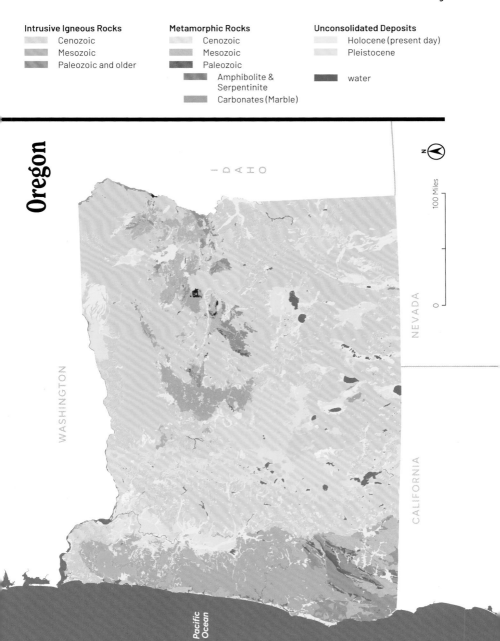

Oregon

IDAHO

WASHINGTON

NEVADA

CALIFORNIA

Pacific Ocean

N

0   100 Miles

Introduction
Every Rock Is a Story

CHAOS. QUIET. COLLISIONS. Separations. Eruptions. Erosions. Catastrophes. Stillness. The rocks beneath our feet speak of all these things. The Pacific Northwest is a region world-famous for its volcanic arcs and flood basalts, but beneath these layers lies a more cryptic geologic history, one that begins with neither Oregon nor Washington existing at all.

Instead, blue. Two hundred million years back. A deep ocean off the supercontinent of Pangea, which was just beginning to break apart. Spokane, Washington, is a Jurassic beach town on Pangea's sandy coast. During this time, the Oregon and Washington coastline grows slowly. But eventually, far out to sea, the ocean floor begins to split apart—erupting lava, which builds deep-sea volcanoes. Some grow so large, they become chains of islands. The new crust forming where the seafloor is splitting also forces older crust toward the continents like a conveyor belt. What happens when oceanic crust moves toward a continent? Do the two collide? Or do they slip past each other, one floating, the other sinking beneath? In the history of Oregon and Washington, it turns out, a little bit of both. As the moving ocean crust dives below the edge of our continent, its island chains and seafloor sediments get caught up underneath. These oceanic rocks glue themselves to the continent, and more land gets created. Accreted terranes, geologists call them. Exotic terranes, others say. Land that came from somewhere else.

In the creation story of the Pacific Northwest, some of these terranes rode straight in from the ocean crust conveyor belt. Others were dragged up the coast by land masses sliding past each other on faults (much like California's San Andreas fault that exists today). All this action results in a spectacularly complex geologic history, one that geologists still labor to unfold. To complicate their work, vast amounts of volcanism—molten rock erupting at the surface—have buried many of these terranes during the chaos created in their collisions with our continent. Apart from earthquakes and eruptions, the process happens on a time scale no human could possibly live long enough to witness. When viewed all together, the geological scene is a Jackson Pollock painting. The history can only be told by carefully picking apart each unique smattering of paint.

The special privilege of rockhounding is collecting not rocks but stories. Obsidian in Oregon's Basin and Range Province captures the very moment of catastrophic volcanic explosions. Agates and jaspers found in the Washington Cas-

Inspecting a chunk of translucent agate as it catches the sun.

cades and Oregon's Blue Mountains Province form in volcanic layers after the chaos and tell us of quiet that followed. Forests buried in volcanic ash, like those of the Owyhee Uplands, transformed into petrified wood and exquisite leaf fossils, revealing the ecosystems that came long before our own. Serpentines, jades, and marbles, materials of the North Cascades and Klamath Country, tell us of the squeezing of rocks as ocean crust crashed into the continent. In these deformed materials, geologists can see evidence of oceanic volcanoes and their surrounding sands, albeit altered and recrystallized. Nowhere is this more apparent than in the Olympic Peninsula. In the Okanogan Highlands of Washington and the Blue Mountains of Oregon, we can even find the old Pangean coastline, with its ancient limestones and even older quartzites and sandstones. Even the granites that dominate the North Cascades, Klamath Country, and Wallowa Mountains, washing down mountain creeks, speak of volcanoes long gone. Granites are the basements of volcanoes, deep wells of magma that feed lava to the surface. When the volcanoes erode away, their granitic basements are exhumed. In our recent geologic past, Ice Age glaciers from the north plowed vast amounts of rocky material into the Pacific Northwest, carving canyons, dumping moraines of rubble and windblown loess (the dust that settles after a glacier recedes).

The 200 million years of tectonic action that created the lands of Oregon and Washington is a dazzling gift from the geologic gods. Rockhounds rejoice! In our present day, we can search the beaches, rivers, forests, and deserts of the Northwest for remnants of the past. I firmly believe that a rock's true value lies in its geologic story more than it could ever be based on its gemstone value or perceived metaphysical qualities. To prove this, I have undertaken the very sincere endeavor of guiding you through the cataclysms and epochs of the Pacific Northwest in the form of a rockhounding guide—one I hope will be the best yet in a long lineage of wonderful books.

Though I am not a geologist, I do my best to tell the geological story of each site and expand that story to present-day cultural ideas about rocks. My background is in the sciences, but my profession is in the art of cutting stone. My expertise is locating rock material to use in craft and sculpture, with geology as my guide. I feel adept at translating geological research, but please know that I am only an interpreter of information, not the source. As research into Pacific Northwest geology evolves, information about rocks and fossils will change. Our understanding will only become more interesting and refined.

Whether you are a geology enthusiast or a die-hard rockhound, a fine arts jeweler or a lifelong pebble puppy, I wrote this book with every type of rock-lover in mind. Out here, interesting rocks are everywhere. Let's go find them.

Universal Rules at a Glance

ALLOWED	PROHIBITED
Rocks, minerals, and metals	Vertebrate fossils (bones, teeth, coprolites)
Plant fossils (petrified wood, leaves)	Artifacts (stone tools, arrowheads, pottery)
Invertebrate fossils (molluscs, crustaceans)	Trash older than 100 years (or 50 years at designated historic sites)

- Collecting is for personal use only. A contract, lease, or mining claim is required to sell rock material.
- Rockhounds are required to adhere to daily collecting limits set by each agency.
- Rockhounding is a privilege, not a right. Agencies may close an area to rockhounding if too much damage is done.
- Agencies prefer surface collecting over digging. Holes must always be backfilled. In many places, panning or sluicing for gold in waterways is prohibited.
- Only archaeologists and paleontologists with permits may dig for artifacts and fossil bones.

Collecting Rules and Ethics: Live by Them

This guide features beautiful and productive rockhounding localities on public lands in Oregon and Washington. The act of collecting rocks on public land means you are taking rocks that belong to all of us and turning them into something that belongs only to you. It's hard to make a case that rockhounding is ethical in this light, and downright impossible when you consider that the land we collect on is only available to us because it was forcibly taken from its original inhabitants, the Indigenous peoples of North America. Rockhounding, despite its veneer as a wholesome hobby, is a perpetuation of the legacy of taking.

What I ask is that you let these truths guide you in the choices you make while out collecting. Before taking something, ask yourself: What will I do with this rock? Will I display or gift it in a meaningful way? Will I make something interesting or beautiful with it? If the answer is yes, and you are in a place where it is legal to do so, keep it. If the answer is no, leave it. If the answer is maybe, definitely leave it. It's the maybes that tilt the scale toward heavy-handed collecting.

Rockhounding with the intent to build a meaningful collection is the ultimate goal of the hobby. Filling your garage with thousands of pounds of rocks is not. These days, most of the amazing material that made the Pacific Northwest so famous is no longer in the ground. Legendary green petrified logs of Hampton Butte are piled in lonesome ranch yards. Warty gray thundereggs of Succor Creek are stockpiled in old timers' garages. Maury Mountain moss agate is buried under tarps behind shuttered rock shops. Ellensburg blue agate is hoarded away in shoeboxes in closets. Eventually these collections will distribute themselves through estate sales, but they'll never end up back in the ground. Visitors who head out to these collecting sites today are met with nearly empty trenches and little hope of finding anything akin to the spectacular specimens of the past.

All is not lost, though. In this guidebook, I've chosen to give a rest to areas that have been damaged by overcollection. It's my hope that readers of this book will take great care when visiting the locations I've chosen to share in their place.

Unless noted, every site in this book is on public land. Public lands are overseen by several agencies, and each has different rules about collecting. Rockhounds are required to know collection laws and follow them, but I encourage you to consider your impact beyond what public agencies allow us to take. Treading lightly in rockhounding areas preserves not only their beauty but also their longevity as a location where interesting material can be found. In the landscape, these rocks live every night under stars. For millennia they watch season after season pass by. If you take a rock from the landscape, think about this: Can you offer it a future any better than that?

Public Lands Agencies and Their Rules

There are essentially three tiers of public land control in the United States: land managed by the federal government, land managed by state governments, and land managed by local governments like counties, cities, and towns. (The remainder is Indigenous land and private property, which are always off-limits.) Oregon has twice as much public land acreage than Washington and therefore more land area in which to rockhound. Federal and state lands are managed by several different agencies that, dizzyingly, decide various types of conservation statuses in which rockhounding is or isn't allowed.

There is a general set of rules that applies universally about what rockhounds can collect on public land where rockhounding is allowed. It's the amount of material we're allowed to collect that changes from agency to agency. It's every rockhound's responsibility to know the universal rules by heart and to make a concerted effort to learn the various limits set by each agency.

Collection Limits by Agency

Lands owned by the federal government are managed by the Bureau of Land Management (BLM), the US Forest Service (USFS), the US Fish & Wildlife Service (USFWS), and the National Park Service (NPS). In Washington, state-owned lands designated for recreation are managed by the Washington State Department of Natural Resources (WDNR), Washington Department of Fish & Wildlife (WDFW), and Washington State Parks (WSP). In Oregon, state lands designated for recreation are managed by Oregon State Parks (OSP), Oregon Department of Fish & Wildlife (ODFW), and Oregon Department of Forestry (ODF). Counties and towns may also own land with public access, but rules regarding rockhounding are harder to ascertain.

Remember: Hobby collecting only. Vertebrate fossils and artifacts are always off-limits.

	Agency	Regulations
FEDERAL	**BLM** Bureau of Land Management	BLM regulations state that the public may collect "reasonable amounts" of rocks, minerals, and plant and invertebrate fossils for hobby purposes only. Commercial sale of collected material is prohibited. "Reasonable amounts" are up to the interpretation of regional and district offices. Most offer guidance that defines "reasonable amounts" as up to 25 pounds per person, per day, with a maximum of 250 pounds per year.
		Petrified wood collecting limits, specifically, have been codified into law. The Petrified Wood Act allows collection up to 25 pounds per person, per day, with a yearly maximum of 250 pounds, and must be for personal use only. Many BLM state and district offices use the Petrified Wood Act limits as their basis for all rockhounding guidance.
		On BLM land, digging is prohibited in designated wilderness areas and wilderness study areas, but surface collecting may be allowed. Always call district offices for information.
		Rockhounding is prohibited within paleontological ACECs (Areas of Critical Environmental Concern) that encompass large areas around Clarno, Kimberly, and Mitchell, Oregon.
		Rockhounding on mining claims without permission is advised against. Consult the BLM's Mineral & Land Records System online map to see current mining claims on public lands (see Appendix 3: Resources).

Collection Limits by Agency *continued*

FEDERAL		
BLM *continued*	Note: BLM collecting limits used to be higher. In the 1990s Oregon and Washington BLM released guidance that allowed recreational collecting limits by the truckload, or up to 250 pounds per day. That directive has since expired.	
USFS US Forest Service (national forests)	Surface collection of rocks, minerals, and common plant and invertebrate fossils is allowed. Reasonable collection is up to 10 pounds per person, per day.	
	Activity that involves digging with hand tools or mechanized equipment requires a permit. Rockhounds note: this means permits are required to dig holes on USFS land.	
	A Northwest Forest Pass is required in all national forests except Malheur, Ochoco, and Rogue River-Siskiyou National Forests.	
	Collecting is off-limits in Forest Service wilderness areas, Mount Saint Helens and Newberry National Volcanic Monuments, Hells Canyon National Recreation Area, and the Columbia River Gorge National Scenic Area.	
	Consult the Wilderness Areas in the United States online map for boundaries (see Appendix 3: Resources).	
USFWS US Fish & Wildlife Service (wildlife refuges)	In Hart Mountain National Antelope Refuge and Sheldon National Wildlife Refuge, hobby collecting is allowed at 7 pounds per person, per day with limits for the year.	
	Collecting is not allowed in other Oregon and Washington national wildlife refuges.	
NPS National Park Service	Collecting is forbidden in national parks and national monuments overseen by NPS. In Oregon and Washington, these are Olympic National Park (exception: one handful of shells and pebbles is allowed to be taken from beaches), Mount Rainier National Park, North Cascades National Park, Oregon Caves National Monument, Crater Lake National Park, and John Day Fossil Beds National Monument.	

Collection Limits by Agency *continued*

FEDERAL	**USBR and USACE** US Bureau of Reclamation and US Army Corps of Engineers	Rock collecting is prohibited within any USBR or USACE property boundaries, which encompass dams and reservoirs.
WASHINGTON STATE	**WDNR** Washington Department of Natural Resources (state trust lands and state-owned aquatic land)	WDNR authorizes noncommercial gathering of rocks, minerals, and non-vertebrate fossils for recreation, research, or educational purposes on public trust land with some exceptions. . . . . Rockhounding is prohibited in creeks and rivers, which WDNR refers to as "typed waters." Collecting is also forbidden on talus slopes, in caves, and along cliffs. . . . . A Discover Pass is required on all Washington state recreation lands (see Appendix 3: Resources).
	WDFW Washington Department of Fish & Wildlife (wildlife areas)	The removal of rocks, minerals, petrified wood, and artifacts from wildlife areas is prohibited. This includes Umtanum Creek Canyon in the Wenas Wildlife Area, a historically popular area with rockhounds. . . . . A Discover Pass is required on all Washington state recreation lands.
	WSP Washington State Parks and Beaches	Rockhounding is prohibited in all Washington state parks. . . . . However, state law allows the collection of beach sand up to 3 pounds. Collection of driftwood is prohibited. Metal detectors must register with each park office. Some state beaches may allow pebble and shell collecting. . . . . A Discover Pass is required on all Washington state recreation lands.

Collection Limits by Agency *continued*

OREGON STATE		
OSP Oregon State Parks and Beaches	Collection amounts for state parks within Oregon's interior are not explicitly set. However, the guidance states a "reasonable amount" may be collected from the surface and that digging requires written permission.
	On Oregon state beaches, collection of pebbles and shells is limited to 1 gallon per person, per day, with a yearly maximum of 3 gallons total. Sand and cobbles have slightly higher limits: 5 gallons per person per day, with yearly limits of 20 gallons (sand) and 10 gallons (cobbles), respectively.
	Fossils may be collected on Oregon state beaches if they are loose or in cobble form. Removal of fossil material from solid bedrock (wave benches, cliffs) is prohibited.
ODFW Oregon Department of Fish & Wildlife	While statewide guidance on removal of rock and mineral material on ODFW lands does not exist, agency staff recommend contacting the managers of specific wildlife areas to discuss if rock collecting is possible.
ODF Oregon Department of Forestry (state forests)	Visitors to state forests may collect rock material, but it is limited to "naturally occurring scattered boulders only, no river rock, crushed rock, or rock from stockpiles." Rockhounds may collect loose rock material from dry forest land at volumes up to 12 cubic feet, or the equivalent of 16 grocery bags.
	Note: River rockhounding is not allowed in Oregon state forests. This means that the Nehalem River and Wilson River in Oregon's Coast Range are off-limits to rockhounding, even though they are often included in other rockhounding guides.

Navigating Mining Claims on Federal Public Land

In your rockhounding adventures, you may come across mining claims on public land. Mining claims tend to be clustered in areas where valuable resources crop out. People stake claims so they can mine and sell precious metals, opals, crystals, and so on. Mining claims don't always have obvious signs of digging, especially placer claims for gold along rivers. In open desert, mining claims are easier to spot. You'll know you're near a claim when you wander into an area with many unofficial-looking posts sticking out of the ground. These posts mark the corners of the claim—20-acre parcels of public land in which someone has exclusive rights to almost every rock and mineral within it.

The most important aspect of a mining claim is that the land remains public even if someone else has staked the mineral rights. You can hike through or camp on the claim; you just can't collect rocks on it. There are two types of mining claims: lode and placer. Generally, lode claims are for solid veins of minerals and metals, and placer claims are for dispersed minerals, which is material that has traveled far from its source, like gold found in rivers. Both types of mining claims are a standard size, approximately 20 acres. Lode mining claims are always rectangular, 1500 feet long by 600 feet wide, to be exact. If a discovery spans an area larger than 20 acres, miners can stake multiple claims, but each 20-acre parcel must be marked individually. Each corner is indicated with a marked post—the northwest corner reads "NW corner," and so forth. A fifth post, known as a landmark, is sometimes placed in the center. The landmark post will have a tube or jar attached with the claim owner's notice inside. If you wander into an area with mining claims, the best thing to do is read the marker on the closest post to figure out where the 20-acre rectangle sits in the landscape. From there you can assess the boundaries and stay outside of the claim.

Mining claim posts can be made of any material: metal rebar, PVC pipes, or wood, like this one.

Not every type of rock or mineral material is claimable. Common materials like sand and gravel require leases instead of claims. Petrified wood is excluded from mining claim laws, and technically, the public can still collect petrified wood in an area with claims. However, no one would advise this, as some miners can become litigious over such matters. My guidance? Stay outside of people's mining claims and stay out of trouble.

Importantly, there is always a chance that a site listed in this guide could be claimed in the future. The best way to stay abreast of current mining claims ahead of time is to consult the BLM's Mineral & Land Records System (MLRS) Real-Time Map (see Appendix 3: Resources) when preparing for a rockhounding trip. The MLRS map is a wonderful online tool that shows you current and expired mining

Rockhounding and Leave No Trace

Even though the act of removing rocks from the landscape doesn't exactly align with the "leave what you find" principle of Leave No Trace, you can still follow these principles in all other ways anytime you're out collecting. The seven principles of Leave No Trace are:

- Plan ahead and prepare: Study the collecting and other regulations ahead of time and always let someone know when you are going and when you plan to return.
- Travel and camp on durable surfaces: Stick to trails when possible and if not, be mindful of where you're stepping to avoid crushing delicate plants.
- Dispose of waste properly: The most fundamental of the principles, this one comes down to pack it in, pack it out. Bury human waste at least 6 to 8 inches deep, 200 feet from water, and pack out your toilet paper and hygiene products.
- Leave what you find: Other than the rocks you collect, leave plants, flowers, and other natural objects alone so they can be enjoyed by the next person.
- Minimize campfire impacts: If you're camping, pay careful attention to fire regulations and use a campstove instead of a fire whenever possible, regardless.
- Respect wildlife: This means not only should you keep your distance but also carry and store your food properly so you don't attract unwanted visitors. Keep dogs on leashes at all times.
- Be considerate of other visitors: Quiet voices, no loud music, and just being courteous go a long way toward helping everyone enjoy their outdoor time.

claims in an area you wish to visit. To see how it works, try it out with a site in this book. Enter the coordinates listed for Rabbit Basin, Site 57, into the MLRS map to view all of the mining claims that surround the public sunstone collection area. You'll notice that the public collecting area is free of claims. There is a short learning curve to using the MLRS system, but like all good maps, everything you need to understand it is in the map legend. Consulting the MLRS map is an essential step for rockhounds who want to venture off the beaten path and discover new areas to collect material.

Tools of the Trade

To collect rocks, all you truly need are **pockets**. Surface hunting is king: it's the least destructive form of rockhounding and the method I hope to instill in your heart. My two most beloved collecting tools are an old canvas fly-fishing vest with slouchy pockets and a collapsible canvas bucket. Buckets are kind of like purses, though. The bigger they are, the more you stuff them with things you don't need. If you're out wandering with a deep bucket, try to keep a very selective mind when

A Note on Rock Dust

Whether you're hard-rock mining in the desert or carving stones at home, know that all rock dust is hazardous to the lungs. Lung tissue is unable to dissolve or eject rock particles, and over time scar tissue builds around minerals, which impedes pulmonary functions and can lead to several lung diseases. Silica dust from common rocks never leaves the lungs and can lead to silicosis. The same goes for asbestos minerals, commonly found in serpentines, known to cause both mesothelioma and lung cancer.

In dusty mining situations, always wear a face mask. Paper N95 masks that filter out 95 percent of airborne particulates are easy to wear outside in hot weather. P100-rated respirators that filter out nearly 100 percent of particles are superior, especially for indoor studio spaces. Mining and carving stones is a joyful pursuit and can be done safely if you take the hazards seriously. In any situation where you are creating rock dust, take all precautions to keep it out of your lungs and the lungs of others.

This specialty rockhounding tool is made to claw away at dirt and tip specimens out of the ground.

taking rocks. Make space to carry a **spray bottle** of water, which can be helpful for cleaning specimens in desert places.

A majority of the rockhounding sites in this book are along rivers. For these sites, I highly recommend bringing along **wellies**, water shoes, or waders. You can also bring a **hiking pole** to keep your balance on slippery rocks. When wading, always stay out of fast-moving water. Rockhounds should avoid wading into rivers during winter and spring for two reasons: water levels are fast and high, and in rivers with outlets to the sea, anadromous fish like salmon swim up them to spawn. We need to leave the river free of human disturbance so they may complete their epic reproductive journey. The best season for river rockhounding is late June through October. When the rains return, water levels can rise quickly.

In drier climates, finding rocks may often require digging. In these situations, **gloves**, a **garden claw**, and **hand shovel** are your best friends. Not big ones, but rather small ones you don't mind hiking with. These will help you tip stubborn rock specimens out of the ground. Perhaps even more excellent is a **specialized**

pick that looks less like a hammer and more like a blunt garden spade. One side is designed for clawing away dirt, and the other is for chipping away at hard-packed clay with more precision. This tool is not made for hitting rocks. It's made for moving earth out of the way, which it does with great efficiency.

When it comes to breaking rock apart—or hard-rock mining—specialized hand tools are required. A **geology pick** looks the most similar to a nail hammer. These are made to knock portions of rock off a larger outcrop—but not with precision. They're mostly used by geologists to collect hand specimens for observation. Blows from a geology pick tend to shatter rock indiscriminately, but they're very useful for prying a rock from packed dirt.

For precision in hard-rock mining, use two hand tools: a **chisel** and a **drilling hammer**. Drilling hammers are small sledges. A 2- or 3-pound drilling hammer is the ideal weight for hard-rock mining. When shopping for chisels, you'll notice a variety of tips. Pointed chisels are superior to flat chisels for breaking hard rock. They focus the power of your hit into a single point. Flat chisels spread that power out and are better for splitting soft, layered stones like limestone and slate along a plane. When swinging a hammer at a chisel, it's important to have control but also a relaxed grip. If you're squeezing the hammer, your hand will absorb most of the impact, which can lead to strain and injuries. Loosen your grip a little and remain focused on your swing. When working stone out of earth, always wear **safety glasses** or goggles. Rocks shatter when hit.

Most rockhounds use a variety of tools: hammers, chisels, pry bars, and geology picks. Gloves and eye protection are essential.

For splitting slabs of softer stones like mudstone or limestone, I like to use a **small hammer** and a **paint scraper** with a blunt end on the handle. I tap around the slab's circumference until I gently split layers apart. This helps reveal delicate fossils like leaves or insects. Some rock shops also sell special **fossil-splitting wedges**, which work wonderfully but aren't easy to come by. For small slabs of stone, just delicately working the sedimentary layers apart with a pocket knife can do the trick. It's also nice to have a **jeweler's loupe** or hand lens. These are small magnifiers that help you see fine details in rocks and fossils. As I've become more adept at identifying rocks, my hand lens has become indispensable.

Travel and Preparedness

Preparedness on the road is essential on all rockhounding journeys. Despite your best planning, challenges can always arise: the weather turns, dirt roads wash out, or tires flatten. Many of the locations in this book are a good distance from cities and large towns, and some are in truly remote areas, far from food and fuel, with rugged roads and no cell service. When venturing out, it's important that your vehicle is well stocked with food, water, tire-changing equipment, extra fuel, a first-aid kit, and maps. All of these. Always. When planning forays, refer to The Mountaineers' go-to list of the Ten Essentials (see sidebar). Furthermore, someone at home needs to know where you've gone and when you intend to return.

Some locations in this book, particularly those in the Oregon desert, are so remote they merit camping overnight. Before traveling to a site, consider its distance from your home and bring everything you need beyond the Ten Essentials. Washington and Oregon's eastern deserts can be unforgiving environments for pets and young children. Due to the tragic invasion of non-native annual grasses like medusahead and cheatgrass, it's always wise to leave pets at home. These grasses are known to be very harmful to our furry friends. Summer heat and a lack of shade can also provide risks, so plan desert trips with care.

What's more, wildfire season seems to grow longer every year, and it impacts rockhounding areas immensely. Invasive grasses like medusahead and cheatgrass exacerbate the risk. Due to fires started by people, famous rockhounding areas have been closed to recreation. Fire is not just a danger in forested areas; desert landscapes are vulnerable too. Dryland fires can move just as swiftly as those that engulf forests. There are three simple things you can do to avoid starting a wildfire: never have a campfire, don't smoke outdoors, and never drive overland—which means driving off designated routes into dry grass, brush, or forest understory. The underside of your vehicle is capable of starting fires by friction; many tragic fires have started this way.

Many locations in the guide will take you to remote areas with unpaved roads. Dirt road travel brings its own level of spice into the mix. If you're new to this kind of travel and wayfinding, here are my essential tips for getting around remote areas.

First, preparedness starts at home. Before heading out on a trip, I do a lot of research on the web. I estimate mileage to locations, I look up rural gas stations and call them to make sure their pumps work (many are old), and I look at dirt roads via satellite imagery on Google Earth. Digital resources are fun at home, but they can be hard to take on the road. While I do use GPS apps in the wild, they're a supplement to my main resource: paper maps. Before leaving, I always mark the places I intend to go on a paper map so if my GPS device fails (if the battery dies, if I leave it on the roof, if I drop it in the river), I'm still in good shape.

When you're out in rural areas, never rely on digital technologies or apps that require cell service to get around. Even if you have service, don't ever ask Google for directions on logging roads or in the desert. The better approach is to compare the driving directions given in this book with an up-to-date paper map. Map reading is an essential rockhounding skill, and your experience will be all the richer for it. Recreation maps specifically are going to provide the kind of detail you want. Some brands publish state-wide gazetteers that highlight recreation access, points of interest, and dirt road conditions. My paper atlases are dog-eared, drawn on, highlighted, and spilled on because I use them so much. I can refer back to everywhere I've been over the years. See the Resources section at the back of the book for my recommendations of navigation apps and paper atlases.

On dirt roads, the quality of your tires matters the most. High clearance and four-wheel drive are helpful against rough road and slippery terrain, but the real hazard is flats. Tires graded only for pavement driving (or any type of worn-out tires) flatten much easier than tires graded for all terrains. Seasoned backcountry drivers always carry a full-size spare and boards to place under their car jack. Why? On unpaved roads, jacks can sink into the dirt, making it impossible to lift the vehicle. Placing boards underneath the jack distributes the weight and prevents it from sinking, while stacking the boards prevents them from snapping. I carry a few one-foot-by-two-foot scraps of plywood in my trunk for this purpose. Plus, tire irons that come standard with your vehicle can make removing lug nuts a real chore. Instead, I suggest carrying a breaker bar to quickly remove lug nuts. If you're unfamiliar with them, have someone at the auto shop show you why they're so great. This is all to say: before you go dirt roading, you need to know how to change a tire. If you've never done it before, practice at home with an experienced friend. Really!

The Ten Essentials

The point of the Ten Essentials, originated by The Mountaineers, has always been to answer two basic questions: Can you prevent emergencies and respond positively should one occur (items 1–5)? And can you safely spend a night—or more—outside (items 6–10) if needed? If you're sticking close to your car, then you can likely leave most of this there. But if you'll be wandering farther afield in search of your perfect rocks, then always take a small pack with these items:

1. Navigation
2. Headlamp
3. Sun protection
4. First aid
5. Knife

6. Fire
7. Shelter
8. Extra food
9. Extra water
10. Extra clothes

Seasoned backcountry drivers also carry a portable air compressor so they can reduce their tire pressure for long drives on rocky roads or deep sand and fill back up when they get back to pavement. If you get stuck in sand or mud, there are a few ways to get out. I keep traction mats to put under the tires if I get stuck in mud or deep sand. Other people keep rolls of scrap carpeting, strips of plywood, or even use the floor mats from the vehicle. I always have a small folding shovel or two as well. Some people let a little additional air out of their tires, but not too much or you'll end up with flats! Sand is easier to get out of than mud. Mud is something I truly don't mess with. If I see a lot of it on the road ahead, I turn around.

When exploring a place that is new to you, park your vehicle in an obvious location with good visibility so you can find your way back to it. If you're wandering through a forest, try to follow a drainage (dry creek or river) the entire time so you can follow it back to your car. In the high lava plains of Oregon, vast juniper forests cover level ground. This environment in particular is easy to get lost in. Keep landmarks as you hike, or better yet, bring a compass or fully charged GPS unit and mark your starting location. My preference is to use a digital device where I can drop a pin on my starting location and use it to find my way back.

In this book, I have chosen many sites where material is only a short stroll from the parking area. However, some of the more remote locations require backcountry

A group uses shovels and picks to dig for petrified wood at Dendrite Butte near Congleton Hollow in central Oregon.

hiking, up to a few miles, to find the best material. Few of these locations have established trails. Your task is to explore at your whim. If you visit sites in this book that are new to you, always stop to take stock of where you are when you first arrive. If you know how you found your way in, both driving and hiking, you'll be able to find your way out.

Think Before You Post

The age of social media has had a profound impact on the rockhounding community. It's turned some avid rockhounds into low-level celebrities and inundated some of Oregon and Washington's most famous rockhounding sites with hoards of new visitors. I love watching our hobby grow, but I'm sad to see the lack of essential information–like collecting rules and ethics–entirely missing from the frenzy of rockhounding social media accounts.

Through sharing, we have an opportunity to make our hobby better. If you decide to post about your wonderful rock finds, I hope you'll also consider sharing information about rock collecting rules, what you find special about the land, and why it matters that we collect lightly. Including messages of stewardship may feel like value-signaling, but such messages have real-world impacts. When you model responsible outdoor recreation, others will follow. If you happen to visit a rockhounding site that feels truly special and possibly vulnerable to the social media machine, perhaps it's best not to post about it at all. Let it live in your memories, safe and sound.

How to Use This Guide

The locations selected for this book are clustered into geographical regions that have unique geological qualities. These geo-regions have been established through decades of geological research and insight into how Oregon and Washington's rocks came to be. The regions define a specific story in the Pacific Northwest's epic history. Each of the sixty locations has been carefully considered and chosen after visiting hundreds of sites in Oregon and Washington. I based my choices on the abundance of material available, safety of travel, safety at the site, and most importantly, geological interest. Sites that had limited material, dangerous roads, unstable cliffs, or damage from previous rockhounding activity were omitted. Furthermore it is with great sadness that there are no locations within the Oregon Cascades included in this book. The western slope from Portland to Roseburg has been decimated by large wildfires over the last several seasons, and the river corridors in which we all love to rockhound have been closed to several types of recreation as the forest ecosystems take time to recover.

In this book, site names are based on real place-names used in established maps of the Pacific Northwest. There are several sites listed in this book that have never been published in any other rockhounding guides and do not have official names. For the purposes of this guide, I have given these areas names based on their immediate surroundings or, in three cases (Martin's Bar, Site 7; Deb's Spot, Site 41; and Lars's Stock Pond, Site 46), I have named them after the people who introduced me to these places and whom I consider important to the rockhounding community.

Location descriptions begin with a history of the rocks, minerals, or fossils found in that place and why they are worthy of finding. If you run into terminology that is new to you, there is a glossary of geological terms in Appendix 1, which I hope will be helpful.

For each recommended rockhounding area, I also provide the following at-a-glance information:

What you'll find: This is a list of the most common rocks you'll find at the location. It is not exhaustive. You are also not guaranteed to find everything I found during my own visits. If you are adept at identification, it's likely you may find uncommon rocks that I did not list.

Geologic age: This is a description of the age of the rocks based on current research. Geologic time is divided into the three major eras of life on earth: the Paleozoic (life begins), the Mesozoic (reign of the dinosaurs), and the Cenozoic (the age of mammals). Each of these eras is divided further into units called periods, and periods are further divided into units called epochs. These divisions of time are agreed upon by international consortiums and used as a standard around the world. In this guide, all given geological ages of rocks are approximate and are based on available research.

Tools: These are the most essential tools to bring with you to the site. These include hand tools, accessories for rivers, and essential digging safety equipment like goggles and gloves—don't leave home without them.

Agency: This is the public land agency or private owner who manages the site. The agency listed is who you should contact with any questions. They have the

A Note about Safety

Safety is an important concern in all outdoor activities. No guidebook can alert you to every hazard or anticipate the limitations of every reader. Therefore, the descriptions of roads, trails, routes, and natural features in this book are not representations that a particular place or excursion will be safe for your party. When you follow any of the routes described in this book, you assume responsibility for your own safety. Under normal conditions, such excursions require the usual attention to traffic, road and trail conditions, weather, terrain, the capabilities of your party, and other factors. Because many of the lands in this book are subject to development and/or change of ownership, conditions may have changed since this book was written that make your use of some of these routes unwise. Always check for current conditions, obey posted private property signs, and avoid confrontations with property owners or managers. Keeping informed on current conditions and exercising common sense are the keys to a safe, enjoyable outing.

—Mountaineers Books

final word on site accessibility and collecting rules. See Appendix 3: Resources for contact information for agency headquarters.

Limits: This is the amount of rock or fossil material you are allowed to collect on each visit. On public lands, these rules must be strictly adhered to. Some are quite generous, but I encourage you to collect lightly. Take home only a meaningful amount of material that you have an actual purpose for: displaying, gifting, cutting. Please, don't let these special items languish in a bucket in your garage. They will outlive you, and your survivors will be forced to deal with them. Furthermore, overcollection strips an area of beautiful rocks and diminishes the site's value to future visitors.

Location: These are given as coordinates in decimal degrees as determined by WGS 84 datum for ease of entering into common mapping apps. Coordinates are always two numbers separated by a comma. The first is latitude and the second is longitude. When typing coordinates in, remember that in the Pacific Northwest, our latitude is north of the equator and therefore a positive number. Our longitude is west of the Prime Meridian and therefore a negative number. You may copy coordinates into a web browser, an app on your phone, or a GPS device. If a deposit of rocks is extremely specific, the coordinates will take you directly to it. If the collecting area is broad, the coordinates will take you to either the center of the collecting area or the safest parking area near the center. If parking is far from the collecting area, coordinates for both are given.

Vehicle: Sites that are safe to reach in any vehicle are simply marked "any." To pass the "any" test, a small, low-clearance vehicle like a Toyota Prius can make it safely to the site. Next, there are vehicles with "some clearance." These are sportier cars like Subarus and small SUVs that also have all-wheel drive. The final category is "high clearance," which includes trucks and SUVs that have excellent ground clearance and four-wheel drive. If a site says "some clearance recommended," it means there are obstacles in the road that a Prius would struggle with, but a Subaru could get through just fine. If a site says "high clearance recommended," it means that it has some obstacles a Subaru may struggle with, but a large SUV or truck could overcome. If a site says "high clearance and four-wheel drive required," it means that the road is truly rugged and only experienced backcountry drivers with a high-clearance truck or SUV should attempt it.

Seasons: This is the window of time when it is worthwhile to visit a site. I took into account seasonal weather like snowpack, rainfall (especially for high water in rivers), sensitive animal uses such as spawning and ground nesting, high summer temperatures, and wildfire risks. Please note that severe weather may impact your use of these sites during the window of time I have recommended visiting.

MAP LEGEND

5	Interstate highway	=	Bridge
20	US highway	⊷	Gate
251	State route	▲	Mountain/peak
5501	Forest road	▪	Point of interest
	Paved road	··········	Federal/state boundary
	Dirt/gravel road	☐	Private property
·············	Site access trail	▨	Mining claim site
----------	Other trail	〜	River/creek
⊗	Rockhounding site	▬	Waterbody
℗	Parking	⌐--⌐	Dry lake
P	Alternate parking	☐	Park/forest/wilderness
Ⓐ	Campground		boundary

Directions: Driving directions are based on mileage numbers I took in my own vehicle when visiting each site. I then compared them to distances on mapping applications to ensure their accuracy. Road conditions always change, and dirt roads especially are subject to washouts and closures. Some roads listed in this book are subject to seasonal closures. If so, I have noted it. Always, always carry a paper atlas with you in remote areas.

Hiking directions are given if a route is required to get to a collecting area from a parking area. Only a few sites have notable hikes (Rainbow Creek, Site 8; McGraw Creek, Site 37).

At the site: This is a description of what to expect upon arriving, what types of rocks you'll find, and any special considerations about safety or challenges to expect at the site. Descriptions of hikes (if required) are also given in this section.

Maps: Use the maps provided to ascertain the relationship of the rock collecting area to the parking area. Collection areas are marked with crossed hammers, and the icon repeats throughout the area if material is widely dispersed. Use the maps to assess boundaries of public land with private land as well. Important features such as roads, gates, fences, diggings, waterways, and drainages are also included.

Rock and Mineral Treasures of Oregon and Washington

Agate, Jasper, and Chert

These are rocks that form after-the-fact in volcanic and sedimentary deposits rich in silica. They're very hard, fracture conchoidally, and don't weather easily. These qualities make them wonderful lapidary materials.

Opal

Opal is a hydrated silica and commonly forms in volcanic ash deposits as they chemically weather. Opal is a cousin to agates and jaspers but looks waxier and is less dense due to its water content. It is brittle and fragile.

Petrified Wood

Petrified wood is most often fossilized by silica. The process happens when trees are buried in sediments rich in volcanic ash. Silica from the ash invades the tree and precipitates as opal, agate, and quartz.

Obsidian and Pumice

Obsidian and pumice are volcanic glasses that erupt in extremely viscous lava flows rich in silica. The high viscosity prevents crystals from forming, thus their fabric remains chaotic or "glassy." Obsidian has no gas bubbles, while pumice is made almost entirely of them.

Rhyolite and Tuff

Rhyolite is a lava rock from volcanoes that are highly enriched with silica. Tuff, or a rock made of volcanic ash, is commonly found in tandem. These volcanic rocks are a rich source of agate, jasper, and opal, which form as these volcanic rocks cool and chemically weather.

Basalt and Diabase

Basalt is a lava that is low in silica and rich in iron and magnesium. It cools into dense, dark rocks that can form impressive columns. Basalt covers large swaths of Oregon and Washington. Diabase is a basalt that cools shallowly within the crust and is common in Oregon's Coast Range.

Greenstone

Greenstone is a common product of old volcanic rock encountering heat and pressure during tectonic events. It is named for its color and often contains veins of other minerals like quartz, epidote, and metals. It is commonly found among exotic terranes.

Peridotite, Jade, and Serpentine

Peridotite is the stuff of the mantle, rich in the green mineral olivine. Jade and serpentine form when peridotites are altered by hydrothermal fluids that permeate active tectonic zones. Craftspeople use caution: serpentine contains chrysotile asbestos.

Epidote

Epidote is a chartreuse-green mineral associated with hydrothermal alteration of rocks and metamorphism. It's commonly found among metavolcanic rocks like greenstone and in quartz veins in basement rocks like granite and gneiss.

Granite and Her Sisters

Granite and her sisters are the crystalline cores of continental volcanic systems. They form when a melt cools within continental crust. Granite is its own chemically distinct rock on a spectrum of sisters such as granodiorite, tonalite, and diorite.

Gneiss

Gneiss is the basement rock of the continents and the most deformed rock on Earth. Gneiss occurs where intense heat and pressure deform deep rocks like granite and very old sedimentary rocks that have been forced deep into continental crust.

Sandstones and Mudstones

Sandstones and mudstones build up as sediments in valleys and riverbeds on land, beaches, and seafloors. They can range from fine clay siltstones to pure quartz sandstones to coarse conglomerates of cobbles.

Quartzite, Phyllite, and Schist

Quartzite is sandstone that has been recrystallized by metamorphic heat and pressure. Phyllite and schist are baked mudstones (ancient clays) that can exhibit dark-gray iridescent layers or sparkling bands of mica.

Limestone and Marble

Limestone is a deposit made of calcium carbonate from ancient reefs that became stone over time. Limestones are often fossiliferous. With heat and pressure, limestone's calcium carbonates can recrystallize into marble.

Rockhounding Recommendations

If you're new to the hobby of rockhounding, picking just one location from a book of sixty interesting sites could feel overwhelming. Each site in this book has something wonderful to offer, and some are easier to get to than others. Perhaps you have kids in tow. Perhaps they don't care much for rocks but love fossils. Or perhaps you're a geology buff looking to see something unusual. Or maybe you're like me, out hunting for rock material to use in your craft. Here are my recommendations for where to get started based on the type of rockhounding trip that best suits your time and curiosities.

FUN FOR FAMILIES

These sites are close to towns or located at well-developed campgrounds, have on-site parking, offer plentiful material, and are great for school-aged children under the supervision of adults.

Site 11: Stillaguamish River (Washington)
Site 14: Stonerose Fossil Quarry (Washington)
Site 20: Beverly Beach (Oregon)
Site 26: Rogue River (Oregon)
Site 38: Fossil (Oregon)

COLLECTING FOSSILS

These are locations where rockhounds are guaranteed to find interesting specimens. However, some labor to unearth them is always required.

Site 14: Stonerose Fossil Quarry (Washington)
Site 20: Beverly Beach (Oregon)
Site 34: Saddle Mountain (Washington)
Site 47: Beulah Reservoir (Oregon)
Site 49: Sand Hollow (Oregon)

A young rockhound searches for fossils behind Wheeler High School in Fossil, Oregon.

SCULPTURE-QUALITY STONE

These locations provide large cobbles and small boulders of sculptable material such as limestone, marble, peridotite, granite, and gneiss. Please note that locations within national forests have a recommended daily collection limit of 10 pounds.

Site 7: Martin's Bar (Washington)
Site 24: Elk River (Site A, Oregon)
Site 29: Rough and Ready Creek (Oregon)
Site 36: Hurricane Creek (Oregon)
Site 37: McGraw Creek (Oregon)

LAPIDARY CRAFT MATERIAL

These locations have an abundance of silicate rocks like agate, jasper, and chert. These are hard rocks that take a nice polish.

Site 27: Meyer Creek (Oregon)
Site 42: Eagle Rock Quarry (Oregon)
Site 45: Warm Springs Reservoir (Oregon)
Site 51: Haystack Rock (Oregon)

BACKCOUNTRY ADVENTURING

These remote and beautiful sites may require several hours of travel to reach. Some require backcountry driving experience. At minimum, good tires are essential for all of these sites. Bring camping supplies and navigation tools, and plan to spend a few days exploring.

Site 43: Congleton Hollow (Oregon)
Site 52: Twin Springs and Grassy Mountain (Oregon)
Site 54: Birch Creek (Oregon)
Site 55: Glass Buttes (Oregon)
Site 57: Rabbit Basin (Oregon)

UNUSUAL GEOLOGY

The Pacific Northwest is covered in volcanic rocks of the Cenozoic era. However, there are some locations where one can view rocks whose stories are a wonderful departure from the landscape of endless lavas.

Site 5: Shipwreck Point (Washington)
Site 6: Fossil Creek (Washington)
Site 10: Sauk River (Washington)
Site 30: Josephine Creek (Oregon)
Site 56: Harney Lake (Oregon)

WASHINGTON
Olympic Peninsula

The rugged and remote Olympic Peninsula is a quieter domain for rock and mineral hunters, but it is not without its prizes. Olympic National Park dominates its interior, and rock collecting is not allowed in the park's forests. However, plenty of other public land awaits. The Olympic Peninsula is a site of active accretion, a term geologists use to describe rock material from the ocean getting glued onto our continent. As the oceanic plate dives under our own continental plate, ocean seafloor crust gets bunched up into a formation called an accretionary wedge. The entire Olympic Peninsula is an accretionary wedge. Rockhounds can explore rivers on the east side for red breccias and marbled green-stones altered in the bunching process and along the north coast for marine fossils uplifted in the action.

Searching the gravels of the Hamma Hamma River on a winter's day

① Hamma Hamma River

"Nothing ever really goes away—it just changes into something else," writes novelist Sarah Ockler, "something beautiful." High in the crested mountains that rise above the Hamma Hamma River, swaths of old, unremarkable marine rocks have been metamorphosed into bands of colorful, gemmy greenstone. These altered rocks were born as dark basaltic lavas from massive undersea eruptions that occurred offshore around 56 million years ago. After the eruptions ceased, a great deal of material eroded from the basalts, piling up in submarine landslides. Over time these sediments compacted on the seafloor into a dark gray sandstone called graywacke. Today, the basalts and graywackes are known to geologists as a terrane called Siletzia, which has been folded up into an entirely new landmass—the Olympic Peninsula.

Plate tectonics have been forcing the submarine rocks of Siletzia from the depths of the sea onto the edge of the North American continent in a process called accretion. Most Olympic bedrock is composed of Siletzian basalt and gray-wacke that have been untouched by metamorphosis in their journey. But here and there, baked and squeezed areas of altered rock crop out and tumble into the peninsula's rivers. These metamorphosed rocks show up on the leading edge of what geologists call the accretionary wedge. The rocks on the peninsula's steep, eastern flank have borne the brunt of the forces that have lifted them from sea-floor into mountain range. Friction, shearing, faulting, and the invasion of hydro-thermal fluids have altered these formerly black and gray rocks into beautiful teal rocks called greenstones.

In the metamorphosis of basalts and their sands, dark pyroxene crystals are replaced with chlorite and epidote. These new minerals impart a green color to the rock, and geologists generally refer to all greenish basaltic rocks as green-stones. The presence of chlorite and epidote are indicative to geologists that the metamorphosis of these rocks happened at somewhat low temperatures and low pressures. This means they were squeezed and cooked a bit while being shoved around at shallow depths in the crust, but they have never been forced deep down into the crust, where temperatures and pressures rise rapidly and heavily deform rocks into gneiss or melt them altogether. Greenstones are lightly metamorphosed rocks in comparison.

Colorful greenstones, epidote, and white quartz are easily found here.

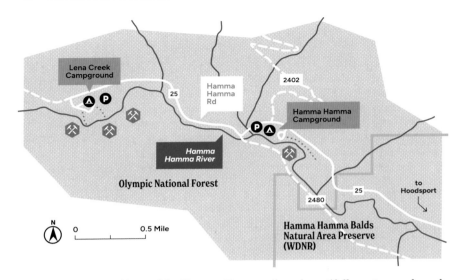

Among the gravel bars of the Hamma Hamma, these beautifully metamorphosed rocks tumble downstream among large volumes of their basalt and graywacke parents. Dark-teal greenstones, rich in chlorite, appear in abundance among the cobbles. Some have veins of white quartz and chartreuse epidote within them. Other rocks are solid chunks of bright, swampy epidote. These rocks are particularly wonderful material for lapidary work, though few rockhounds care to seek them out. I have always thought that if I reincarnated as a rock, I would want to be epidote. I would be beautiful and largely left alone.

WHAT YOU'LL FIND: Epidote, quartz, greenstone	**LIMIT:** Up to 10 pounds per person, per day
GEOLOGIC AGE: Cenozoic era, Paleogene period	**LOCATIONS:** **Hamma Hamma Campground:** 47.595056, –123.122861 **Lena Creek Campground:** 47.597583, –123.151250
TOOLS: Wellies, waders, or water shoes; a hiking pole for balance	
	VEHICLE: Any
AGENCY: US Forest Service, Olympic National Forest. A Northwest Forest Pass is required (see Appendix 3: Resources). A fee is required to camp at Hamma Hamma and Lena Creek Campgrounds.	**SEASONS:** Summer and early fall. Warning: Avoid the river in winter and spring. High runoff poses a danger to you, and you pose a danger to spring-spawning fish.

DIRECTIONS → Make your way to the intersection of State Route 119 and US Highway 101 in Hoodsport, Washington. From here travel north on US 101 for 13.8 miles. Turn left (west) onto Hamma Hamma Road (Forest Road 25) and drive 6 miles to the Hamma Hamma Campground. On foot, follow the established trail that leads southeast from the campground approximately 300 feet to the river's edge. To get to Lena Creek Campground, continue up Hamma Hamma Road for another 1.7 miles. At the campground, several established footpaths lead down to the gravel bars along the river.

AT THE SITE → The river runs somewhat narrow at Hamma Hamma Campground, but during low-water months in summer, some gravel is exposed. Farther upriver at Lena Creek Campground, the river meanders, resulting in larger gravel bars that offer up plentiful material. At both sites, search the gravel bars for dark-teal greenstone, milky quartz, and bright-green epidote. Look particularly for chunks of epidote that are smooth and with few fractures if you are collecting material for lapidary work.

② Dosewallips River

The Olympic Peninsula is a mass of marine rocks caught up in the chaos of subduction—when one plate slides underneath another. About 56 million years ago, a massive, young seamount of basaltic lava known as Siletzia "docked" with the North American continent. It was far too massive to neatly sink into the subduction trench under North America, and so bits of it were forced up against the continent. Big bits. Some geologists see evidence that Siletzia was enough of a wedge that it put the brakes on subduction altogether. Tectonic forces eventually got things moving again, and when it did, great amounts of seafloor sediments (sandstones and mudstones) began piling up behind the Siletzia terrane as subduction along the trench continued. This accretionary process created the Olympic Peninsula and the coast ranges of Oregon and Washington that exist today.

Siletzia is characterized by an extraordinary mass of basalt that erupted under the sea a few million years before it docked with North America. Some of the basalt that was forced upward in the creation of the Olympic Peninsula has been altered into greenstone—a beautiful dark-teal rock with veins of white quartz and chartreuse epidote. Plenty of these rocks can be found here in the Dosewallips River. Theoretical models used by geologists suggest that the Yellowstone hotspot (yes, the big scary thing that sits underneath Yellowstone National Park) may be responsible for the birth of Siletzia. How could this possibly be?

Cobbles of bright-green epidote and red jasper stick out among the dark basalt and graywacke.

Hotspots seem to be stationary points of powerful upwelling in Earth's mantle. But ocean plates and continents on the surface move (they always move), and as they do, they drift over the hotspot, leaving a trail of volcanic chaos in their wake. Think of it like Whac-A-Mole in a wobbly line. Plates bounce around a bit as they move, like bumper cars, so their trend over hotspots is rarely straight. Researchers have been able to trace this wobbly line of incredible hotspot volcanism through time and space, suggesting the first eruption of Siletzia occurred under the sea about 56 million years back. North America would eventually plow over the hotspot, resulting in the eruptions of the Tillamook Volcanics, then the Crooked River Caldera, and after that the unprecedented eruptions of the Columbia River flood basalts and simultaneous explosive calderas of southeastern Oregon. The passage of time would see more calderas erupt in northern Nevada and Idaho, marching ever eastward. The hotspot, still active, now sits under present-day Wyoming and Montana, in America's most visited national park.

Opposite: A quiet spot on the Dosewallips River in summer

WHAT YOU'LL FIND: Greenstone, epidote, graywacke, glacial drift	**LIMIT:** Up to 10 pounds per person, per day
GEOLOGIC AGE: Cenozoic era, Paleogene period	**LOCATION:** 47.737277, –123.025781
	VEHICLE: Any
TOOLS: Wellies, waders, or water shoes; a hiking pole for balance	**SEASONS:** Summer and early fall. Warning: Avoid the river in winter and spring. High runoff poses a danger to you, and you pose a danger to spring-spawning fish.
AGENCY: US Forest Service, Olympic National Forest. A Northwest Forest Pass is required (see Appendix 3: Resources).	

DIRECTIONS → Make your way to the town of Brinnon, Washington, to the intersection of US Highway 101 and Dosewallips Road. Turn west onto Dosewallips Road (Forest Road 2610) and drive for 7.1 miles to a turnout along the edge of the river. When parking in the turnouts, you must leave room for other cars to pull over. The road is narrow, and the turnouts are required for safe passing. There are short footpaths from the turnouts that lead down to the gravel bars. If there is no room to park, continue 0.3 mile to another turnout downriver. Avoid sections of private property along the river (see map). You may also park at the Dosewallips River trailhead at the end of the road and make your way down to the river from there.

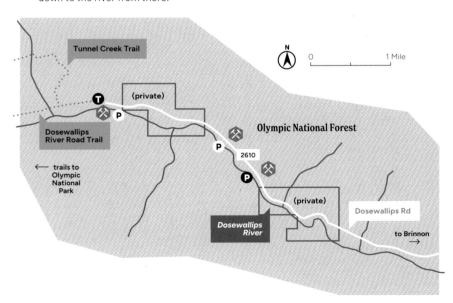

AT THE SITE → Some bushwhacking may be required to get down to the river, which runs shallow and calm in summer and early fall. Bring good water shoes or waders to explore this stretch of the river. Make sure to walk downstream from the parking area, since a small parcel of private property encompasses the river upstream. The Dosewallips River trailhead, which leads up into Olympic National Park, is 1.2 miles farther up the road. Search the river's gravel bars for green epidote, red jasper, milky quartz, and possible agates. Avoid wading in the river during winter and spring when the water is deep and swift.

③ Dungeness Forks

The Dungeness and Gray Wolf Rivers drain the high peaks of the Olympic Peninsula. The range's stunning mountains are composed of old seafloor that has been forced up from the deep in its collision with North America. Sandstones, mudstones, and old lava rock all drain down the rivers, and much of this material

A wonderful variety of native Olympic rocks as well as rocks from afar left by glaciers can be found in the riverbed.

has been somewhat metamorphosed during the great collision that began about 50 million years ago.

Our continent, North America, has been colliding with oceanic plates for a long time. Oceanic plates sink under continents, rather than merge, because they are made of rocks that are much denser. Continents essentially float in comparison. The process of one plate sinking below another is called subduction, and a deep trench forms at the margin of the down-going plate. The process is messy, and a great deal of seafloor sediments and seamounts made of basaltic lava crumple up against the overriding plate, unable to make the plunge with the rest of the plate. With nowhere to go, they glom onto it, eventually being uplifted as new land.

These glommed-on rocks make up the dominant cobbles and gravels at Dungeness Forks. Among them, travelers from an entirely different origin are mixed in. Occasionally, you'll find granite-like rocks or a wavy gneiss in the riverbed. These are materials that originated in the Canadian Rockies and North Cascades. So how did they get here on this isolated peninsula surrounded by water? The answer is glaciers.

Welcome to the Pleistocene, which began 2.5 million years ago. You know the Pleistocene well. You're likely familiar with the tail end of it, a chunk of time known as the Ice Age. During its time, global ice sheets grew and retreated numerous times until their finale several thousand years ago. They covered the poles and reached down into the temperate latitudes. The ice that blanketed the North Cascades, Puget Sound, and the Olympic Peninsula is known as the Cordilleran ice sheet. In its slow, forceful advance, it dragged all sorts of rocks along with it. At its most triumphant, it was over a mile deep and had profound impacts on the mountains and valleys being crushed underneath its weight. Rocks were dragged hundreds of miles from their origins. This glacial drift arrived on the Olympic Peninsula long after the emergence of the old terrane rocks that its peaks are made of.

WHAT YOU'LL FIND: Greenstone, graywacke, glacial drift	**LIMIT:** Up to 10 pounds per person, per day
GEOLOGIC AGE: Cenozoic era, Paleocene through Pleistocene epochs	**LOCATION:** 47.974641, -123.113816
	VEHICLE: Some clearance recommended
TOOLS: Wellies, waders, or water shoes; a hiking pole for balance	**SEASONS:** Summer and early fall. Warning: Avoid the river in winter and spring. High runoff poses a danger to you, and you pose a danger to spring-spawning fish.
AGENCY: US Forest Service, Olympic National Forest. A Northwest Forest Pass is required (see Appendix 3: Resources).	

Opposite: The Dungeness River carves through the steep flanks of the Olympic Mountains.

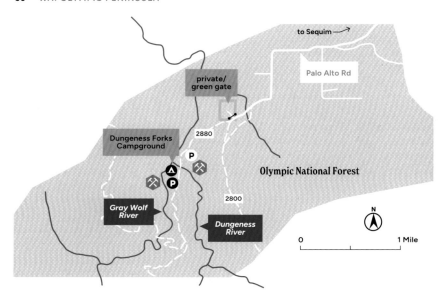

DIRECTIONS → Make your way to the Olympic Peninsula town of Sequim, Washington. In the town's center, at the intersection of Washington Street and Sequim Avenue, drive south on South Sequim Ave for 0.5 mile. Turn left to merge onto US Highway 101 East and drive for 2.7 miles. Turn right (south) onto Palo Alto Road and drive for 7.8 miles to a fork. Palo Alto Road turns to dirt and becomes Forest Road 2800 (on some maps as 28) at this point. Stay right and drive for 0.2 mile to a second fork. Stay right again to take FR 2880 for 0.8 mile down to Dungeness Forks Campground. (*Caution: There is a private driveway with a green gate at the second fork that can be mistaken for the road. FR 2880 comes just after it.*) FR 2880 is steep and rutted. Some clearance and all-wheel drive/four-wheel drive recommended. If the campground is open, drive through it and park in the large lot at the back of the campground along the river. The gravel bar is adjacent to the parking area. If the campground is gated, park along the road and walk down to the river.

AT THE SITE → The Gray Wolf and Dungeness Rivers meet at the Dungeness Forks Campground. The gravel bars on the Gray Wolf fork tend to be larger, and I recommend starting your search at the campground and wading upriver. The dominant rocks are Siletzian graywacke. Colorful red breccia, altered volcanic greenstone (once-upon-a-time basalt), white quartz, chartreuse epidote, and sparkly schist can be found here—all accretionary rocks. Rocks dragged in by glaciers such as altered granite and gneiss show up, too, but are far less abundant. Avoid the rivers in winter and spring during high runoff and fish spawning.

④ Murdock Beach

Travelers from afar—rocks of glacial drift—mix with rocks eroded from the Olympic peaks in the piles of fine gravel that line the high-water mark on Murdock Beach. It's a pebble collector's dream, with a colorful array of material to find. As the tide recedes, a different rock scene emerges. Cobbles of limey mudstone concretions, cloaked in green algae, cover the beach. These cobbles erode from the old Pysht and even older Makah Formations that guard the north Olympic coast. Occasionally, the concretions from the Makah Formation may contain glendonites. These strange diamond-shaped ghosts are remnants of large crystals that formed along deep-sea vents where strange life-forms ate up methane gas spewing from the crust. In some rare instances, other concretions found on Murdock Beach

High tide at Murdock Beach on a winter's day. Colorful stones of glacial drift can be found high up on the beach.

At low tide the ancient marine sediments and their concretions are exposed.

contain fossils of that methane-eating world: clams, snails, tubeworms, and crabs. There's also evidence that not all the mud balls on Murdock Beach hail from the deep-sea vents. Some may be coming from the shallower marine formations too. In recent paleontology news, some concretions have been broken open to reveal the holdfasts of kelp from 30 million years ago, helping to place this royal algae on an evolutionary time scale that was previously only guessed at.

Before you get too excited about the dazzling concretions of Murdock Beach, know that the reality here is that most concretions are just limey mud balls that have coalesced around tiny specks of seafloor material. Cracking them open often yields . . . not much. But at least they're cool limey mud balls that formed 30 million years ago? To improve the chances of finding a worthy specimen, search for concretions that are already broken or have a crack propagating through them. WDNR, which manages the

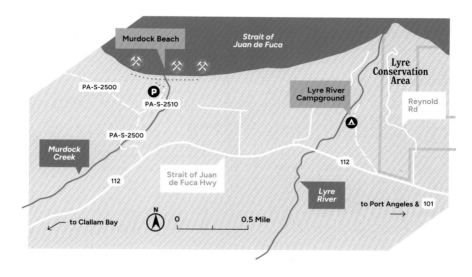

site, wants you to know that extracting a fossil from concretions takes patience. "Use a rock hammer and chisel to break the rock along the plane of weakness created by the [fossil or glendonite]. If this doesn't work, soak the concretion in a bucket of water for a few days to soften it before trying to break it open. Finally, use a smaller chisel to flake off the remaining rock," exposing its treasure.

There's an art to exposing fossils that goes beyond splitting concretions open. Serious enthusiasts and fossil preparators use diamond tools and precision sandblasters to artfully remove the calcified mud away from the specimen within. The process is done in a studio, often under a large magnifying glass, and takes days to complete. Fossil preparation seems to be a common hobby among retired dentists, if that gives you a sense of the intricacy of the craft. Members of the North America Research Group (NARG), a paleontologist hobby club in Oregon, are particularly famous for their preparation of fossil crabs. They artfully work around the diminutive 30-million-years-dead crustation, seemingly animating it back to life. Claws are artfully freed from stone, and the crab practically crawls out from its epic hibernation.

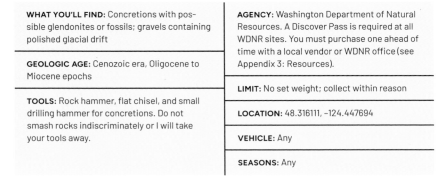

WHAT YOU'LL FIND: Concretions with possible glendonites or fossils; gravels containing polished glacial drift

GEOLOGIC AGE: Cenozoic era, Oligocene to Miocene epochs

TOOLS: Rock hammer, flat chisel, and small drilling hammer for concretions. Do not smash rocks indiscriminately or I will take your tools away.

AGENCY: Washington Department of Natural Resources. A Discover Pass is required at all WDNR sites. You must purchase one ahead of time with a local vendor or WDNR office (see Appendix 3: Resources).

LIMIT: No set weight; collect within reason

LOCATION: 48.316111, –124.447694

VEHICLE: Any

SEASONS: Any

DIRECTIONS → Make your way to the intersection of First Street and South Lincoln Street (US Highway 101) in Port Angeles, Washington. Take US 101 West for 5.5 miles. Turn right onto Strait of Juan de Fuca Highway (State Route 112 West) and drive for 16.2 miles. Turn right into an unmarked gravel road (PA-S-2500) and drive 0.3 mile. Turn right at the fork onto PA-S-2510 (also unmarked) and proceed downhill for 0.3 mile to the Murdock Beach trailhead. Park and walk the mellow trail approximately 500 feet to the beach.

AT THE SITE → Low tide is the right time to come to Murdock Beach. Colorful Olympic rocks and glacial till scatter the gravel bars of the high-tide line, and round concretions scatter the low-tide zone. The best way to find fossils and glendonites in concretions is to search for ones that are naturally broken or have an existing crack. Remember that most concretions are only mud balls with no treasure inside. If you do decide to break concretions open, gentle hits around the circumference of the stone should be enough to get it to crack neatly in half. Do not leave rejected shards strewn on the beach. Toss them into the waves to preserve the natural scene.

⑤ Shipwreck Point

Exposed on a narrow strip of shoreline on the northwestern coast of the Olympic Peninsula are remarkable and unusual rocks from the deep that were laid down some 30 million years ago. Here, marine sediments from the Makah Formation yield blocks of limestone that once precipitated around deep-sea vents where gases were escaping through faults in the ocean crust. Strange life-forms congregated

Searching for concretions at Shipwreck Point during low tide

A ghost of a glendonite emerges from a naturally broken concretion.

around these seeps, birthing a deep, watery ecosystem that survived without a single photon of light.

Today these uplifted rocks erode round concretions (balls) of calcified mud that once formed around the vents. Most are wonderfully spherical, some are oval, and others are like hot dogs. Shipwreck Point is a designated conservation area, so you can only look at these rocks, not keep them. Still, the geology here is so unusual that just a visit to look is worth it. If you find concretions that have naturally broken in half, most will reveal just more mud. But a few will reveal a prismatic rock inside, shaped like a diamond on a playing card. These are cross sections of glendonites, a fascinating and obscure thing from the deep.

Once upon a time, before these glendonites were encased in concretions, they were remarkable, elongate crystals of aragonite, a kind of calcium carbonate. They formed in beautiful clusters in proximity to vents of methane gas welling up from the ocean crust. Over time, calcium carbonate sediments within the muds congealed around the glendonites and preserved their shape as the original crystal itself dissolved. What caused their dissolution is a mystery, considering they are made of the same mineral that now encases them. In 1975, glendonite pioneer Sam Boggs Jr. examined several specimens from Washington and found that crumbly granular calcite, another variety of calcium carbonate, and fine bits of organic debris had filled in the voids left behind by the original glendonite crystals. He suggested that what we see in the concretions today are *ghosts of glendonites*, or pseudomorphs, minerals that replace and take the shape of their predecessor.

Intact glendonite crystals from a locality in Australia. The glendonite ghosts found at Shipwreck Point were once crystals like these. (Photo courtesy of The Arkenstone)

The geologic situation that would allow the growth of such crystals in deep-sea muds is not entirely clear, but it may be linked to the unusual chemistry of the marine rocks that encase them. Studies have shown that most of the sedimentary rocks at Shipwreck Point hail from deep water, up to 2000 feet. Hydrogen gas was escaping through deep faults in the crust, mixing with dissolved carbon, resulting in methane. A great deal of carbonate minerals precipitated around these ancient methane seeps, which influenced the chemistry of the rocks and seawater around them. This chemical oasis at-

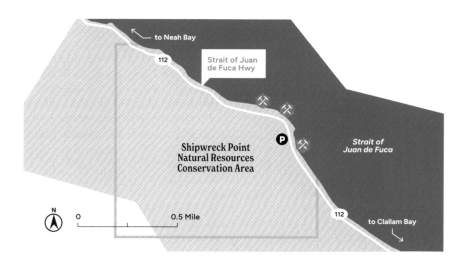

tracted only the freakiest sea life that could withstand the toxicity. Extremophile species of clams, snails, and tubeworms thrived near the seeps. Today their fossils are found in blocks of limestone on the beaches at Shipwreck Point among the strange concretions.

WHAT YOU'LL FIND: Concretions, some with glendonites; occasional fossil shells in limestone (for looking, not keeping)	**AGENCY:** Washington Department of Natural Resources. A Discover Pass is required at all WDNR sites. You must purchase one ahead of time at a local vendor or WDNR office (see Appendix 3: Resources).
GEOLOGIC AGE: Cenozoic era, Oligocene epoch	**LIMIT:** Removal of rocks not allowed
TOOLS: None. Do not break rocks in the conservation area.	**LOCATION:** 48.316111, –124.447694
	VEHICLE: Any
	SEASONS: Any

DIRECTIONS → Make your way to the intersection of Frontier Street and State Route 112 in Clallam Bay, Washington. Sunsets West Co-op Grocery will be on the corner. Drive west on SR 112 (Strait of Juan de Fuca Highway) for 10.4 miles to a pullout on the right at a small interpretive sign for Shipwreck Point. Park here. Walk a few yards onto the beach. You will see blocks of rock emerging from the tidal zone.

AT THE SITE → Time your arrival at Shipwreck Point for low tide. Round concretions nest among the blocks of old marine sedimentary rocks in the intertidal zone. Most concretions are just mud balls. The best way to find glendonites is to search for concretions that are already naturally broken. Time and luck are the key to success. If you find some, take a photo then leave them in place.

WASHINGTON
North Cascades and Okanogan Highlands

The jagged peaks and narrow river canyons of Washington's northern territory do little to simplify the geologic story of our region. Thanks to glacial sculpting, this rugged, snowcapped, and darkly forested terrain puts the complexity and chaos of the Pacific Northwest's history on full display. The advance and retreat of massive Pleistocene ice sheets carved away the earth here. In their wake, basements of volcanic arcs and exotic terranes—land from somewhere else—crop out among the Okanogan Highlands and North Cascades with their crystalline granites, sparkly schists, and wavy gneisses. Patches of old seafloor lie bare on mountaintops, and marine fossils tumble into forested creeks. In some places this old seafloor has even been altered into spidery serpentines, which yield elusive pockets of nephrite jade. Occasionally, remnants of younger volcanoes dot the bedrock, and plant and animal fossils can be found in their ashes. The ultimate place to find interesting rocks in this cold, rainy region is in its rivers and streams.

Opposite: Icy creeks drag a variety of rocks
down the slopes of the North Cascades.

⑥ Fossil Creek

In the creation story of Washington, a great deal of the land that sits here now was originally born somewhere else. Some was carried in from ancient oceans and forced up onto our continent in the process of accretion. Accretion glued island chains, oceanic crust, and seafloor sediments to the margins of North America, creating new land. Evidence of accretion is readily observable at Fossil Creek, high up in the glacial North Cascades. Ancient seafloor sediments tumble downstream in dark, murky blocks. Laid down in the Jurassic (during the reign of the dinosaurs) these seafloor sediments reflect a once quiet, offshore place. Over the millennia, this scrap of seafloor was squeezed and somewhat baked as it was tectonically forced from the ocean floor onto dry land, a process that took millions of years.

Geologists refer to this ancient chunk of seafloor as the Nooksack Formation. Cobbles of Nooksack Formation erode into Fossil Creek, which runs into the north fork of the namesake Nooksack River. Both the creek and its confluence with the river are excellent places to search for these ghostly fossils. Upon first glance, the ancient marine rocks look dark and unremarkable. It takes some perseverance,

Dark blocks of Nooksack Formation rocks tumble down Fossil Creek at Site A.

Fossil bivalves in Nooksack Formation rock

but once you spot a fossil or two, you will start seeing them everywhere. Some rocks are filled with fragile bivalve shells from a lineage of ancestral clams. Their shells make fine graceful arcs in the rocks. Other chunks hold torpedo-shaped belemnites, the bodies of diminutive Mesozoic squids. Many of the fossils themselves have recrystallized into a coarse white marble (baked calcium carbonate). Others have completely eroded away, leaving only a trace fossil in their wake. The strange holes and tubes found in the rocks here are molds of these long-gone creatures.

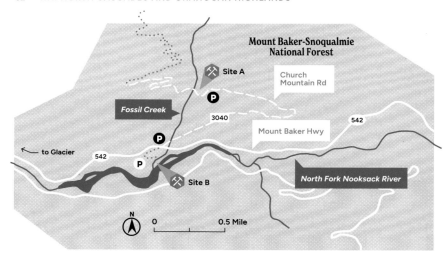

To get acclimated to how these fossils appear in the host rock, start at Site A. This is where the Nooksack Formation crops out. Visit the gravel bars of the North Fork of the Nooksack River below (Site B) to continue your search. The Nooksack River is a battlefield of basement rocks like granite and gneiss from upstream, diluting the presence of fossiliferous rocks. Still, plenty of Nooksack Formation material tumbles out of Fossil Creek to make the search worth it.

WHAT YOU'LL FIND: Jurassic bivalve and belemnite fossils	**LIMIT:** 10 pounds of rock and fossil material per person, per day
GEOLOGIC AGE: Mesozoic era, Jurassic period	**LOCATIONS:** **Site A, Fossil Creek:** 48.911755, –121.847638 **Site B, North Fork Nooksack River:** 48.903950, –121.860081
TOOLS: Geology pick; wellies, water shoes, or waders; a hiking pole for balance	
	VEHICLE: Any
AGENCY: US Forest Service Mount Baker–Snoqualmie National Forest. A Northwest Forest Pass is required (see Appendix 3: Resources).	**SEASONS:** Summer and fall. Warning: Avoid the river in winter and spring. High runoff poses a danger to you, and you pose a danger to spring-spawning fish.

Opposite: Fossiliferous rocks of Fossil Creek mix with an ocean of granite and gneiss at Site B.

DIRECTIONS → **Site A, Fossil Creek:** Make your way to the US Forest Service's Glacier Public Service Center at 10091 Mount Baker Highway (State Route 542), Glacier, Washington. From the Glacier Public Service Center drive east on SR 542 for 5.2 miles to Church Mountain Road (Forest Road 3040). Turn left onto Church Mountain Road and drive 2.3 miles to where Fossil Creek goes over the road on a concrete slab. There is safe parking on the left side of the road a few yards from the creek.

Site B, North Fork Nooksack River: From Site A, head back down Church Mountain Road for 2.3 miles to its intersection with SR 542. The Nooksack River runs along the south side of the highway, and there is a pull-off across from Church Mountain Road where cars can park. Park here and use the established footpath from the parking area, which leads along the top of the steep riverbank and eventually down to the Nooksack River's gravel bars. If this parking area is occupied, you can turn west onto SR 542 and drive a few hundred feet to another pull-off on the south side of the highway. Your goal is to get to gravel bars that are downstream but still close to the confluence of Fossil Creek and the Nooksack River.

AT THE SITE → **Site A, Fossil Creek:** On first inspection, the rock material will not look obviously fossiliferous. Metamorphic pressure has destroyed the most obvious evidence, but on closer inspection, you will start to notice lumps and voids in the rock. Some chunks do contain visible shells of *Buchia crassicola*, a bivalve, and others contain long torpedo-shaped belemnites. A geology pick can be useful for breaking material apart, and you will see evidence of previous visitors working the stone.

Some fossils have gone entirely missing, leaving beautifully preserved holes in the Jurassic rocks.

Site B, North Fork Nooksack River: Fossil Creek dumps into the Nooksack. Here, fossiliferous material mixes with the granite and gneiss that dominate the river's gravel bars. Many fossiliferous specimens can be found on these gravel bars, which are broad. And many of the fossil rocks contain trace fossils, or voids where the fossil has eroded away. The Nooksack is a dynamic system draining a steep and glacial mountain range. Take great care navigating the piles of loose cobbles along the gravel bars.

Searching through the cobbles on the North Fork of the Nooksack River

⑦ Martin's Bar

As we walked along the shady trail to a secluded gravel bar on the upper reaches of the Nooksack River, my friend Martin Holden, a once-upon-a-time geologist, told me of the Japanese tradition of *suiseki*, in which a rock, unchanged by human hands, is displayed on a simple pedestal and appreciated for its intrigue. He felt this particular gravel bar was a good place to find rocks for suiseki because of their size and beauty. As we emerged from the forest, we found ourselves in a river of basement rocks—granite, gneiss, and schist—that had been forced from deep in the crust to the peaks of the North Cascades. For lapidary artists like myself, these materials are particularly difficult to work with. Most of us would scoff at the notion of collecting rocks like granite and gneiss. But here we were.

Martin held up a large cobble—wavy, dark, and sparkling. "These rocks have been through a lot of trauma. First at the beginning of their lives, and then again a lot later." He was referring to a deep magma chamber where this rock was born and the eventual chaos it endured as Earth shifted her tectonic coat around. Gneisses are the most deformed rocks on Earth, undergoing intense heat and pressure. Martin said that the trauma they endured was "necessary in order to gain the wisdom these rocks needed to live." This animism—the attribution of a life to a rock—was Martin's way of seeing Earth through an otherwise unknowable expanse of time.

Researchers have been able to deduce that the basement rocks that tumble into the Nooksack River melted and deformed sometime in the last 40 million years.

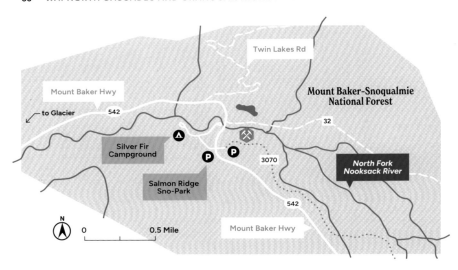

The parent rocks from which they melted and cooled were born as many as 200 million years before that, hundreds of miles south along a proto-Pacific coast. Over the millennia they ended up here, high in the North Cascades. It's an astonishing story that has been pieced together through laboratory investigation of hardy crystals like zircon, element isotopes, and magnetic minerals. The journey undertaken by the ancestors of these river rocks may never fully be known, since melting and recrystallizing is a form of erasure and rebirth. For geologic minds like Martin's, the practice of suiseki opens a portal to the reincarnation of rocks. The rock rests on its altar, a placeholder for the unknowable.

WHAT YOU'LL FIND: Granite, gneiss, and schist	**LIMIT:** 10 pounds of rock and fossil material per person, per day
GEOLOGIC AGE: Cenozoic era, Paleogene period	**LOCATION:** 48.904947, –121.692876
	VEHICLE: Any
TOOLS: Wellies, waders, or water shoes; a hiking pole for balance	**SEASONS:** Summer and fall. Warning: Avoid the river in winter and spring. High runoff poses a danger to you, and you pose a danger to spring-spawning fish.
AGENCY: US Forest Service Mount Baker–Snoqualmie National Forest. A Northwest Forest Pass is required (see Appendix 3: Resources).	

Ancient granite, schist, and gneiss sparkle in the sun.

DIRECTIONS → Make your way to the US Forest Service's Glacier Public Service Center at 10091 Mount Baker Highway (State Route 542) in Glacier, Washington. From the Glacier Public Service Center, drive east on the SR 542 for 13.1 miles to Forest Road 3070 on the left. This is the entrance to the Salmon Ridge Sno-Park and will present itself as a massive parking lot rather than a road. Drive across the large lot and park at the information kiosk. The trail to the North Fork of the Nooksack River begins here. Walk northeast on this established trail for 600 feet to a large gravel bar on the edge of the river.

AT THE SITE → This gravel bar is characterized by large cobbles of basement rocks. Speckled granites, streaked gneisses, and wavy schists dominate the gravel bar. Remember that the Forest Service collecting limit is 10 pounds. If you are here to build your suiseki collection, you may max out at two or three cobbles.

Viewing Stones: Scholar's Rocks and Suiseki

by Martin Holden

MAYBE YOU'VE HAD the experience of finding an interesting stone on one of your adventures, one that "spoke" to you for some reason. Maybe you brought it home and placed on a table or a windowsill, where you could admire it from time to time. If so, you have rediscovered the ancient tradition of collecting "viewing stones," known since ancient times in China as gongshi, and in Japan as suiseki.

Scholar's Rocks

People have collected interesting stones since the beginning of time, of course. But it was during The T'ang Dynasty in China (618–907 CE) that stone appreciation really took off. It was a relatively stable and prosperous time, during which a rich court life developed, full of music, poetry, and art. T'ang scholars found much inspiration in nature, including the stones called gongshi, also known as "scholar's rocks" or "viewing stones." The most desirable of these were the limestone *lingbi* and *taihu* stones, wildly twisted and pitted with holes. Their forms recall the romantically rugged landscape of South China, so often depicted in classical Chinese paintings. This "karst" landscape is characterized by fantastically tall pillars of limestone, deeply eroded crevasses, and caves. Gongshi are smaller products of the same processes.

Traditionally, large gongshi might be placed in a formal garden, and smaller ones used to create miniature landscape compositions with plants (an art form known as *penjing*). The best stones were given fitted wooden bases, often elaborately carved. Collectors rated stones according to strict criteria, such as openness, texture, perforations, asymmetry, and even resonance (when struck like a gong). In addition to the classic limestone gongshi, "stones" of different kinds often made an appearance in a scholar's study, including twisted root burls, shipworm-eaten driftwood, coral, and so on. Some were actually manufactured, using ceramic, bronze, or even paste-glass.

Placed in a scholar's study or family courtyard, these stones became objects of quiet contemplation. Artists painted portraits of the more remarkable stones, and poets wrote verses about them. Many be-

A rock sheds its ordinariness when it becomes a viewing stone

came quite famous and were passed down through the generations. The appreciation of scholar's rocks has waxed and waned in China over the centuries, subject to historical disruptions (such as the Proletarian Cultural Revolution of the 1960s). However, there has been a resurgence of interest in recent years, both in China and around the world.

Suiseki

The art of suiseki is essentially a Japanese reinterpretation of the Chinese gongshi, introduced to Japan by emissaries from the Chinese Imperial court. Initially, it was the penjing (miniature landscapes) that were most popular in Japan, dovetailing nicely with ancient animist traditions celebrating the spiritual aspects of nature. By the Kamakura period (1183–1333 CE), a new appreciation of singular stones was developing, influenced by Zen Buddhism. Zen thought centered simplicity of expression, and an acknowledgment of the transience of things, giving rise to the aesthetic ideas of wabi (subdued, austere beauty) and sabi (rustic patina), among others.

The complex limestone forms favored by Chinese scholars are rare in Japan, partly due to these aesthetic concepts, and partly to the different geology of the islands. Suiseki tend to be simpler and more equidimensional than scholar's rocks, collected from eroding mountain slopes, riverbeds, and the seashore. The definition of what constitutes a proper suiseki has varied over the centuries, but the trend seems to be toward including more and different forms. This inclusiveness has helped the art form gain popularity around the world. We find the following five categories of suiseki (developed by contemporary scholar Morimae Seiji) to be useful.

Sansuiseki (landscape stones) are the stones that most people think of when they think of suiseki. Their forms suggest mountains, plateaus, waterfalls, islands, and rugged coastlines; there are as many kinds of sansuiseki as there are natural landforms. Some are quite intimate, such as a pool in a mountain stream. Others suggest a more remote perspective, such as a mountain range viewed from a great distance. Sansuiseki are the most popular form of suiseki, both in Japan and worldwide.

Sugataishi (figure stones; also keishoseki, object stones) are also very popular. Their forms may suggest (sometimes very subtly) the shape of a human, an animal, a boat, a house—anything, really. This is the most playful form of suiseki. Fun fact: the many American rockhounds who collect food-shaped rocks are also collecting sugataishi! The Chichibu Chinsekikan (Hall of Curious Rocks) in Chichibu, outside Tokyo, houses the worlds largest collection of jinmen-seki, stones that look like human faces. A visit will confirm that nature has randomly created stone versions of both Elvis Presley and Edvard Munch's The Scream.

Monyoseki (patterned stones) don't necessarily have figural forms but rather display surface patterns suggestive of natural phenomena, such as flowers, grasses, or trees; rain, lightning, or snow; the stars, the moon, and so on. These textures may be caused by crystalline inclusions, veins, or even fossils.

Biseki (beautiful stones) represent a surprising departure from the quiet calm of the wabi-sabi aesthetic. Biseki may display multiple, contrasting colors and are often polished to better reveal their bling. Sometimes a natural mineral specimen, such as a crystal cluster, will be mounted as a biseki.

Our favorite form of suiseki are the *chusho-yoseki* (abstract stones). It might seem like cheating to designate as a suiseki a stone that doesn't look like anything in particular! Yet these viewing stones can be some of the most powerful of all. Since they don't reference a specific form, they affect us on a deeper level, asking us to pause and consider their meaning. Chusho-yoseki return to the original idea of the scholar's rock: a mysterious object for quiet contemplation. A perfectly spherical stone might fall into this category, for example.

In some quarters, modifying a suiseki is frowned upon. It is thought to be disrespectful to the *kami*, or spirit of the rock. Others feel that stone appreciation is more of an art form than a spiritual practice, and that a little tweaking is fine. Usually, this just means trimming the base of the stone so that it sits properly, but sometimes, it means carving an entire stone from scratch. Traditionalists also hold that suiseki benefit from being handled, and especially from being passed down through the generations. An old suiseki is best!

To show off your stone to the best advantage, it helps to place it on a pedestal, which in this case is called a *dai*. A dai can be as simple as a block of wood. However, most collectors prefer a *daiza*, a custom base carved to fit the irregularities of the individual stone. Sometimes, stones are set in a ceramic (*suiban*) or bronze (*doban*) tray or bowl, where they "float" in either water or sand. Any of these may then be placed on a *shoku*, a small wooden table made especially for such displays. In the traditional Japanese home, suiseki and other special objects of artistic merit might be displayed in the *tokonoma* (or *toko*) a recessed alcove made expressly for this purpose.

In our opinion, the best place to look for suiseki is close to the source, but also far enough away. In the mountains, look in the riverbed just downstream. On the coast, look on the rocky beach below a rugged headland. The stones there will retain some character, but weathering will have smoothed away the rough edges. Let nature do some of the work for you!

Viewing stones are not just quaint miniatures. They can be seen as an example of the fractal symmetry of nature itself. The mountain and the stone scale from large to small, and back again, all the while retaining their basic geometry. The deep perforations of a scholar's rock reiterate the caves in the limestone hills. Suiseki capture the essence of the landscape where they were found. You might collect a beautiful, weathered slab of basalt from the base of a plateau in the desert. At home, placed in a tray of sand, the stone once again becomes the mountain—if the light is just right. All you have to do is squint a little.

Rocks from the rivers of the North Cascades artfully arranged by Suiseki enthusiast Martin Holden

⑧ Rainbow Creek

Rainbow Creek might as well be the drain of time. Though it coalesces along the flanks of a large volcano, it drags much more than lava rock down its path. The volcano, known as Mount Baker, is the youngest in a series of volcanoes that have erupted here over the past 1 million years. Each time Mount Baker erupts, it surrounds itself with its detritus, building itself up into a cone. Because it is a young volcanic system, a lot of the ancient crust it pokes up through is not yet buried under lava.

The bedrock that Mount Baker has invaded is composed of Permian seafloor—volcanic basalt—dating back almost 300 million years. Over eons of tectonic action, this old seafloor ended up here as an accreted terrane, and much of its basalt has been metamorphosed into a beautiful greenstone, which is streaked with white mineral veins of calcite, quartz, and pockets of translucent agate. Some of it has streaks of chartreuse-colored epidote, a mineral associated with hydrothermal alteration. Geologists refer to these old Permian rocks as the Chilliwack Formation,

Dark-teal greenstone, with beautiful white mineralized veins running through it

and Mount Baker pokes through it like a chimney. Among the Chilliwack lies patches of younger seafloor sediments known as the Nooksack Formation. These rocks date back to the Jurassic, around 140 million years in the past. They ended up on the continent through the process of accretion as well. It's possible you may find some of its almost-black fossiliferous rocks in Rainbow Creek, but the Permian greenstone and fresh andesite lava from Mount Baker (an unremarkable gray material) dominate the creek bed.

It's important to note the incredible unconformities, or chunks of missing time, between the three rock formations that crop out along Mount Baker: the Chilliwack rocks of the Permian that are 300 million years old, the Nooksack Rocks of the Jurassic that are 140 million years old, and the Mount Baker lavas of the present-day. Between each of these formations, Earth experienced incredible evolutions and devastating extinctions. In each of these eras, the arrangement of the continents would be unrecognizable from one another. The flora and fauna that dominated the land and sea would look entirely alien, if compared with each great age, as if they were from different planets. But they are all from the same place, just from very different times. Much like the rocks themselves, Earth births, pressures, and destroys its creatures, only to start the process of creation all over again.

WHAT YOU'LL FIND: Greenstone and agate; perhaps some epidote, fossiliferous shale, and andesite lava	**LIMIT:** Up to 10 pounds of rock and fossil material per person, per day
GEOLOGIC AGE: Paleozoic through Cenozoic eras	**LOCATION:** 48.767321, –121.664016
	VEHICLE: High clearance recommended
TOOLS: Wellies, waders, or water shoes; a hiking pole for balance	**SEASONS:** Summer and fall. Warning: Avoid the river in winter and spring. High runoff poses a danger to you, and you pose a danger to spring-spawning fish.
AGENCY: US Forest Service, Mount Baker–Snoqualmie National Forest. A Northwest Forest Pass is required (see Appendix 3: Resources).	

DIRECTIONS → Make your way to the intersection of North Superior Avenue and the North Cascades Highway (State Route 20) in Concrete, Washington. At this intersection stands the town landmark, shuttered cement silos that rise like a monolith from the landscape. At the silos, head north on North Superior Avenue for 0.3 mile where it comes to a T-junction with Burpee Hill Road. Turn left (west) on Burpee Hill Road and drive 3.9 miles to its intersection with Baker Lake Road. Turn right (north) onto Baker

Opposite: Misty Rainbow Creek on a drizzly summer's day. A steep ridge on the flank of Mount Baker rises in the background.

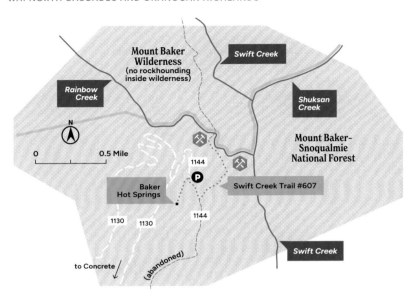

Lake Road and drive 11.6 miles. (You'll cross a bridge shortly before your next turn.) At 11.6 miles turn left onto Forest Road 1130. This dirt road features treacherously deep potholes the remainder of the way. Follow FR 1130 for 3.9 miles to a fork. At the fork turn right onto FR 1144 and drive 0.5 mile to its end. The lot where FR 1144 terminates is the trailhead for Rainbow Creek, Swift Creek, and Baker Hot Springs (it's warm, not hot). The short trail for Baker Hot Springs meanders southwest from the parking lot for 0.2 mile. The trail for Rainbow Creek and Swift Creek heads due south on an overgrown road from the parking lot. Follow the old road on foot for 0.3 mile. You will come to a trail sign for Swift Creek Trail #607. Turn left here and hike 0.5 mile downhill to Rainbow Creek. Bush-whack a few paces through forest to get out to the water. This spot is about a thousand feet upstream from the convergence with Swift Creek.

AT THE SITE → Rainbow Creek is an impressive drainage on the flanks of Mount Baker. It is also the boundary line for the Mount Baker Wilderness. No rock collecting is allowed on land above the waterline on the opposite side of the creek. Take great care navigating this waterway, as its rocks are loose and jumbled. I highly recommend bringing a hiking pole along to keep your balance. Stay above the rushing waters and explore the extensive gravel bars for interesting greenstones, epidotes, and small agates.

9 Cascade River

The Cascade River drains dense, crystalline rocks from the peaks and slopes of the glacially sculpted North Cascades. These rocks were once the basement of early Washington—crumbling granite, squeezed schist, and wavy gneiss. The squeezed and baked rocks of old terranes such as marble, quartzite, and serpentinite show up in the river too. It takes a trained eye to discern these from the dominant granite and gneiss of the gravels.

Two stories unfold in the stones of the Cascade River: one of an accreted terrane and the other of a very hot melting episode that helped stitch the terrane to the continent. The terrane is known to geologists as the Chelan Mountains terrane, and its origins were most likely that of an island arc, far out to sea. Imagine something like Japan, with its steep volcanoes and elegant coastline. The Chelan terrane islands were probably beautiful in the Permian and Triassic, and now their remnants are buried here as quartzites, schists, and marbles, high in the North Cascades. It's amazing how swiftly Earth's surface rearranges itself, eats itself, renews itself.

Pebbles and cobbles of igneous and metamorphic rocks line the riverbed.

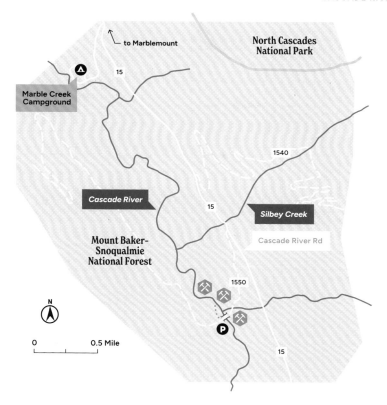

In the rock cycle, there's a difference between baking and melting. Many of the accreted terranes were compressed and cooked by the friction of colliding with our continent. Accretion isn't just the phenomenon of getting glued to the land, though. It's a side effect of the larger action at play. It happens as a whole conveyor belt of ocean crust dives beneath the continent. The accreted rocks are a jumble of oceanic sediments and crust that get caught up with the continent as they make the plunge underneath. Some material detaches at the surface (it *delaminates*) and others get forced down into the subduction trench. These trench rocks undergo some heat and even more pressure, which permanently alters them. At the boundary between the original rocks of the continent and the accreted terrane rocks, bodies of magma can invade from the mantle. In general, bodies of magma that invade the crust and cool are known as plutons, and if they invade the fault

Opposite: A misty autumn day on the serene Cascade River

between a terrane and another rock body, they're known as stitching plutons. As the invading magma solidifies, it forms a rock called granite or her sisters: granodiorite, tonalite, and diorite, to name a few. Over time, these deep plutons warp under intense pressure, resulting in the beautiful gneiss found in the riverbed. The rocks on this stretch of the Cascade River reveal the heart of a collision between a lonesome island chain and a continent that took it forever in its arms. The continent is only now beginning to release it through the slow tumble of erosion down rivers and back out to sea.

WHAT YOU'LL FIND: Granite-like rocks, gneiss, schist, quartzite, marble, serpentinite	**LIMIT:** 10 pounds of rock and fossil material per person, per day
GEOLOGIC AGE: Paleozoic to Mesozoic eras	**LOCATION:** 48.501179, −121.250316
TOOLS: Wellies, waders, or water shoes; a hiking pole for balance	**VEHICLE:** Some clearance recommended
AGENCY: US Forest Service, Mount Baker–Snoqualmie National Forest. A Northwest Forest Pass is required (see Appendix 3: Resources).	**SEASONS:** Summer and fall. Warning: Avoid the river in winter and spring. High runoff poses a danger to you, and you pose a danger to spring-spawning fish.

DIRECTIONS → Make your way to the intersection of North Cascades Highway (State Route 20) and Cascade River Road in the small town of Marblemount, Washington. Turn east onto Cascade River Road (Forest Road 15), which crosses over the Skagit River. Drive for 10.2 miles. Turn right onto FR 1550, a narrow, single-lane, dirt road that dips down into the woods, and drive for 0.8 mile, crossing over a one-lane bridge. Pull over and park after crossing the bridge and follow a well-worn footpath a few dozen yards to the gravel bar next to the bridge.

AT THE SITE → The Cascade River is swift but shallow. Bring good water shoes or waders so you can make your way from gravel bar to gravel bar. Granite-like rocks, gneiss, and schist dominate the riverbed, but occasionally interesting metamorphic rocks like quartzite, marble, and serpentinite can also be found. Avoid the river during heavy rainfall and spring runoff.

Finding Stones for Sculpture

by Carl Nelson, past president of the Northwest Stone Sculptors Association

EACH SPRING, snow melting off the Cascade Mountains brings down a delightful assortment of rounded and fractured stones and cobbles that only nature can prepare for the coming months of the various rivers' ongoing garage sale. As the meltwaters recede and expose the year's offerings, my fellow stone carvers and I trek to our favorite rivers in the foothills of the mountains to look for carvable stones such as peridotite, serpentine, granite, jade, and whatever else may have washed down from the Cascades' complex geology to inspire our sculptures.

There is much to be said for stones like granite and jade, but one of my favorite stones to find in the rivers is peridotite composed of the mineral olivine. Cobbles of this rock are tan on the outside and a beautiful variety of greens on the inside. When sculpted down to a delicate thinness and highly polished, the material can become translucent. These olivine-rich rocks are more commonly known as dunite because their exterior, or rind, is always oxidized, resulting in an orange-tan dun color. These dun-rinded cobbles are what sculptors like myself look for along the rivers in the North Cascades. However, they don't appear just anywhere, so we seek out sections of river where glaciers and snowmelt are eroding material from known geological deposits of peridotite rocks.

There are so many inspiringly shaped stones along the rivers that it is easy to feel greedy and want to take them all home. Restraint is advised. Have the wisdom to know that there are more stones making their way down the river for you to discover, and remember that you have only so much time to carve before they arrive. Furthermore, the rivers of the Cascades are important salmon habitat. Stones should be taken from above the waterline and not from the river channel itself until spawning season is over. Consult the Washington State "Gold and Fish" pamphlet for information regarding salmon seasonality (see Appendix 3: Resources). The rules set by federal and state agencies to not disturb salmon habitat are real and important.

When looking for stones, I sometimes see a small cobble with an interesting shape, and it will speak to me that it's a bowl or a platter, and the tan rind of the stone will become the dish's rim. Other times I might see the head of a critter like a rabbit. Or perhaps I am thinking of carving something for someone special going through chemo and in the stone I find the form of a frog. Sometimes I find a pleasing-shaped stone that speaks to me, but I don't yet see its shape within, so I take it home and wait to see what it will eventually become.

Dunite is not a stone to be directly shaped with a hammer and chisel. It is a hard stone (5 to 7 on the Mohs scale), dense and heavy, with a variety of crystal sizes and a propensity to split along a hexagonal fracture pattern.

It is a stone that works best with what we affectionately call spinning diamond tools. These are angle grinders, die grinders, and rotary tools that have diamond blades, diamond burrs, and diamond cup wheels to shape and form. After all the grinding, sculptors use diamond pads and diamond paste to bring the final shine out of the stone. These tools come from the granite countertop and lapidary worlds and do a very nice job sculpting olivine-rich rocks like dunite. I learned to use these tools at the Northwest Stone Sculptors Association annual symposiums. These events are the best places to meet other stone sculptors and learn to carve stone (see Appendix 3: Resources).

For me the most joyful discovery about dunite has been its translucency. If you have the patience to create a surface that is one-eighth inch (or less) thick, the light will come through, revealing the stone's matrix and small olivine crystals. To be successful in creating a thin sculpture, you will need a stone that has enough integrity to hold together as you are working to thin it. One of the nice qualities about cobbles specifically

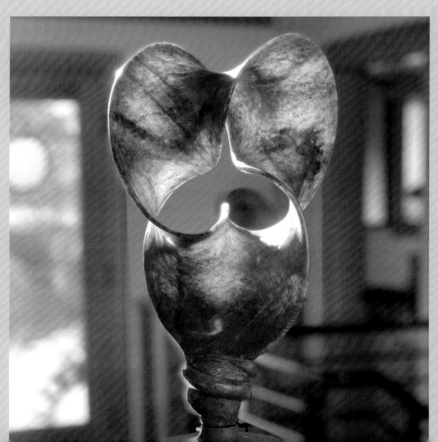

is that to survive the bumping and tumbling of the river, the rock has to have integrity. When I found a particular cobble with no cracks or fractures, which became *Unity—Woven As One* (pictured), I was pretty confident that I had the right stone. The other key to success for a thin-surface sculpture is to have a curving form and avoid long flat surfaces. I developed a möbius form for the *Unity* piece to represent the interweaving of the elements a community needs to provide its members to flourish: basic human needs, the foundations of well-being, and opportunity.

Making the stone thin reveals the variation and nature of the specific piece of stone. Dunite from a quarry or an outcropping may have much more variation, and its nature has to be respected, carefully considered, and worked around. This material has not yet been tested for durability by glacial sculpting and the tumbling of the rivers. Glacial deposits left by advancing and retreating glaciers underlie the abundance of rounded river rocks. The rivers are a convenient and ever-changing place to find durable rocks, but there are other excellent places where people's activities have revealed them. Although not as glamorous, a visit to an old gravel pit or a working mine (always with permission) can be a treasure hunt with inspiring finds.

In Washington State, the Northwest Stone Sculptors Association has a long-standing relationship with a dunite quarry and has been able to arrange a guided trip once a year for its members to collect rocks for sculpting. On one visit, while scrambling up a hillside, I found an interestingly shaped 100-plus-pound boulder of dunite that had an orange rind and a band of large olivine crystals woven through its midsection. I could only guess what I would find inside and around the band of crystals. After some help from fellow stone carvers to get it off the hillside and lug it home, I was not disappointed. After many hours of grinding and meticulous work to thin it, the pattern revealed what looked like a kelp forest of dark and light greens beneath the orange rind.

The forests of the Pacific Northwest help set the stage for the awe you can experience when foraging along the rivers for stones. The sound of the birds, the water in eddies and riffles as you walk along the banks, the endless variations—size, color, and revealed geology of the stones, especially when there's a light mist and the rocks go from faint pastel grays to colorful reminders of their potential. In this environment, it is easy to have a rock catch your eye and pull you toward it.

The intuition of a connection to a stone can be difficult to describe, especially why you choose it, how you might eventually carve it, or why it seems to choose you to find the form within. That moment in time, that choice, is the sum of all your past experiences and your hopes coming together in an encounter, which can be inspirational and awesome. It changes what you do with your time, energy, and these few breaths you have been granted in this life. Seeking stones is a path worth following for many reasons. When taking the time to listen quietly—carefully—and reflect, much can be found within.

Opposite: *Unity—Woven As One* by Carl Nelson

A misty day in early summer on the Sauk River

⑩ Sauk River

This is a strategic location for rockhounds to search for an unusual family of rocks: the serpentines. On this stretch of the Sauk, Clear Creek—a small tributary—dumps its load of serpentinized rocks into the river. Serpentinization occurs in the abyssal places where new crust is born: deep ocean rifts. In these places, dark, dense minerals are released from Earth's mantle to birth new crust. Interaction with seawater is inevitable, and it invades the new rock, stewing and expanding it. The original minerals crystallized in the mantle (mostly olivine and pyroxene) are transformed into soft, glossy serpentinite. The process of serpentinization also occurs during subduction when soaked ocean crust is forced under a continent and burped back up again (still solid, never melted).

Serpentinites themselves can also undergo further alteration, especially when tectonically shoved up against other types of rock bodies as they are forced onto the continent. A wide variety of interesting minerals forms on the margins of these contact zones and, in the right circumstances, jade and jade-like minerals appear:

nephrite jade, hydrogrossular garnet, diopside, idocrase, and a rock called rodingite (a mixture of everything), to name a few. Each of these can form hard, dense specimens with beautiful green translucence that can range from light to dark. At this location, nephrite jade and her sisters crop out along the contact between a serpentine body and old, baked seafloor sediments that were long-ago metamorphosed into phyllite—a dark, shiny, and flakey mineral similar to schist. Outcrops of phyllite can be easily observed where Clear Creek drops into the Sauk River, and plenty of it can be found in the gravel bars.

Of the serpentine family of rocks, serpentinite is the easiest to find in the river. It yields dark, gemmy, green-to-black cobbles with spiderwebs of white veins running through them. Relatively soft, serpentinite is an easy material for lapidary work and sculpture. However, precautions must be taken: the rock's white spider webbing can contain the fibrous mineral chrysotile, a form of asbestos. In nature,

A webbed cobble of rodingite

serpentinites are safe to look at and touch, but taking them home and creating airborne dust from them is hazardous. Hard-rock mining in serpentine deposits is equally hazardous. If you find serpentinite, don't smash it. Instead, scratch the surface with a pocket knife to test for its telltale softness.

In the river, nephrite jade and her hardy sisters are far less abundant. The jade is the singular prize for most collectors, and the presence of mining claims up Clear Creek is a good sign for rockhounds in the gravel bars below. Unless it is bright green, know that nephrite jade can be extremely difficult to distinguish from her sister minerals. Often microscopic analysis is required. "Experience is the best tool for identifying jade," writes Lanny Ream in his book *Nephrite Jade of Washington and Associated Gem Rocks*. Ream recommends making a concerted effort to research images of Washington jade samples and handling them if you have access. "The best way to find jade and identify it in the streams is to go jade hunting and get experience finding it."

WHAT YOU'LL FIND: Serpentinite, phyllite, and possibly nephrite jade and jade-like rocks; basement rocks like gneiss and schist are common in the gravel	**LIMIT:** 10 pounds of rock material per person, per day
	LOCATION: 48.220840, –121.570344
GEOLOGIC AGE: Paleozoic to Mesozoic eras	**VEHICLE:** Any
TOOLS: Wellies, water shoes, or waders; a hiking pole for balance	**SEASONS:** Summer and fall. Warning: Avoid the river in winter and spring. High runoff poses a danger to you, and you pose a danger to spring-spawning fish.
AGENCY: US Forest Service, Mount Baker–Snoqualmie National Forest. A Northwest Forest Pass is required (see Appendix 3: Resources). An additional camping fee may be required at Clear Creek Campground.	

DIRECTIONS → Make your way to the town of Darrington, Washington. In the center of town, at the intersection of State Route 530 and the Mountain Loop Highway (Forest Road 20), head south on the Mountain Loop Highway for 3 miles to the entrance of the Clear Creek Campground. Park here and make your way to the river that runs alongside the camp. If the Clear Creek Campground is full, or access is closed for the season, drive for another 0.2 mile and park at the pullout just before the Clear Creek Bridge and hike down to the water. There is additional river access another 0.4 mile down the road at the Sauk River trailhead. Park there and follow the Sauk River Trail about 500 feet out to the gravel bars.

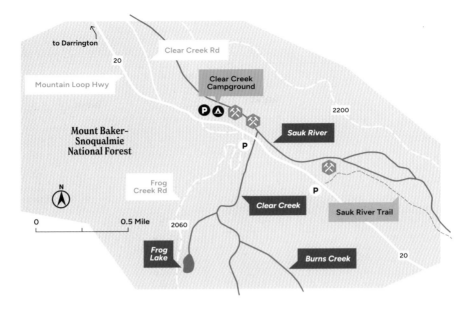

AT THE SITE → Gravels of the Sauk River are best exposed during summer and early fall. They are composed dominantly of basement rocks traveling from farther up the river corridor. In your search for serpentine rocks, you'll encounter a great deal of gneiss, schist, phyllite, some granite-like rocks, and some baked sedimentary rocks that look unremarkable. The serpentine rocks stand out as a dark-green rock with a spidery web of lighter veins running throughout. A knife blade will scratch it because of its softness. Nephrite jade and her sisters are very hard, unscratchable stones and tend to have a rind that is either white, brown, or almost black.

⑪ Stillaguamish River

The misty and serene Stillaguamish River drains high mountains of ancient marine sediments that have been compressed and baked into a beautiful array of stones: sandstone into quartzite, mudstone into argillite, plankton blooms into chert: all metasedimentary rocks. The story of sediments is a story of entropy over time. It's the story of epic mountains crumbling, sending their remnants down rivers, onto beaches, and eventually into the quiet of the deep sea. Generations

The Red Bridge spans the serene Stillaguamish River.

of plankton bloom in the stormy oceans and die off. Their remains sink to the seafloor, joining the ranks of memories recorded in the deep. Over the millennia, the stuff that piles up on the quiet seafloor may be forced up into mountains once again, eventually fated to erode their way back toward the sea.

In the Stillaguamish River, cobbles of metasediments composed of once-simple sediments are grinding their way down to their original form in a circular journey. The late poet Pablo Neruda wrote an entire volume of poetry reflecting on the cyclical life of rocks. He posited everything, even the living, even us, all eventually arrive at stone. Becoming a rock is inevitable for all of us. Though we may be freed from it for a moment, as a living being, or as a liberated sediment, stone is our shared destiny. In the Stillaguamish River, we watch as these metasediments are freed from their stone bodies into chunky cobbles, finer gravels, specs of sand, and infinitesimal clay. But eventually they will all harden back into stone, someday, somewhere, somehow.

This is the joy of rockhounding: to intercept a stone mid-journey. To commune with its present and try to understand its past. Because stones don't speak (they are the "mute word of Earth," says Neruda), geologists must deduce information about their history by observing their finer parts. In sedimentary rocks, these fine parts are clasts: grains of sand, fragments of clay. Geologists have been able to surmise that the metasediments in the mountains above the Stillaguamish were laid down in a proto-Pacific Ocean, during the Jurassic and Cretaceous—the reign of the dinosaurs. It wasn't until the dawn of the age of mammals that these marine sediments had become mountains.

The quartzites here are made of ancient sand grains—fossil beaches—compressed into a hard, shiny, translucent stone. The argillite, beautifully banded in green and ecru (pictured), is composed of fine layers of deep marine clays. Jasper-like rocks found in the river here are cherts, the remnants of ancient radiolarians. Radiolarians are tiny zooplankton that build ornate shells of silica. As their populations bloom and die off, the microscopic silica shells sink to the seafloor, coating it in a radiolarian ooze. Over time these radiolarian layers harden into chert as they become interbedded with the mudstone of the seafloor. Each of these rocks tells a story of long-gone mountains eroding away, of oceanic floras and faunas blooming and disappearing. Neruda would say that these stones were here before the wind, man, or dawn. That their first movement was the first music of the river.

With some hunting, beautifully banded and nicely silicified mudstones can be found here.

WHAT YOU'LL FIND: Quartzite, chert, argillite, breccia, greenstone, granite, schist, gneiss	**LIMIT:** 10 pounds of rock and fossil material per person, per day
GEOLOGIC AGE: Paleozoic to Mesozoic eras	**LOCATION:** 48.070445, –121.654493
TOOLS: Wellies, water shoes, or waders; a hiking pole for balance	**VEHICLE:** Any
AGENCY: US Forest Service, Mount Baker–Snoqualmie National Forest. A Northwest Forest Pass is required (see Appendix 3: Resources). An additional camping fee may be required at Red Bridge Campground.	**SEASONS:** Summer and fall. Warning: Avoid the river in winter and spring. High runoff poses a danger to you, and you pose a danger to spring-spawning fish.

DIRECTIONS → Make your way to the town of Granite Falls, Washington. Near the center of town, at the intersection of East Stanley Street and North Alder Avenue, drive north on North Alder Avenue, which will turn into Mountain Loop Highway (Forest Road 20) after 0.3 mile. Drive a total of 18 miles to the entrance of Red Bridge Campground, which will be on your right. Park here and walk a few paces down to the gravel bars that skirt this river-bend camping area.

AT THE SITE → The Red Bridge Campground sits on a bend in the river, and a gravel bar wraps around its entire flank. I suggest bringing good water shoes or waders so you can cross the river in some places to explore other gravel bars. Only do so in summer and early fall

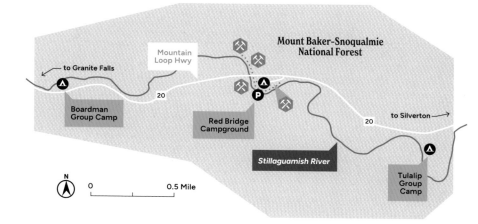

when the water levels are low. The Stillaguamish River drains several rock formations in addition to the beautiful metasediments. You'll find gneiss, schist, granite, volcanic lava rock, and breccia here as well.

12 Methow River

Welcome to the Methow Domain. The rocks found here are from a very different Earth, two in fact. The worlds that existed when rocks of the Methow were born held vibrant ecosystems, with strange and beautiful flora and fauna that would be unrecognizable today. (The arrangement of the continents would be unrecognizable too.) Sadly, both of these former worlds met the bitter fates of mass extinction.

The oldest rocks in the Methow region, heavily deformed, appeared on Earth almost 300 million years ago in the final stretch of the Paleozoic, a time called the Permian. (If the Paleozoic is a book, then the Permian is its final chapter.) The arrangement of the continents into the supergiant Pangea may have halted global circulation of oceanic currents that moderated a stable climate. Or more likely it was huge fissures that opened up in Siberia, releasing untold volumes of lava

A colorful variety of igneous and metamorphic rocks from the Methow Domain

and greenhouse gases like sulfur dioxide and carbon dioxide. (Or perhaps it was a meteor, much like another that was sure to come.) Whatever the cause, enough carbon entered the atmosphere to elevate global temperatures and acidify the oceans. Geologists estimate that up to 90 percent of Earth's species disappeared by the end of the Permian, ending the Paleozoic entirely, and dawning a new, trembling era: the Mesozoic.

The majority of rocks in the Methow Domain hail from this new era, when the fragile remains of Earth's life began to rebuild a new world. Eventually life would triumph, yielding extraordinary royalty: the dinosaurs and birds, the flowers, the bees. When the next shattering extinction event would draw the Mesozoic to an end (a 6-kilometer-wide meteor), all but one of these groups would eke out a way to survive. The birds, flowers, and bees would usher in the age of mammals—the Cenozoic—which we live in today. Tragically, humans are releasing enough greenhouse gases to compete with those of the Permian extinction, and the tender balance of life on Earth is heading in an ominous direction.

The gravel bar on the north side of the Burma Road bridge

In the Paleozoic and Mesozoic, the Methow Domain was likely the floor of an open ocean. The ancient rocks that make up the land here were forced against the continent during the Mesozoic—the process known as accretion. As this happened, a section of ocean was slowly closed in. Geologists have been able to document the appearance of a Mediterranean-like sea, naming it the Methow Ocean. It would eventually disappear, cut off by incoming terranes from the west and slowly filling in with sediments from the high, eroding continent to the east. Evidence of the rivers and currents that carried these sediments show up in the form of conglomerates (rocks made of river rocks). Old chunks of Methow Ocean crust known as the Hozomeen terrane crop out along the valley. In the river, you'll find evidence of the terrane in the form of porphyry, a dark basalt flecked with elongate, white plagioclase crystals, and greenstone, basalt cooked into a beautiful teal rock with veins of white quartz and chartreuse epidote running through it.

Basement rocks are found in Methow River gravels in abundance: ancient gneisses from the Paleozoic are found mixed into the copious granite-like rocks of the healing Mesozoic world. Granite and her sisters (such as granodiorite, tonalite, and diorite) are abundant in the river. Some are colored a salmony orange from the rich presence of potassium feldspar. Granite and her sisters hail from the interiors of old volcanic arcs and plutons—melts that occurred during the chaos of accreting terranes. Any of the rocks in the Methow River that would record evidence of the Permian mass extinction would be sedimentary marine rocks. These rocks, now deformed into schists, quartzites, and marbles, show up in the gravels too. They are so deformed that no evidence of the tragedy of their former world travels with them.

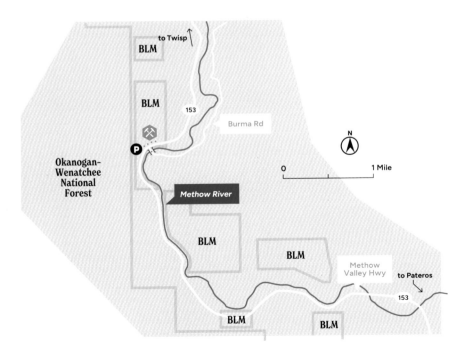

WHAT YOU'LL FIND: Porphyry, epidote, gneiss, granite, schist, conglomerate	**LIMIT:** A reasonable amount of rocks may be taken for personal use only. A reasonable amount is often defined as up to 25 pounds per person, per day, with a maximum of 250 pounds per year. Do you need 25 pounds of rocks? Probably not. Collect lightly and with intention.
GEOLOGIC AGE: Paleozoic to Mesozoic eras	
TOOLS: Wellies, waders, or water shoes; a hiking pole for balance	
AGENCY: Bureau of Land Management, Spokane District Office	**LOCATION:** 48.100919, –120.020377
	VEHICLE: Any
	SEASONS: Summer and fall. Warning: Avoid the river in winter and spring. High runoff poses a danger to you, and you pose a danger to spring-spawning fish.

DIRECTIONS → Make your way to the town of Pateros, Washington, to the intersection of US Highway 97 and the Methow Valley Highway (State Route 153). Drive west on the Methow Valley Highway, which follows the Methow River, for 8.5 miles. Pull over in the designated safe parking areas on the side of the highway just before the Burma Road bridge. The gravel bar is on the west side of the river. There is a small footpath to the river from the Burma Road bridge.

AT THE SITE → This quaint gravel bar sits on a small parcel of BLM land on the west side of the river. Explore the dry rocks high on the gravel bar. The Methow River runs swiftly here. You'll find cool-red conglomerate (rock made of a lot of other rocks), chartreuse-green epidote, speckled porphyries (dark rocks with a scattering of light-colored crystals), granites rich in pinkish-orange feldspar crystals, and wavy-banded schists. Most of the cobbles here are the size of big potatoes.

⑬ Similkameen River

The scenic Similkameen River, which flows out of British Columbia into the northern reaches of Washington State, drags 200 million years of rocks downstream, each specimen showcasing the geologic forces that built the Pacific Northwest. Along the banks of the Similkameen, you'll find dominantly plutonic rocks like granites: the basements of ancient volcanoes and accreted terranes. Some of these plutonic rocks have a fantastic amount of potassium feldspar, which color the rock a bright, salmony pink. You'll also find a lot of gneiss—granite that has been squeezed into wavy bands of dark and light crystals. These granites and gneisses give geologists clues about the creation story of Washington, in which oceanic island chains slowly crashed into the North American continent as the ocean plate they were riding on subducted underneath, resulting in all sorts of volcanism at the surface.

In this remote region of Washington, one of these ancient island chains sits exposed at the surface—the famed Quesnellia terrane. The Similkameen River drains swaths of Quesnellian rocks that were altered and squeezed as they were forced onto North America. Before accreting, the islands of Quesnellia were a volcanic arc surrounded by shallow limestone reefs (think Japan or the Aleutians). As Quesnellia collided with North America, the volcanic rocks were squeezed—or metamorphosed—into a material geologists call greenstone. You'll find a lot of this dark-green rock streaked with beautiful white quartz and chartreuse epidote. The limestone reefs of Quesnellia were squeezed into marbles, and its shallow mudstones were squeezed into slate and phyllite—a flashy, flaky, silvery-black rock similar to schist. All of these metamorphic materials show up among the rocks in the river.

Granite, gneiss, and schist dominate the riverbed.

The scenic Similkameen River winds through ancient terrane rocks and glacial drift from the last Ice Age. (Photo by Greg Shine, BLM)

On this section of the Similkameen, you won't see outcrops of granites or greenstones, even though they are abundant in the river. These basement rocks are dragged downstream from higher up in the watershed. Instead, the slopes here are composed of fine sediments carved into spire-like badlands, a startling and unexpected sight. These badlands are piles of glacial outwash. Over the last 2.6 million years, a colossal ice sheet advanced and retreated several times over northern Washington. Known as the Cordilleran ice sheet, it was responsible not only for the epic sculpting of the North Cascades but also for the phenomenal amount of sediment raked from the mountains during advancement and dumped into valleys during retreat.

The Cordilleran ice sheet is famous for its rapid melting, which caused such catastrophic events as the Missoula floods. The ice sheet is estimated to have met its end about 14,000 years ago as global temperatures quickly warmed. Around the planet, sea level is estimated to have risen up to 3 meters. Imagine that—enough water to raise the surface of all Earth's oceans by almost 10 feet! That's an unfathomable amount of water. Geologists study the footprint of the Cordilleran ice sheet in northern Washington to develop a framework of sea level rise to compare to the

current-day melting of two extraordinary ice sheets: Greenland and Antarctica. It is likely the sea level rise from their retreat will be similar to that of the Cordilleran. The world may need to prepare for inundation.

WHAT YOU'LL FIND: Greenstone, phyllite, granite, gneiss	**LOCATION:** **Site A, Miners Flat:** 48.97985, −119.53000 **Site B, Similkameen Recreation Site:** 48.9868, −119.5679
GEOLOGIC AGE: Mesozoic era–aged rocks, Cenzoic era–aged detritus from glaciers	
TOOLS: Wellies, waders, or water shoes; a hiking pole for balance	**VEHICLE:** Any
AGENCY: Bureau of Land Management, Spokane District Office	**SEASONS:** Summer and fall. Warning: Avoid the river in winter and spring. High runoff poses a danger to you, and you pose a danger to spring-spawning fish.
LIMIT: A reasonable amount of rocks may be taken for personal use only. A reasonable amount is often defined as up to 25 pounds per person, per day, with a maximum of 250 pounds per year. Do you need 25 pounds of rocks? Probably not. Collect lightly and with intention.	

DIRECTIONS → Make your way to the town of Oroville, Washington. From the intersection of Main Street (US Highway 97) and Central Avenue in Oroville, head west on Central Avenue (which turns into the Loomis-Oroville Road) for a total of 6.5 miles to Site A: Miners Flat. There are a few places where you can get down to the river here, and the site also has gorgeous views of the sedimentary badlands upslope. Once you've had your fill of exploring at Miners Flat, carry on another 2 miles on Oroville-Loomis Road to Site B: Similkameen Recreation Site, which you might find to be a more preferable spot with its broader river access.

AT THE SITES → Explore the edges of the river for the various rock treasures. The Similkameen moves swiftly, so avoid wading too deep. At Miners Flat you can hike into the badlands composed of glacial drift across the highway from the recreation area. Take great care crossing Loomis-Oroville Road.

⑭ Stonerose Fossil Quarry

Welcome to the Eocene epoch, a time of chaotic volcanism in northeastern Washington's history. We'll travel approximately 50 million years into the past. Here, lakes glimmer in the valleys below the Sanpoil volcanoes, which tower above the landscape. Dramatic faulting has caused blocks of earth to drop downward, forming valleys, allowing lavas to escape through the faults' fractures—building volcanoes. Over the Sanpoil's eruptive history, volcanic ash flows into the valley's lakes, and autumn leaves sink into the lake-bottom muds. Microscopic plankton called diatoms bloom and die off, sinking as well. Insects and fish join them. Over time so much sediment flows into the lakes that they fill in and disappear.

Fast-forward to the present. The lakebeds are turned to stone, the Sanpoil volcanoes have eroded away, geothermal fluids from the days of volcanism have altered much of the re-

Andy Brockett of the Stonerose team helps a group of youngsters get the hang of splitting rock. (Photo by Simon Curtis)

A rich variety of plant fossils can be found if you're willing to put in some elbow grease.

maining bedrock, and earth has been crumpled upward into high, forested mountains. Ice Age glaciers have advanced and retreated, and the humans indigenous to this place have been forced off their land to make way for a boomtown of miners: the altered rock from the days of the Sanpoils is enriched with gold. Little attention is paid to the bountiful deposits of leaves from the old lake-bottom sediments . . . until the gold runs out. In the 1980s, as the riches begin to dwindle, a deposit of lacustrine, or lake-bottom, sediments is unearthed on the north end of the boomtown. Leaves, twigs, insects, and fish are found in abundance. One day, a fossil rose—a stonerose—is uncovered, and the rest is history.

The late poet Lindley Williams Hubbell saw such delicate fossils as if they were like frost crystals on glass. Permanently, forever, he surmised. In the fine mudstone layers of the lacustrine sediments, ancient plants are preserved as delicate carbon films of their former selves. With each split, visitors to the dig site reveal these leafy ghosts to a sun they haven't seen in 50 million years. How the world has changed since the days of their last photosynthesis! It's hard not to feel deeply moved by the ability to reach across the veil with such ease. To connect to the autumn leaves of a single, unfathomably long-ago season. Many people have felt this way about digging here, and so the Stonerose Interpretive Center was born.

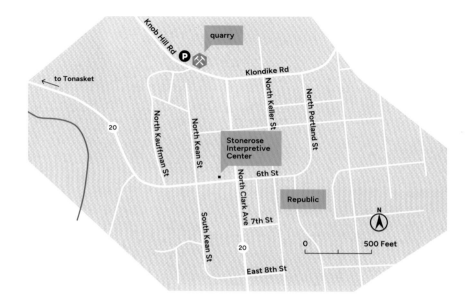

Located a few blocks south of the diggings, the center hosts a gorgeous collection of plant and animal specimens unearthed at the site. They welcome visitors to dig for a small fee and provide tools and instructions. Material is abundant, and everyone will leave with a small memento of Eocene life.

WHAT YOU'LL FIND: Fossil fragments of leaves and sticks, possibly insects or fish	**LIMIT:** Visitors can choose three of the fossils they found to keep.
GEOLOGIC AGE: Cenozoic era, Tertiary period, Eocene epoch; approximately 50 million years old	**LOCATION:** Stonerose Interpretive Center, 15 N. Clark Ave., Republic, WA 99166; 48.650417, –118.740028
TOOLS: Small hand tools required for splitting layers: hammer, flat chisels, paint scraper, pocket knife; safety glasses and gloves	**VEHICLE:** Any
AGENCY: Stonerose Interpretive Center & Eocene Fossil Site. Interpretive center free; fossil site admission required. Check website for rates (see Appendix 3: Resources).	**SEASONS:** The gift shop is open year-round, with holiday closures. Diggings open seasonally. Call ahead to ascertain business operations (see Appendix 3: Resources).

DIRECTIONS → Make your way to the Stonerose Interpretive Center in Republic, Washington. Note: You must check in at the interpretive center to pay the fee before heading to the quarry. After paying the fee, head north on North Clark Avenue for two blocks, then turn left on Knob Hill Road (Klondike Road). You'll see the quarry on your right in 0.1 mile. Park at the concrete barriers.

AT THE SITE → The Stonerose fossil quarry is a small area where a great deal of material has already been removed from the hillside. Begin your search by collecting slabs of sedimentary rock that litter the slope and bring them to one of the splitting benches available at the site. With great care, split the rock along bedding planes using hand tools to reveal new fossil material. The hosts at the interpretive center can give you a demo on how best to split rock before you head up to the quarry. Plant fragments are common. Complete leaves take more patience to find. Flowers, seeds, cones, fish, and insects are more rare.

Washington geologist George Mustoe published a thorough survey of the site in 2015. He notes that there are three distinct layers at the Stonerose quarry. The bottom is fine diatomaceous silt that fractures brittlely, which limits the quality of the specimens. The middle zone consists of easy-to-split mudstones that are rich in fossils. The upper part of the deposit, which is too high to reach safely, is composed of coarser, sandier sediments, and fossils are mostly limited to wood fragments and twigs.

Washington Cascades

The Cascade Range volcanoes are strung like pearls among mountaintops, neatly demarcating a phenomenal boundary of plate tectonics. From Lassen Peak to Mount Baker, each snowcapped volcano is a vent for magma derived from the mantle above ocean crust that is sinking below the North American continent and giving off hot water. *Subduction* is the term geologists use when an oceanic plate runs into a continental plate and slides beneath it. A volcanic arc forms above, reliably venting molten rock and gases to the surface. The volcanism of the Cascades produces a variety of lavas, but the predominant form is andesite. The silica from these lavas eventually yields beautiful agates, jaspers, and wood petrified in volcanic eruptions. In this rainy, mountainous terrain, creeks and rivers are the ideal places to discover the treasures of the Cascades.

Opposite: Volcanic sandstone containing Leisegang banding is common among the gravel bars.

Mist shrouds the mountains along the Cowlitz River.

⑮ Cowlitz River

The mighty Cowlitz River is a volcano drain. Along its misty, meandering path, it captures creeks and streams that run off the flanks of Mount Rainier, the Goat Rocks, Mount Adams, and the explosive celebrity that is Mount Saint Helens. On this broad stretch of the Cowlitz, the river is predominantly made of rocks from the southern flank of Mount Rainier. It has yet to intercept the tributaries running off of her sister volcanoes.

The rocks that tumble down the Cowlitz erode from volcanic lavas, ashfall deposits, and pyroclastic flows laid down over the eons. The Cascade Volcanic Arc started erupting about 37 million years ago, however each of its jewel-like volcanoes is a fresh and young edifice. Volcanic peaks come and go rather quickly on geological time scales. If the Cascade Range were a piano, each volcano is merely a single key, pressed for just a moment in time, a vent for volatile material making its way to Earth's surface.

The dominant material erupting from Cascade volcanoes is andesite lava, an unremarkable gray material that is less metallic than basalt, but also less silica-rich than rhyolite. In the lava family, it's the middle child. Amid the Cowlitz's ocean of andesite, rockhounds can find other colorful rocks derived from volcanic ash that has weathered into teal and red claystones and volcanic sandstones that exhibit a type of wavy banding that looks just like a landscape.

The interesting banding in picture stones likely occurs after the rock has formed. The process is still somewhat debated by researchers, but the most accepted theory is that fluids pass through porous rocks and precipitate bands of iron oxides in their wake. We see this type of picture-stone banding occur most commonly in volcanic ash and sandstone, both porous materials. Because you asked, the process of mineral banding in porous stones is referred to as the Ostwald-Liesegang-supersaturation-nucleation-depletion cycle.

Picture stones, jaspers, porphyries, and altered claystones are common among the gravel bars.

Fluids, say groundwater from above or hydrothermal waters from the deep, seep into a rock formation that is porous. The rocks already have iron in their matrix, and the invading fluid may bring more. Fluids can only hold so much dissolved matter. As the fluid passes through the rock, enough dissolved iron builds up that it reaches saturation (part one of the cycle). Upon reaching supersaturation, the iron must come out and does so by precipitating, or nucleating (part two of the cycle), leaving a band of solid iron-oxide behind. Because a lot of iron came out of the fluid, it is now depleted of iron (part three of the cycle). As the fluid continues to pass through the rock, dissolved iron builds up again, and it eventually saturates and precipitates out of the fluid, leaving another depositional ring or band behind. The process continues onward and results in the landscape-like rings and bands we witness in the stone.

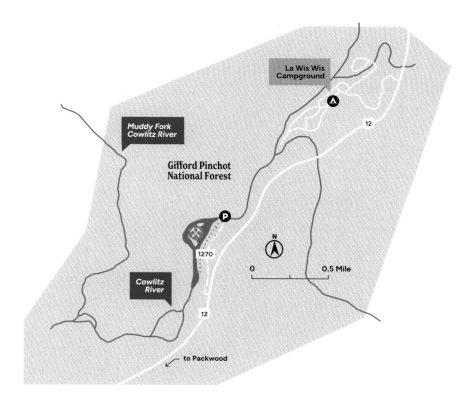

WHAT YOU'LL FIND: Picture stones, breccia, jasper	LIMIT: 10 pounds of rock and fossil material per person, per day
GEOLOGIC AGE: Cenozoic era, Paleogene to Neogene periods	LOCATION: 46.663637, –121.602623
	VEHICLE: Any
TOOLS: Wellies, water shoes, or waders; a hiking pole for balance	SEASONS: Summer and early fall. Warning: Avoid the river in winter and spring. High runoff poses a danger to you, and you pose a danger to spring-spawning fish.
AGENCY: US Forest Service, Gifford Pinchot National Forest. A Northwest Forest Pass is required in the Gifford Pinchot National Forest (see Appendix 3: Resources).	

DIRECTIONS → Make your way to the town of Packwood, Washington. At the intersection of Willame Street and US Highway 12, head northeast on US 12 East for 4.9 miles. Turn left onto Forest Road 1270 and drive 0.5 mile to its end. Park here and hike a few dozen yards down to the gravel bar that flanks the riverbed.

AT THE SITE → The gravel bars on this part of the Cowlitz River are massive. There's no shortage of collecting opportunities here. FR 1270 terminates at a dead end where the river runs narrow and deep, a wonderful area for swimming. (Many people camp here in vans.) Walk west from the parking area through a small grove of conifers to get to the large gravel bars. Avoid the river in winter and spring during high runoff.

16 Cispus River

The Cispus River winds through the misty evergreen slopes between Mount Adams and the Goat Rocks Wilderness. It eventually merges with the swift Cowlitz River that drains the colossal Mount Rainier. The mountains that drain their sediments into the Cispus River are made of volcanic rock, all laid down well into the age of mammals. Eruptive episode after eruptive episode, lava flows and ash falls buried this landscape. All of the rocks in the gravel bars of the Cispus River record these catastrophic volcanic events.

The majority of volcanic rock found in the river gravels is an unremarkable gray andesite, the stuff of stratovolcanoes. Stratovolcanoes are the kind we all imagine: gargantuan cones that plume smoky ash and rocky debris. Among the gray cobbles of andesite lava, bright bits of red, teal, and yellow turn up. The color within these rocks forms as the volcanic rock chemically weathers—its minerals

A misty day on the rushing Cispus River

break down into other minerals. The red rocks are colored by the oxidation of irons. The yellow rocks erode have interesting banding patterns in them caused by pulses of precipitating iron oxides. Many rockhounds refer to these as "picture stones," and they can make for wonderful lapidary specimens. The bright-teal stones are amalgamations of feldspar minerals altering into various forms of clay. Eventually all of these volcanic rocks will break down into sand and clay. But for now, they're still rocks.

In the Cispus River, you'll also find breccia (pronounced: *breh-cha*), which is a rock made up of angular fragments of rocks. These breccias are formed in landslides and pyroclastic flows. Pyroclastic flows are violent eruptions of searingly hot ash, rock, and gas, which flow down the flanks of volcanoes at tremendous speeds. When they cease, the ash and rock fragments fuse together in their own heat. One of the greatest dangers posed by the active Cascade volcanoes is to nearby communities that may lie in the path of a possible pyroclastic event. The ancient Roman city of Pompeii was buried under one such flow. It erupted from Mount Vesuvius in AD 79, rushing into town at 60 miles per hour. "We thought we had enough time to get out," says Pierce Brosnan's character in the 1997 volcano thriller *Dante's Peak*. In this particular scene, Brosnan is attempting to explain to the town's sexy mayor how a pyroclastic flow dashed his dreams of marriage. "Unfortunately, we were wrong. We got too close to the show." Following the theatrical release of *Dante's Peak*, the village of Plymouth on the island of Montserrat would be overtaken by several pyroclastic flows and buried forever.

Opposite: Colorful stones of the Cascade volcanoes dominate the gravel bars.

WHAT YOU'LL FIND: Picture stone and breccia, possibly agate and jasper	**LIMIT:** Up to 10 pounds per person, per day
GEOLOGIC AGE: Cenozoic era, Paleogene to Neogene periods	**LOCATION:** 46.443142, –121.780806
	VEHICLE: Any
TOOLS: Wellies, water shoes, or waders; a hiking pole for balance	**SEASONS:** Summer and early fall. Warning: Avoid the river in winter and spring. High runoff poses a danger to you, and you pose a danger to spring-spawning fish.
AGENCY: US Forest Service, Gifford Pinchot National Forest. A Northwest Forest Pass is required (see Appendix 3: Resources).	

DIRECTIONS → Make your way to the small town of Randle, Washington. In town at the intersection of US Highway 12 and State Route 131, drive south on SR 131 for 1 mile. Turn left onto Cispus Road and drive for 11.5 miles to a pull-off along the right side of the road. (At 8.1 miles, Cispus Road turns into Forest Road 23.) At the pull-off there is an established footpath that will lead you to the river, which runs close to the road. If the pull-off is occupied, you can backtrack 0.6 mile to the North Fork Campground, which has access to the North Fork Cispus River.

AT THE SITE → This section of the Cispus River is a chaos of boulders, cobbles, and gravels. Take great care when navigating the gravel bars. I recommend a hiking pole or walking stick to help with balance. Avoid the river in winter and spring when runoff is high.

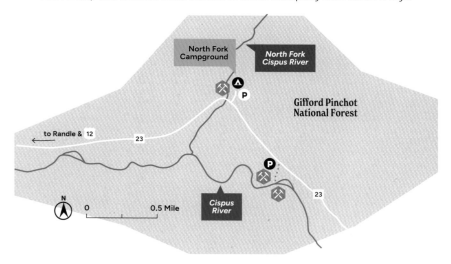

⑰ Quartz Creek

When a volcano of the Cascade Range explodes, its peak blasts into smithereens, sending fragments of rock soaring into the sky. The old lavas that skirt the volcano's flanks are merely thin laminations, easily shaken loose by the quakes that precede an eruption. When the volcano blows, these layers break loose forming landslides and mudslides (called lahars), which race down the mountain. (And if the rocks are superhot, they are called pyroclastic flows.) The combination of broken rock hurling downslope and hot, fragmental rock falling from the skies produces a new geologic layer surrounding the volcano. When all of this exploded and re-deposited stuff eventually solidifies, it becomes breccia, a cemented material composed of sharp, angular fragments of other rocks. Here in Quartz Creek, the gravels are made of it.

The Cascade Range is known to geologists as a subduction arc. The neat front-line of volcanoes that dot the range like a string of pearls is venting hot, volatile material caught up in the action of an oceanic plate (the Juan de Fuca) slipping

A bridge spans the shallow Quartz Creek in late autumn.

beneath our own (the continent of North America). Subduction happens because the broken plates of Earth's crust are always on the move. Upwelling of hot material from the mantle at oceanic ridges, or perhaps the tipping of cold ocean plates back into the mantle, drives the perpetual motion. But what caused Earth's plates to break up and start drifting around in the first place is a source of passionate and controversial debate among geologists.

The convection that powers plate tectonics is one of the most unique phenomena in our solar system. Only a few bodies that orbit the sun have hot interiors that cause volcanism at their surfaces: Venus, Earth, Mars, and Jupiter's moon Io. (Perhaps Mercury, our Moon, and Saturn's moon Enceladus may also qualify, though they have long been quiet.) The remainder of planets and moons are cold to their cores. However, while Venus, Mars, and Io have volcanoes, their surfaces aren't broken up into plates that move. There is growing evidence that at some

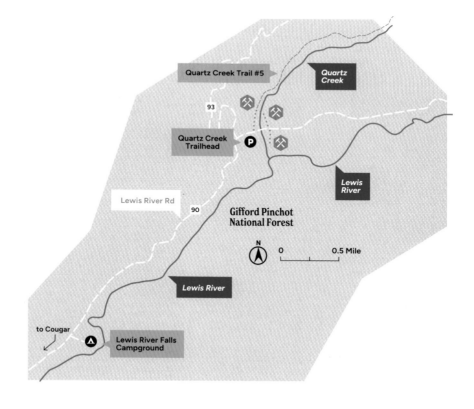

Breccias, rocks made of exploded rocks, dominate the creek bed.

point Mars may have had plates that moved around, but today its surface is still. Thus, the movement of plates, and the subduction arc volcanoes that ribbon them, are unique to a singular body in the solar system: Earth. Remember this as you pick up the colorful, fragmental breccias in Quartz Creek. They are evidence of a dynamic and tectonic planet, singularly special in a cold and quiet universe.

WHAT YOU'LL FIND: Volcanic breccia	**LIMIT:** Up to 10 pounds per person, per day
GEOLOGIC AGE: Cenozoic era, Oligocene epoch to present	**LOCATION:** 46.182056, –121.847750
	VEHICLE: Any
TOOLS: Wellies, water shoes, or waders; a hiking pole for balance	**SEASONS:** Summer and fall. Warning: Avoid the river in winter and spring. High runoff poses a danger to you, and you pose a danger to spring-spawning fish.
AGENCY: US Forest Service, Gifford Pinchot National Forest. A Northwest Forest Pass is required in the Gifford Pinchot National Forest (see Appendix 3: Resources).	

DIRECTIONS → Make your way to the post office in Cougar, Washington, at 16745 Lewis River Road. From here, drive northeast on Lewis River Road (State Route 503) for 35.6 miles to the Quartz Creek trailhead, which will be well marked on the right side of the road. (Note: 3.4 miles outside of town, Lewis River Road becomes Forest Road 90.) Park at the trailhead. You may access the river from trails at the trailhead, or you can walk along the road, crossing the bridge that spans Quartz Creek, to get to large gravel bars on the other side.

AT THE SITE → Quartz Creek runs shallow and clear most of the year. The gravel bars here are rich with colorful volcanic breccias from repeated Cascade eruptions. Hiking upstream will yield interesting specimens of this cool, fragmental rock. Downstream, Quartz Creek quickly dumps into the swift Lewis River, where rockhounding is not as easy.

18 Dry Creek

Nestled between the fabled Wind River and Trapper Creek Wilderness, a gentle stream pulses through the forest, quietly unnoticed. Dry Creek meanders through the steep drainages southeast of Mount Saint Helens, sweeping rough and crumbling volcanic rocks downstream. Veins of clear agate and white quartz decorate these rocks, the eroded remnants of lavas that have blanketed this landscape for millions of years. Mount Saint Helens is one of several volcanoes in the Cascade Range. Each is a vent that releases molten rock and gas rising from the deepest parts of the crust. The plate that makes up the ocean floor off the Oregon and Washington coast is sliding underneath our continent, tipping downward into the mantle. The oceanic plates contain a great deal of water, which superheats as it approaches the infernal mantle. This fuels the volcanic burping of hot, explosive rock at the surface. Estimates put the first eruptions of the Cascades about 37 million years back, and they continue to this day.

In Dry Creek, it's likely the rocks here are composed of ashy debris from eruptions that were somewhat rich in silica. Many rocks are mottled with pockets of agate and white quartz, and some erode large, hard lumps of these materials into the river. Agate and quartz are common materials that develop as volcanic ash changes over time. They are both forms of the mineral silica (silicon dioxide, SiO_2). The crystals in agate are extremely tiny, so geologists refer to agate as cryptocrystalline. Quartz crystals tend to be somewhat larger, and geologists refer to them as macrocrystalline. (Sometimes they are even big enough to see with the naked eye! This is the stuff you find in gem shops.) I have never found any large crystal

Autumn leaves blanket the gravel bars on Dry Creek.

points of quartz in Dry Creek. Rather, the rocks here tend to have veins of clear agate surrounded by rough white quartz and sometimes a coating of druzy. *Druzy* is a rockhounding word for sparkle that covers a rock. Under a microscope, you can see that the sparkle is caused by a carpet of tiny quartz points. So, quartz points in Dry Creek? Yes. Just very, very tiny!

WHAT YOU'LL FIND: Agate and quartz in pockets of volcanic rock	**LIMIT:** 10 pounds of rock and fossil material per person, per day
GEOLOGIC AGE: Cenozoic era, Oligocene epoch to present	**LOCATION:** 45.884306, –121.977222
	VEHICLE: Any
TOOLS: Wellies, water shoes, or waders; a hiking pole for balance	**SEASONS:** Summer and fall. Warning: Avoid the river in winter and spring. High runoff poses a danger to you, and you pose a danger to spring-spawning fish.
AGENCY: US Forest Service, Gifford Pinchot National Forest. A Northwest Forest Pass is required in the Gifford Pinchot National Forest (see Appendix 3: Resources).	

DIRECTIONS → Make your way to the intersection of Hot Springs Avenue and Wind River Highway in the center of Carson, Washington. From here, drive north on Wind River Highway (which changes to Wind River Road/Meadow Creek Road) for 13.4 miles. Stay straight to continue onto Mineral Springs Road. Drive 0.5 mile and turn right onto Little Soda Springs Road. Drive another 0.3 mile to the Trapper Creek trailhead, and park. A

A lava rock revealing a pocket of agate and quartz

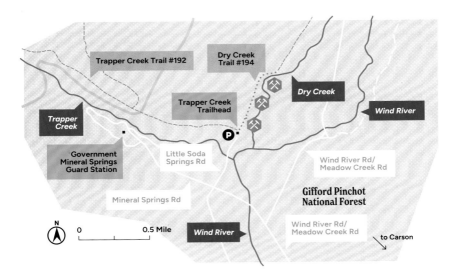

sign at the parking lot kiosk marks the main trail: Trapper Creek Trail #192. Follow this trail into the forest for a few yards to a second sign that marks several diverging trails. Stay to the right to follow Dry Creek Trail #194. Walk 0.1 mile, keeping your eye out for an established footpath leading down to the creek. Use this short footpath to gain easy access to Dry Creek's large gravel bars.

AT THE SITE → Make note of where you drop down into Dry Creek so you can find your way back to the trail, especially in the summer when plant growth hides small paths. The gravels of the creek are dominantly a crumbling andesite lava filled with gemmy inclusions. White agate and white quartz are common. I recommend wading upstream to stay within Dry Creek, which runs shallow most of the year. Around a few bends, the water has carved pools deep enough for swimming. Downstream, Dry Creek quickly dumps into Wind River, which is dominated by crumbly breccias and soft volcanic claystones that are quite colorful: teal, purple, and red.

Oregon Coast Range

Oregon's Coast Range stands guard over the edge of the continent. Its low mountains consist of accreted and uplifted rocks, the oldest comprising ancient seafloor basalt, which erupted some 55 to 50 million years ago. This huge mass of lava was accreted onto the continent shortly after erupting, becoming a terrane known as Siletzia.

Up in the Olympic Peninsula, Siletzian rocks are on full display. But here in the Coast Range they are totally buried. Slightly younger volcanic rocks, known as the Tillamook Volcanics, erupted here about 46 to 40 million years ago covering the freshly accreted Siletzian rock with lava. Swaths of diabase, a basaltic magma that didn't quite make it to the surface, formed dikes and sills within the crust. A great deal of diabase is now exposed in the upper reaches of the range.

Most notably, the Coast Range is a topographical feature that's being shoved upward as the oceanic Juan de Fuca plate subducts beneath our continent. This region used to be much more low lying, with the coastline sitting farther inland. Over time, enormous tracts of coastal marine sediments buried the Siletzian bedrock too. Now a great deal of them have been uplifted into the slopes and terraces that line the scenic coast. Fossils of early whales and dolphins as well as abundant shells and fish bones erode down the slopes and back out to sea.

Opposite: A fossil-filled cobble of Astoria Formation rock

⑲ Short Beach

A towering cliff of eroding basalt looms over a secluded beach on the Oregon coast. Charismatic sea stacks made from the same old lava rise from the sea. If you can believe it, this lava flowed here about 16 million years ago from the remotest corner of eastern Oregon. At the time, the continent was drifting over a hotspot in the mantle, and a perfect storm of conditions in the crust above it set the stage for all hell to break loose. Fissures several miles long tore open between present-day Enterprise, Oregon, and Walla Walla, Washington, unleashing a torrent of lava that would gradually bury thousands of square miles of the landscape and flow down the Columbia River channel and out to sea. The sea stacks and vertical cliffs of old basalt seen here are remnants of the epic flows.

When you first arrive at Short Beach, look at the rocks around you. You'll notice a lot of "fresh" rock material eroding from the cliff above. It's rough and untumbled, easy to spot among the wave-smoothed cobbles. This material is weathered basalt. It contains large vesicles, called amygdules, filled with zeolites (white fibrous minerals), agate (clear hard lumps), limonite (orange rust), and clay minerals (bright teal and powdery). All of these minerals are secondary, meaning they form as the basalt chemically weathers, or breaks down over time. Most minerals aren't stable forever. All rocks will eventually break down into metals, silica, and clay, and that's exactly what's happening here.

Among the smooth cobbles, agates and jaspers are easy to find, especially if you're willing to dig around. The agates are clear white to carnelian orange. (Carnelians are orange agates.) The jaspers range from murky red to a beautiful teal. Agate and jasper are silicate minerals that are quite hard, and they often have odd, lumpy shapes

Pebble puppies dig through the basalt cobbles at Short Beach.

Small agates and jaspers become easy to find if you put in the time.

compared to the rounded cobbles. They're relatively resistant to erosion. Specimens tend to be small but pretty. For most beachcombers, it's more about the Zen-like search than the actual prize. What makes these ordinary materials special is that they are treasures tumbling from the voids of a far traveling lava. The origin of the flood basalt found at Short Beach is an extraordinary departure from the typical stories of the Coast Range.

WHAT YOU'LL FIND: Agate, jasper, zeolite	**LIMITS:** 1 gallon of pebbles and shells per person, per day, with a yearly maximum of 3 gallons total; 5 gallons of cobbles per person, per day, with a yearly maximum of 10 gallons total
GEOLOGIC AGE: Cenozoic era, Miocene epoch	
TOOLS: A small garden claw; a container for specimens	
	LOCATION: Oregon Beach 30A: 45.47285, –123.96885
AGENCY: Oregon State Parks	
	VEHICLE: Any
	SEASONS: Any

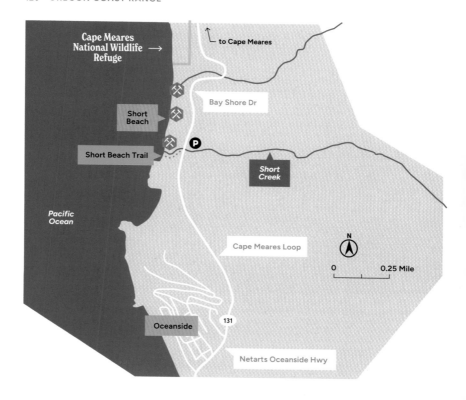

DIRECTIONS → Make your way to the town of Oceanside, Oregon. From the intersection of Netarts Oceanside Highway (State Route 131) and Cape Meares Loop, follow Cape Meares Loop north for 1.2 miles to the Short Beach trailhead. There is no designated parking lot; to park, pull safely off the road. An Oregon State Parks sign marks the trail down to the beach, which is a quick descent on steep stairs cut into the hillside.

AT THE SITE → You'll see many folks wandering the waterline with buckets searching for agates, but the best area to search is higher up on the beach in the gravel bars. Bring a small garden claw to reveal agates and jaspers hidden within the piles of beach rocks. The smaller gravels are easier to move compared to the large cobbles. Some sections of the gravel bar can be quite steep. Do not dig below these. Sit atop the gravel bar and move rocks aside to reveal treasure within. Agates are found easily, as they glow when light passes through them. Keep a keen eye for jaspers, which tend to hide better among the dark basalt. Make sure to fill your digging area back in if you move a lot of rock.

Agate: The Journey Stone

IN ONE OF HIS final collections of poetry, Pablo Neruda turned his gaze on the world of stones. Agates, in particular, captured his attention. He referred to them as the "chastity of Heaven"—delicate, oval, smooth, reborn. "Respectable agate . . . I sing of your fiery modesty." Neruda was in the sunset of his own tumultuous life, and rather than looking inward, he turned his poetic gaze toward stones. He colorfully explained that agates weren't the extravagant hell of the ruby or the celebrity of the emerald. Instead, he said agates were "simple as a dog," street stones, noting their solidness in the continuous traffic of rivers. The agates Neruda collected in Chile, and in his many places of political exile, are no different from the agates found in the Pacific Northwest. They appear throughout the world, tumbling down streams, catching the glow of the sun and the attention of our eyes. It's a humble material, says Neruda, "Earth's root child."

Mystics (and gem wholesalers) would have you believe otherwise. Agate is no street stone. It's a powerful aura stabilizer, a potent preventer of nightmares, especially when charged under a full moon. If held right, these little rocks clear mental blocks and enhance our perception and analytical abilities. Through agates, we become superhuman. Carnelian, the fiery variety, is the warrior stone, which can simultaneously still all tempers and open roads to fertility and sensual awakening. According to purveyors, carnelians provide a direct path to the heavily co-opted spirit realm of Egyptian gods, straight to the office door of Isis herself. People make an awful lot of money selling

us these ideas. They put the stones to work, bestowing upon them the insurmountable responsibility of humanity's fulfillment.

No matter what ideas people try to sell you, know that no stone is capable of such things. Their metaphysical powers are not truths—they are wishes. Their magic appeals to us because we're all so earnestly seeking a way to improve our world and, more importantly, ourselves. To carry an agate or carnelian as a token of these wishes is actually a sweet thing. But it's not the stone that does the work; it's you. The tragedy of the metaphysical world is the erasure of the stone's own history to make way for mystical powers to serve the human ego.

If anything, agate is the journey stone. Its birth is slow, filling voids and cracks in volcanic and sedimentary rocks over eons, carefully gathering silica from the host rock around it. Time passes, and then more time passes, until uplift and erosion free it from its home. It tumbles down desert washes and forest streams, resistant to the destructive forces around it. It journeys onward into gulches, rivers, and onto beaches, where it washes back and forth in the perpetual motion of waves. Its translucence catches the rays of the sun, causing it to glow like a tiny beacon. A traveler through time and space.

Humans can't help but pick up agates. Over the centuries, agates have been carved into talismans, jewels, intaglios, and even exquisite scepters and urns. For thousands of years, huge quantities of carnelian agates have been collected in the Nubian Desert of Africa. These crimson stones were once the calling cards of elite peoples around the

Mediterranean, particularly the Egyptians (hence the metaphysical connection to Isis). Today, museums hoard fragments of esoteric carnelians carved by artists who lived three thousand years ago, refusing to repatriate them.

In the natural world, agates (and carnelians) last for a really long time. They're composed of silica crystals that are so finely interlocked, it takes an eternity of erosion to grind them down. Essentially, they have few zones of weakness. When mineralogists gaze into the fabric of agates, they see cryptocrystalline silica, the smallest possible scale at which silica crystals can hold hands. (A geological term for cryptocrystalline silica is *chalcedony*. Agate is chalcedony. It's a lot of words for the same thing.) Mineralogists may also observe patches of opal, silica's little sister, who still has some water in her crystal matrix. This causes some chaos in opal's structure, which is often amorphous, meaning it is disorganized and glassy. Think of opal as a toddler. Mineralogists might also observe patches of agate's more grown-up sister, macrocrystalline silica, or quartz. These are geometric crystals with a more open, hexagonal crystalline structure, allowing for geometric crystals to grow. Sometimes we can see quartz crystals with the naked eye, but on agates, we most often experience them as a dazzling surface of sparkles called druzy. If you were to look at druzy through a simple magnifying glass, you'd see a tiny carpet of quartz points emerging from the stone. Agates can be pure chalcedony, or they can also carry bits of their sister silicas within them.

The birth of agates in voids and cracks is a subject of great debate among mineralogists. Plenty of logical theories involving the

Remnant of a carved carnelian plaque from an Egyptian bracelet, circa 1390–1352 BC (Photo courtesy of The Metropolitan Museum of Art)

precipitation of silica in voids exist, but few experiments have been able to replicate the process of formation in the lab. Does it all begin as opal and slowly shed molecular water to become chalcedony and quartz? A process of maturation? Or can silica precipitate directly as chalcedony, skipping an opal phase altogether? What chemical processes cause the beautiful banding in some agates and a total absence of it in others? Is this more a question of physics than chemistry? "Practically all aspects of agate genesis generate debate," says researcher Ingrid Kigai. "The time is ripe to clarify the most important enigmas concerning the environments of formation of agates." What is known is that these hardy lumps of silica are survivors. Their cryptocrystalline bodies set them up for an epic journey through the processes of erosion on Earth's surface. They coalesce in rivers and waves undaunted, like Neruda says, "solid in the continuous traffic of water."

⟨20⟩ **Beverly Beach**

Along this stretch of the Oregon coast, sediments from a much older ocean have been uplifted from the seafloor. Sandstones of the Astoria Formation, laid down from 20 to 15 million years back, erode from low cliffs that face the sea. Creeks running down from the forest drag even more of it onto the beaches. The Astoria Formation is richly fossiliferous, meaning it's chock-full of fossils. Its sandstones provide a glimpse into life off the coast several million years in the past.

The dominant fossils are shells left behind by molluscs—a royal family of invertebrates that includes the bivalves, gastropods, and cephalopods. Bivalves are creatures with two shells—think clams, scallops, mussels, and oysters. Gastropods are the familiar whelks, conks, and snails, with their single twisting shells. Cephalopods don't fossilize quite as easily, as many are soft bodied, like the octopuses and squids. (I hear you, *octopi* people. *Cæsar non supra grammaticos.* But *octopus* has its roots in Greek, not Latin. If you really insist, call them octopodes.) Other cephalopods like the nautiloids have better luck fossilizing. Nautiloids have chambered shells that resemble a large snail, but instead of having a slug-like body, they

Wave-smoothed cobbles litter the beach with Cliffs of Astoria Formation sandstone in the distance.

A variety of shell fossils found on Beverly Beach (Photo by Bob Oblack)

are just like a squid. A few fossil nautilus specimens have turned up in Beverly Beach sandstones, but not many. You've likely heard of ammonites, perhaps the most famous fossil cephalopod, but their legacy ended shortly after the disappearance of dinosaurs. Thus, they were long extinct by the time the Astoria Formation ecosystem existed.

Vertebrate fossils show up on Beverly Beach as well. They're far less abundant and take a trained eye to identify. Most fossil bones have become unassuming, round beach cobbles. Paleontologists have cataloged several ancestors of whales, dolphins, seals, sharks, stingrays, and even an ancient albatross. Normally, the collection of vertebrate fossils is prohibited on federal and state lands. However, laws pertaining to coastal beaches overseen by the state of Oregon allow collection of vertebrate fossils *if they are loose or in cobble form and fit in a 5-gallon bucket*. Beverly Beach provides an extraordinary opportunity for fossil enthusiasts to participate in paleontology and contribute to citizen science.

The Astoria Formation contains many fossils that are familiar to us. They were left behind by creatures that would give rise to the generations of sea life that we know so well in our modern world. But among them lie creatures that disappeared somewhere in between their time and ours. The sedimentary outcrops along Beverly Beach have yielded several discoveries of fossils new to science, and nearly all of them have been found and reported by average people like you and me (see sidebar, "Fossil Collecting Along Oregon's Coast" for how to report fossil finds). Perhaps you'll be the next person to make a fascinating discovery that adds to the rich evolutionary history of the Oregon coast!

WHAT YOU'LL FIND: Invertebrate marine fossils, mostly shells	**LIMITS:** 1 gallon of pebbles and shells per person, per day, with a yearly maximum of 3 gallons total; 5 gallons of cobbles per person, per day, with a yearly maximum of 10 gallons
GEOLOGIC AGE: Cenozoic era, Miocene epoch	
TOOLS: Wellies, waders, or water shoes; a small garden trowel to help tip specimens from the sand	**LOCATIONS:** **Site A, Beverly Beach State Park (Oregon Beach 54):** 44.729528, −124.058139 **Site B, Wade Creek Beach (Oregon Beach 54A):** 44.715250, −124.058889
AGENCY: Oregon State Parks	
	VEHICLE: Any
	SEASONS: Any

DIRECTIONS → **Site A—Beverly Beach State Park:** Make your way to the intersection of Oregon Coast Highway (US Highway 101) and Corvallis-Newport Highway (US 20) in the center of Newport, Oregon. Drive north on US 101 for 6.4 miles. Turn right at the sign for Beverly Beach State Park. Drive 0.1 mile on the park's entrance road to the day-use parking lot on your left. From here, hike a short trail that crosses under the highway to the beach.

   Site B—Wade Creek Beach: From Site A, drive south on US 101 for 1 mile. Pull over into a gravel lot on the west side of the highway. You will see a small tsunami hazard sign with a map of the area and beach number 54A. From the south end of the parking area, an old road slopes gently down to the beach. The walking distance is approximately 450 feet.

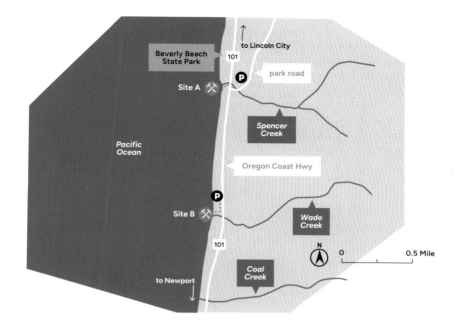

AT THE SITE → Both Spencer Creek and Wade Creek have just enough movement to drag sand off the beach and expose cobbles of Astoria Formation rocks rich in marine fossils. I have found some beautiful scallop fossils at both sites. The creeks are obvious features on the beach, and the paths will dump you out right alongside them. No tools are needed to collect rocks here, though sometimes a small hand tool or trowel can help dislodge rocks from the sand. If you're up for a long stroll, more fossils can be found along the beaches to the north and south. However, the best direction to walk is south of Site B (Wade Creek), where large outcrops of Astoria Formation erode onto the beach.

Only loose rock and fossil material can be collected from the beaches. Do not hammer into large boulders, wave benches, or cliffs. If you think you have found a fossil bone or tooth from a vertebrate, photograph it next to something for scale (sunglasses, a shoe, a pen, anything) and share your images with state park officials and members of the North America Research Group (NARG) based in the Portland area (see Appendix 3: Resources).

Fossil Collecting Along Oregon's Coast

THE CENTRAL COAST of Oregon is an exceptional region to search for fossil material from the ancient sea. Long swaths of uplifted terraces expose over 25 million years of marine and coastal sediments that encase a wonder of fossils. Invertebrate fossils left behind by ancient clams and snails are spectacularly abundant, and fossil bones of ancient fishes and sea mammals can be found too, though they are much more rare. From Lincoln City to Newport, large cobbles containing fossil whale skulls have been pulled off the beaches (pictured) as well as bones from early ancestors of dolphins, seals, and an extinct lineage of coastal predators affectionately called oyster bears. (Imagine a large, slick bear who loves to swim and has a whiskery face like a seal.) Several important fossil discoveries have been made along the Oregon Coast—not by paleontologists, but by average people like you and me. But what about paleontology rules? Don't they prohibit collection of fossil bones?

A partial skull of an ancient whale found on the beach. Note how the bone texture contrasts with the stone. (Photo by Bob Oblack)

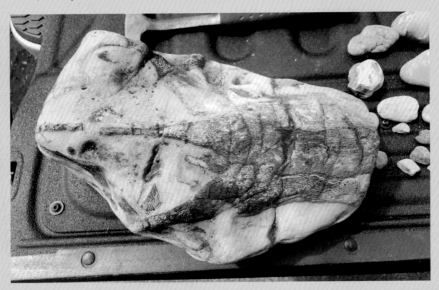

In Oregon, all beaches are public land managed by the state. State rules regarding rockhounding on beaches offer rockhounds a very special opportunity to engage in fossil discovery. Buried in the Oregon Administrative Rules Database is a clause of regulations outlining hobby collecting of rocks and fossils along the state's seashore. These rules are outlined in Chapter 736, Division 21, Section 90 and state that the public may collect rock and fossil material from Oregon beaches for hobby purposes only. No sale of any collected material is permitted.

In the rules, collectible material is divided into three categories: sand, pebble-sized, and cobble-sized. Pebble-sized specimens like agates, shell fossils, and seashells may be collected in volumes up to one gallon per day, with a maximum of three gallons per year. Larger cobbles may be collected in quantities up to five gallons per day, with a maximum of ten gallons per year. Furthermore, the rules state that the public is welcome to take cobbles that contain fossils, and there are no stipulations regarding vertebrate versus invertebrate. This results in a very unusual and special privilege for rockhounds!

There are prohibitions, however. Digging directly into boulders, cliff faces, seawalls, or wave benches to remove embedded fossils is not allowed. Paleontology permits are required in such situations. However, if the fossil exists in the form of a *loose cobble* on the beach and fits in a five-gallon bucket, you may indeed collect it. The regulations also state that cobbles moved out of the way while searching must be returned to their original state. Basically, if you move a bunch of cobbles out of the way to get to others, you cannot leave piles behind. You need to put each rock back in place.

So what happens if you find something that looks like fossil bone on an Oregon beach? The first thing to do is photograph the fossil in place. Fossil bone has a distinct, porous texture and looks and feels different from the sandstone or mudstone that surrounds it. If the fossil fragment is in a loose cobble and fits in your five-gallon bucket, you may keep it. If the fossil is embedded in a cliff or wave bench, note the location of your discovery (coordinates are best) and share that information with staff members of the nearest state park.

You should also engage the broader fossil community about your find. In the Portland region, the North America Research Group (NARG) is a paleontology-focused rock club that works to promote fossil discoveries around the state. NARG is the best community group to connect with regarding fossil finds in Oregon. Sometimes, a discovery is noteworthy enough to be examined by paleontologists and prepared for museum display. The folks at NARG can help with fossil identification and connect you with researchers and institutions. They also host annual paleontology festivals where you can engage with scientists and fellow fossil hunters. Perhaps you should even consider becoming a member yourself!

Fossil hunting along Oregon's beaches offers rockhounds an opportunity to contribute directly to the pool of paleontological understanding. If you discover something cool, reach out and share it.

㉑ Lost Creek

The diminutive Lost Creek has a big story to tell. It trickles across the vast beach, moving just enough sand out of the way to reveal a bed of small agates, jaspers, and fossil shells. The story begins about 55 million years back. The world was hot and steaming. There was no ice at the poles. The age of mammals was just getting started. In Oregon, the Cascade Range volcanoes did not yet exist. The hot climate dumped up to 10 feet of rain on this place, and sea levels were so high, they reached inland toward the domain of the John Day River. The earliest Clarno volcanoes were erupting in central Oregon, with rivers sweeping silica-rich sediments toward the sea. To the south, the mighty Klamath terrane was pulsing sands from its ancient, deformed rocks into the mix. All of these sediments would eventually flush to the seafloor, slumping off the coastal shelf and into the deep. The oldest rocks in Lost Creek hail from these seafloor sediments: the Tyee Formation.

A local rockhound shows beach strollers his treasure from Lost Creek.

Soon after, a massive plateau of undersea basalt called Siletzia would be forced against the continent, relocating the coastline to the west. Global events involving tectonics and volcanism would lead to a period of global cooling, and ice would begin gathering at the poles. Extinctions would occur, and the sea level would retreat from inland Oregon, moving closer to the coastline of today. More sediments would pile up off the coast. The rocks from these events show up in Lost Creek as the Nestucca mudstones, and Alsea and Yaquina sandstones. These formations carry the ashy sediments from the birth of the early Cascades with them. It's likely that the agates and jaspers found in little Lost Creek come from all these old seafloor sediments, which swept a lot of ashy silica off the continent and out to sea. Each of these old marine formations is fossiliferous, too, and some of the shells may end up here as well.

Most of the fossil shells in Lost Creek, however, come from the Astoria Formation, the youngest of the rocks, which started depositing about 20 million years back. How is it, though, that a neat progression of old marine rocks are no longer in the deep? Why are they eroding from mountains of the Coast Range that rise above the sea? The answer is subduction. As the oceanic Juan de Fuca plate dives beneath the continent, a great deal of marine sediments were forced against and under the North American plate, uplifting the surface to form the Coast Range we know today. Erosion eventually removed surface rock to expose the marine rocks beneath. The treasures it holds erode down the slopes, onto the beaches, back out to sea.

WHAT YOU'LL FIND: Fossil clams, agate, jasper	**LIMITS:** 1 gallon of pebbles and shells per person, per day, with a yearly maximum of 3 gallons total; 5 gallons of cobbles per person, per day, with a yearly maximum of 10 gallons
GEOLOGIC AGE: Cenozoic era; Eocene, Oligocene, and Miocene epochs	
	LOCATION: Oregon Beach 62: 44.543833, –124.074194,
TOOLS: Wellies, waders, or water shoes; a small garden trowel to help tip specimens from the sand	**VEHICLE:** Any
AGENCY: Oregon State Parks	**SEASONS:** Any

DIRECTIONS → Make your way to the intersection of Oregon Coast Highway (US Highway 101) and Corvallis-Newport Highway (US 20) in the center of Newport, Oregon. Drive south on US 101 for 7 miles. Turn right at the sign for Lost Creek State Park Day Use Area. Park here and follow the established foot trail a few yards down to the beach.

Opposite: It's hard to believe these seemingly fresh-looking clams could be millions of years old.

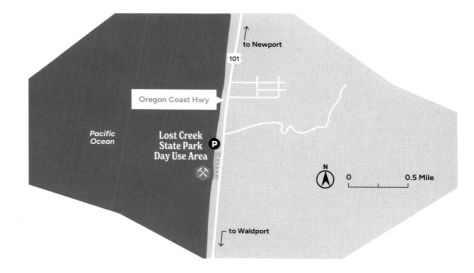

AT THE SITE → The diminutive Lost Creek is visible from the path. A hand tool or small trowel can be helpful sorting through the fine gravels of the creek. Whole fossil clams seem to be the most abundant treasure, but a few agates and jaspers show up too.

22 Big Creek

Big Creek cuts down through the Coast Range forests and dumps its cobbles and pebbles into the sea, but not before spreading them out in a spectacular gravel bar along the beach. From the high points of the Coast Range, pebbles erode from the Tyee Formation, laid down some 55 million years ago along the ancient coastline. In the lower foothills, the creek cuts through the younger Yachats Basalt, which erupted here some 37 million years ago. The Yachats eruptions are tied to that troublesome hotspot over in Yellowstone, if you can believe it. It's theorized by some geologists that the Oregon coast once overrode it, and several eruptions ensued. Along Big Creek you'll find an epiphany of basalt and diabase (basalt's unerupted twin), which is flecked with elongated white feldspar crystals.

Alongside the basalt and diabase, more colorful pebbles show up in abundance. It's likely these were dragged down onto the beach by Big Creek from the Tyee Formation, which consists of long-gone river channels, muddy deltas, sandy beaches, and seafloor stuff. The sediments that make up the Tyee all derived from the ancient Klamath terrane of the southern part of Oregon and the Clarno volcanoes of central Oregon. The Clarno volcanoes are long gone, having been replaced by the monolithic Cascades, but the Klamath Mountains persist to this day, ruling over the southern Oregon coast.

Let's imagine the time of the Tyee's formation. It's the dawn of the age of mammals. Smoldering volcanoes of the Clarnos peek above the horizon to the east. It's hard to say if they are snowcapped, since the time of the Tyee (the Eocene epoch) was ever so hot and steamy. On the horizon to the south, the Klamath Mountains loom, a mass of several accreted terranes that have only recently finished docking with North America. Each of these high mountainous regions sends rocky debris down rivers and out into the ancient Tyee basin. Fifty-five million years pass, and we're back in the present day. The old Tyee basin has been uplifted into the Coast Range. Deep in the past, pebbles and sediments dumped into it, and now it empties everything back out down rivers and creeks, ever propagating the endless cycling of sedimentary rocks.

Sunset on the beach near Big Creek

A small cobble of diabase, which shallowly invaded the bedrock of the Coast Range

WHAT YOU'LL FIND: Basalt, diabase, agate, jasper, quartzite, and sandstone	**LIMITS:** 1 gallon of pebbles and shells per person, per day, with a yearly maximum of 3 gallons total; 5 gallons of cobbles per person, per day, with a maximum of 10 gallons per year
GEOLOGIC AGE: Cenozoic era, Eocene and Oligocene epochs	
TOOLS: Wellies, waders, or water shoes; a small garden trowel to help tip specimens from the sand	**LOCATION:** **Parking, Oregon Beach 90:** 44.169972, –124.116333 **Big Creek:** 44.175500, –124.115861
AGENCY: Oregon State Parks	**VEHICLE:** Any
	SEASONS: Any

DIRECTIONS → Make your way to the intersection of Oregon Coast Highway (US Highway 101) and State Route 126 in Florence, Oregon. From here, drive north on US 101 for 14.8 miles. Turn left at the sign for Muriel O. Ponsler Memorial State Scenic Viewpoint, which is part of Carl G. Washburne Memorial State Park. Park here and take the short path from the overlook down to the beach. Here, the diminutive China Creek runs across the sands. Hike north along the beach for 0.4 mile to Big Creek, which is much larger and rich in pebbles.

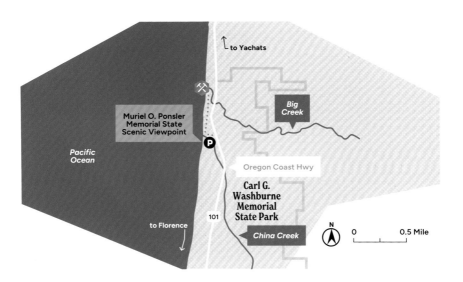

AT THE SITE → Big Creek lives up to its name. During wetter seasons, it can run fast and deep, cutting a sandy ravine in the beach. Search around it and be careful when wading in it. Its sandy edges can give way. Large gravel bars that are safe to dig around in flank the creek's wings. Most rocks here are colorful quartzite and sandstone pebbles from the Tyee Formation. Agates and jaspers appear as well, likely coming from both the Tyee Formation and Yachats Basalt.

㉓ Seven Devils

The colorful, veined pebbles that show up at Seven Devils State Recreation Site come as a bit of a surprise, especially if you've been making your way down the Oregon coast from the north. Here, at Seven Devils, we hit a geological transition zone, where two strikingly different histories collide. To the north, the Oregon Coast Range and beaches are made up of sediments from the Tyee Formation

The creek at Seven Devils during low tide

A variety of rocks from the ancient terranes of the Klamaths as well as the younger rocks of the Coast Range mix together at Seven Devils.

and lava rocks from Siletzia. None of these rocks is much older than 56 million years or so. All of them were born during the Cenozoic—the age of mammals. To the south, though, the Cenozoic rocks give way to much older stuff—the sheared, cooked, and warped rocks of the Klamath country. The Klamath's mountains are a braided rope of exotic terranes—land from somewhere else. Most of the terrane rocks were born long ago (and far away) as undersea lavas and seafloor sediments during the Paleozoic and Mesozoic eras. (Need a refresher on geologic time? Consult the geological timescale at the back of the book!) Over the last 100 million years, they've been forced onto the continent in a mess of crushed and recrystallized rock, but not without almost being swallowed forever by a subduction zone trench.

Of the Klamath terranes, the Sixes River terrane is the youngest, made of sediments that sank to the seafloor about 90 million years ago, during the Cretaceous period. Today, rocks from the Sixes River terrane dump out onto the beach at Seven Devils in the form of marbled argillites, milky quartz, and shiny jaspers. These materials were once mudstones forced into a subduction trench and then uplifted. In the process, they were squeezed and baked—and eventually released—newly shiny, hardened, and metamorphosed. They offer themselves up to us in a dizzying array of colors, and almost all of them make for wonderful lapidary materials.

The Sixes River terrane, Siletzia, and the marine sediments of the Tyee Formation all dump rock material onto the beach at Seven Devils. For several million years now, each geological formation has been eroding its way back toward the sea. The colorful rocks in the diminutive creek at Seven Devils share one destiny: to be beckoned back to their original home in the deep. Consider that when collecting here. These pebbles have made it so close to their great return. By taking them, you are intercepting them in their journey and forever altering their story.

WHAT YOU'LL FIND: Marbled argillite, quartzite, milky quartz, jasper	**LIMITS:** 1 gallon of pebbles and shells per person, per day, with a yearly maximum of 3 gallons total; 5 gallons of cobbles per person, per day, with a yearly maximum of 10 gallons
GEOLOGIC AGE: Mesozoic to Cenozoic eras	
TOOLS: Wellies, water shoes, or waders; a small garden trowel to help tip specimens from the sand	**LOCATION:** Oregon Beach 142: 43.235806, –124.391333
	VEHICLE: Any
AGENCY: Oregon State Parks	**SEASONS:** Any

DIRECTIONS → Make your way to the intersection of State Route 42 and Oregon Coast Highway (US Highway 101) in Bandon, Oregon. Drive north on US 101 for 4.2 miles. Turn left onto Seven Devils Road. Drive for 4.5 miles, then turn left at the entrance of Seven Devils State Recreation Site. Drive 0.3 mile on the entrance road and park near the beach. A short path leads down to the water.

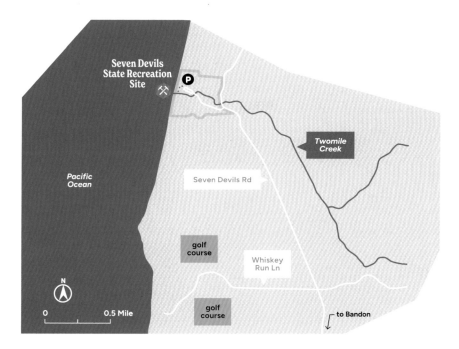

AT THE SITE → Twomile Creek runs along the Seven Devils parking area and spills out onto the beach where it clears away sand, revealing a small area rich in colorful stones. A small hand tool or trowel can be helpful for tipping rocks out of the sand. Coming at low tide is recommended. A fine coating of algae can leave some white rocks looking a bit green. Give them a slight scrub to check. The gray, veined stones are likely graywacke—sandstone derived from basalts that have been altered. Black rocks with veins are likely the metamorphosed mudstones of the Sixes River terrane. Agates and jaspers may hail from any of the formations.

OREGON
Klamath Country

Welcome to a very old part of the Pacific Northwest. A great deal of the
rock that makes up the bedrock here was born as ocean crust in the era
before the dinosaurs (the Paleozoic) and glommed onto our continent
in a series of accretionary events during the dinosaurs' monstrous
and ill-fated reign (the Mesozoic). Marine reefs, rocky island arcs, and
huge swaths of seafloor sediments rode in on the ocean crust conveyor belt and attached themselves (accreted) onto North America as
the conveyor slipped underneath. It was never a tidy process, though,
and a great deal of the rocks were forced deep and burped back up.
The resulting rocks are stunning greenstones (squeezed volcanic
rock), cherts and argillites (recrystallized mudstones), and granites
from rock that melted. This region also holds North America's largest exposure of rock from the mantle in the form of harzburgite and
serpentinite. These rocks provide an extraordinarily rare glimpse into
Earth's inside. In the remote and misty Klamath Mountains, rivers and
beaches are the easiest places to find interesting rocks and minerals.

Opposite: A colorful cobble of red jasper likely from
a chert deposit in the Yolla Bolly Terrane

⑳ Elk River

The Elk River carves its way out of the steep Klamath Mountains, flooding lowland cranberry bog territory before dumping out into the Pacific Ocean. The rocks that make up the darkly forested peaks are remnants of exotic terranes—land that came from somewhere else. Earth's plates are perpetually in motion, colliding into each other in some places and rifting apart in others. The oceanic plate off the coast of the Pacific Northwest has long been colliding with our own. But because the oceanic plate is made of cold, dense rocks, it dives beneath North America, which is quite buoyant in comparison. Continents float. However, the diving—or subduction—of an ocean plate is never tidy. Ocean crusts aren't flat, they have seamounts and plateaus and rifting ridges too. They have deep basins of sediments that originated from the continent. When these masses meet a subduction zone, they make a mess of things.

The majority of rocks tumbling down the Elk River come from a large swath of ancient seafloor muds and sands. These are rocks from the Galice Formation, and they date back to the Jurassic, when North America was setting out on its own after a fresh breakup with Pangea. During this time, the Atlantic Ocean was opening up, forcing a newly single North America to start overriding oceanic plates on her western shores. Think of it as her hot-girl summer. Sands and clay from early west coast rivers were dumping into the sea and piling up on the ocean floor. When subduction brought these sediments back toward North America, they weren't able to continue riding on the downgoing oceanic plate. In their forceful collision with the continent, these old sediments were metaphorically altered into sparkly schists. Now they dominate the upper portion of the river.

Lower down the Elk River, closer to the valley, the riverbed is suddenly invaded by very different materials. Here,

Autumn on the quiet Elk River

Conglomerate and granite dominate the riverbed at Site A.

rusty conglomerates mix into the fold. Even more striking is the appearance of granite-like rocks—diorite—that dominate the gravels. This is the stuff of melting. In the process of subduction, melts from the mantle intruded among the accreting terranes. Called plutons, these melts are often found invading old terrane rocks, essentially stitching them to the continent. They're the glue. The lower stretch of the Elk River cuts through an exposed pluton and drags its light, granitic rocks into the river, where they join the ranks of the old sediments from a bygone world.

WHAT YOU'LL FIND: Schist, conglomerate, granite-like rocks	**LIMIT:** Up to 10 pounds per person, per day
GEOLOGIC AGE: Mesozoic era, Jurassic period	**LOCATION:** Site A: 42.708750, −124.331944 Site B: 42.725694, −124.271278
TOOLS: Wellies, waders, or water shoes; a hiking pole for balance	**VEHICLE:** Any
AGENCY: Rogue River–Siskiyou National Forest	**SEASONS:** Summer and fall. Warning: Avoid the river in winter and spring. High runoff poses a danger to you, and you pose a danger to spring-spawning fish.

DIRECTIONS → **Site A:** Make your way to the intersection of Oregon Coast Highway (US Highway 101) and 8th Street in Port Orford, Oregon. From here, drive north on US 101 for 3.1 miles. Turn right/east onto Elk River Road (Forest Road 5325). Drive for 14 miles and turn left onto a short dirt track down to the river, or pull over and park here and walk the short track down to the water instead. (At the time these directions were compiled, a large boulder at the 14-mile mark on Elk River Road was spray painted red. Keep an eye out for it as a landmark for Site A.)

Site B: From Site A, continue up Elk River Road (FR 5325) for 4.7 miles. (You will pass Sunshine Bar Campground along the way.) Continue straight onto FR 5201 and drive 500 feet. In this very short distance, you'll pass the entrance for Butler Bar Campground. Just after the entrance, pull over by the bridge and park. The gravel bar is just a few paces down a path along the river.

AT THE SITE → The gravels at Site A are dominated by plutonic rocks (diorite and her sisters). Galice Formation rocks from upstream can be found mixed in. The cobbles can be quite large and wonderful for suiseki. The Elk River is also the boundary line for the Grassy Knob Wilderness Area. No rock collecting is allowed on land above the waterline on the opposite (north) side of the river. The same goes for Site B.

Site B is just under the bridge at the northeast end of Butler Bar Campground. Here the rocks are strictly metamorphosed marine sediments of the Galice Formation (flashy phyllite and schist are most abundant). The river meanders slower here, and the rocks are more pebble size than cobble size.

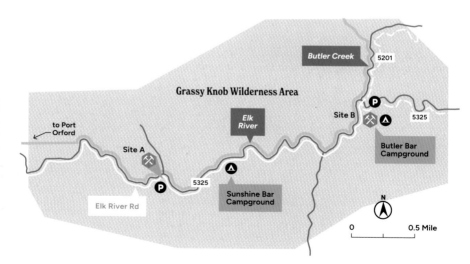

25 Sisters Rocks

Here at Sisters Rocks, dark muddy sediments laid down on a Jurassic seafloor rise like monoliths from the sea, connected to the coast by a narrow bridge of land. The night-colored bodies of the Sisters sea stacks are streaked with veins of milky white calcite and quartz, harboring occasional seams of clear agate. These gargantuan piles of dark mudstone hail from the Otter Point Formation, the bottommost rocks of the puzzling Gold Beach Terrane.

Terranes are travelers, blocks of earth moved around by plate tectonics. In the Pacific Northwest the big story is the accretion of exotic terranes over the last roughly 100 million years. Often, we can imagine accretion as scraps of ocean crust gluing themselves to the continent as they get scraped off of subducting oceanic plates, or glomming onto the underside of the continent as they ride down the subduction trench. But the Gold Beach terrane is different. It didn't come

Sisters Rocks are composed of heavily sheared and silicified mudstone from an ancient seafloor.

The dark mudstones are streaked with veins of minerals like clear agate and milky white quartz.

riding in, saddles ablaze, from the westward open ocean, getting lassoed into a subduction trench. Instead it rode up from the south, ponying up the coastline on an ocean plate that was riding toward the continent at an oblique angle. Imagine a gang of masked robbers trying to overtake a moving train. Their motion is a gallop both toward it and alongside it.

What's exciting about the Gold Beach terrane is how far these rocks have traveled. Analysis of crystal grains and magnetic minerals reveal that its sediments were laid down off the coast of southern California and the Baja Peninsula during the Jurassic, when large reptiles ruled land and sea. These marine rocks began migrating here during the Cretaceous, finally docking with the Oregon coast some 50 million years ago.

Much of the Gold Beach terrane is composed of marine mudstones and sandstones that are nearly intact. In them, we can see ripple marks, cross-bedding, and even fossils. But at the bottom of the terrane, our inky Otter Point Formation has been deformed and altered, run through with a spiderweb of white crystalline minerals. And strangely, small outcrops of rocks like serpentinite (stuff from the mantle) show up among its many faults. For now, more questions than answers surround the stuff of Sisters Rocks. When we gaze into the marbled boulders all we see is mystery.

WHAT YOU'LL FIND: Agate, quartz, deformed mudstone	**LIMITS:** 1 gallon of pebbles and shells per person, per day, with a yearly maximum of 3 gallons total; 5 gallons of cobbles per person, per day, with a yearly maximum of 10 gallons
GEOLOGIC AGE: Mesozoic era, Jurassic to Cretaceous periods	
	LOCATION: **Parking:** 42.592556, –124.397139 **Sisters Rocks, Oregon Beach 168:** 42.593056, –124.404000
TOOLS: Geology pick, safety glasses	
AGENCY: Oregon State Parks	
	VEHICLE: Any
	SEASONS: Any

DIRECTIONS → Make your way to the intersection of Oregon Coast Highway (US Highway 101) and 8th Street in Port Orford, Oregon. From here, drive south on US 101 for 13.6 miles to the Sisters Rocks State Park south trailhead. The gravel parking lot on the west side of the highway is large but poorly marked. From the northwest corner of the parking lot, follow the narrow trail that leads down to both coves, approximately 0.5 mile. Take care in wet weather, as the trail can be slippery.

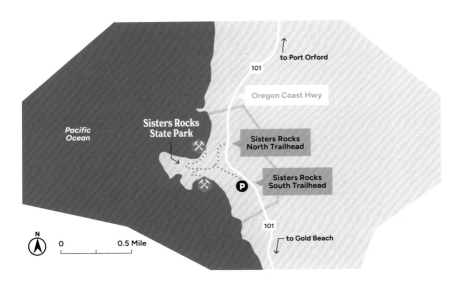

AT THE SITE → The Sisters are flanked on their north and south sides by coves. The beaches here are rich in cobbles, but the prominences of the sea stacks themselves can be worth hunting around in as well. Veins of white minerals and agate streak the ancient black rocks. There's no real need to hammer at boulders down here, since plenty of material covers the ground, but if you do, remember that all rock hammers have an on-off switch. They're called safety glasses.

Rogue River

The Rogue is a rainbow of battered stones. Here, in Oregon's second longest river, every possible rock you could imagine tumbles downstream. These are the mélange rocks of the many terranes buried within the epically large Franciscan Subduction Complex. They were once mountains, riverbeds, seafloors, undersea volcanoes, and even bits of the inside of Earth—not the crust, the mantle! *The inside.*

The majority of rocks in this stretch of the lower Rogue River are sparkly schists—ancient mudstones transformed into their journey from seafloor to mountaintop. Among them, colorful greenstones and epidote from the baked remnants of old undersea volcanoes appear. Spidery, dark-green serpentinites and peridotites, the

A peaceful autumn day on the lower Rogue River

A vertiable rainbow of rocks such as chert, gneiss, peridotite, sandstone, and quartz dominate the gravels.

stuff of the mantle, blend in among the gravels. Bright-red jaspers, which likely hail from old quartz-rich sandstones or opal-rich radiolarian cherts, flash like a siren in the water. Bridal pebbles of white quartz, mottled and felted plutonic rocks, striped sandstones, and ribboned mudstones add to the medley. The whole world is in the Rogue.

Over several million years, these rocks assembled here through epic tectonics. North America was coming into her own after a split up with Pangea. She was traveling west, overriding ocean plates as she went. Most of the rocks here are a mélange of oceanic rocks spit up from subduction trenches during all the action. Other rocks in the Rogue hail from plutons that intruded the crust during subduction. These melts rose from the deepest part of the subduction zone where conditions were right. Melts are buoyant and always find a way upward into the crust. During this time, it is likely there was a volcanic arc above them (like the modern-day Cascades), but it has long since eroded, likely carried out to sea by an ancestral river.

WHAT YOU'LL FIND: Schist, quartz, jasper, chert, serpentinite, peridotite, epidote, greenstone, granite-like rocks, gneiss-like rocks, agate, sandstone, mudstone	**LIMIT:** Up to 10 pounds per person, per day
	LOCATIONS: **Site A, Lobster Creek Campground:** 42.502194, –124.29652 **Site B, Quosatana Campground:** 42.499917, –124.234278
GEOLOGIC AGE: Mesozoic era, Jurassic period; Cenozoic era, Eocene epoch	
TOOLS: Wellies, waders, or water shoes; a hiking pole for balance	**VEHICLE:** Any
AGENCY: Rogue River–Siskiyou National Forest	**SEASONS:** Summer and fall. Warning: Avoid the river in winter and spring. High runoff poses a danger to you, and you pose a danger to spring-spawning fish.

DIRECTIONS → **Site A:** Make your way to the intersection of Ellensburg Avenue (US Highway 101) and 8th Avenue in Gold Beach, Oregon. Drive north on US 101 for 1.3 miles. Turn right onto Jerry's Flat Road and drive 9.7 miles. Turn left at the sign for Lobster Creek Campground and drive 0.3 mile to the boat ramp and beach. Park in the day-use parking area. **Site B:** From Lobster Creek, continue east on Jerry's Creek Road for 4.7 miles to Quosatana Campground. (Jerry's Creek Road changes its name to Agness Road/Forest Road 33 0.1 mile after leaving Lobster Creek.) Turn left into Quosatana Campground and drive 0.3 mile down to the boat ramp and beach. Park in the day-use parking area.

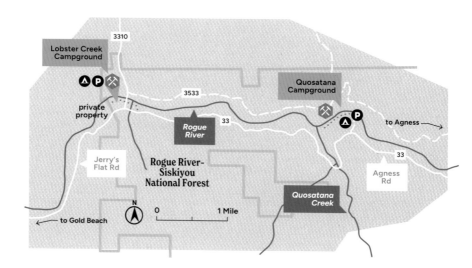

AT THE SITE → Driving onto the gravel bars at both locations is allowed, and you'll see several other people doing it. I recommend parking in the designated day-use parking area near the boat ramp at each site and walking down to the river. There are all sorts of ways to get stuck on gravel bars. Please note that the western half of the massive gravel bar at Lobster Creek Campground is private property (see map). At both sites, search the gravel bars for green epidote, dark green-black peridotite and serpentinite, red jasper, white milky quartz, sparkly schist, and dark-teal greenstones.

㉗ Meyer Creek

Among the prominences of large scenic sea stacks, a small creek runs out of the coastal mountains, across the beach, and into the sea. Named Meyer Creek on some maps and Myer Creek on others and Meyers or Myers on still others, it drags rocks from the Yolla Bolly terrane down with it. The flow of the creek is no match for the power of ocean waves though. With each high tide, the creek is inundated by beach sand and buried from view. It takes several hours of a receding tide for sweet little Meyer Creek to shake the sandy coat off its body. Around low tide, and for just an hour or two after, fiery-red and ochre-yellow jaspers emerge from the creek, before being inundated again.

Jaspers are secondary rocks, meaning they form after-the-fact. *Jasper* is not a scientific term but rather a rockhounding name. *Jasper* is used perhaps much too

Meyer Creek running into the sea at low tide

Red jasper with fine white veins of quartz from the Yolla Bolly terrane

casually for a whole variety of rocks, but most often it describes a kind of colorful, opaque material found in volcanic and sedimentary deposits. It forms as silica mobilizes and redeposits among the host rock. In the case of Meyer Creek, we find a great deal of jasper tumbling down from a metamorphic formation, the Yolla Bolly. It's highly likely these jaspers are breaking off large sedimentary blocks of argillite, a highly silicified metamorphosed mudstone, or a marine chert layer that has been baked and deformed in its journey onto the continent from the bottom of the sea.

Chert has its origins on the seafloor as a layer of radiolarian ooze that builds up as silica skeletons of radiolarian plankton sink to the seafloor. Cherts are well described in the Yolla Bolly terrane, and massive cliffs of them crop out farther south near Brookings. Sure, it's possible this jasper is derived from the abundant argillite too. If so it would be coming from swaths of rock where hot fluids moved large quantities of silica around during the Yolla Bolly's tectonic journey. However, the widespread presence of chert noted on geological maps of the area leads one to suspect that this spectacular radiolarian stuff is the likely origin of these beautiful jaspers. The only trick to collecting them is to act in harmony with the ellipses of the tides.

WHAT YOU'LL FIND: Red and yellow jasper (chert)	**LIMITS:** 1 gallon of pebbles and shells per person, per day, with a yearly maximum of 3 gallons total; 5 gallons of cobbles per person, per day, with a yearly maximum of 10 gallons
GEOLOGIC AGE: Mesozoic era, Jurassic to Cretaceous periods	
	LOCATION: Oregon Beach 182: 42.305917, –124.410083,
TOOLS: Wellies, waders, or water shoes; a small garden trowel can help tip specimens from the sand	**VEHICLE:** Any
AGENCY: Oregon State Parks	**SEASONS:** Any. Note: Meyer Creek is only accessible at low tide.

DIRECTIONS → Make your way to the intersection of Ellensburg Avenue/Oregon Coast Highway (US Highway 101) and 8th Avenue in Gold Beach, Oregon. Drive south on US 101 for 7.9 miles. Pull right into the lot for Meyers Creek Vista Point. (Note: Do not be tricked by "Meyers Creek Beach Viewpoint" which is 0.6 mile north. See map.) Park and walk the short path down to the beach. Meyer Creek is approximately 350 feet to the north. It runs into the sea below the high bridge.

AT THE SITE → Meyer Creek gets inundated with sand at high tide. The creek takes several hours to push the sand away, revealing itself by low tide. A garden of bright red and

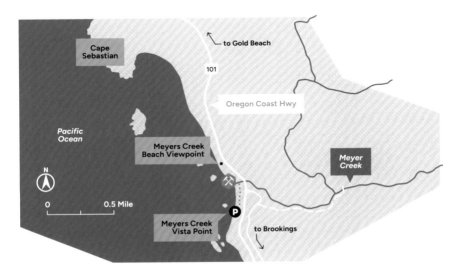

yellow jasper can be found if your timing is right. Make sure to come at low tide or within a one- to two-hour window after low tide. The jaspers tumble down from the Yolla Bolly terrane; however, the scenic sea stacks on the beach are from the slightly younger Otter Point Formation, part of the Gold Beach terrane.

Chetco River

I waded into the Chetco on a cold, sunny day at the start of November. Usually by this time of year, river rockhounding season was over. But the fall rains hadn't made much of a showing, and the river flowed with sanity and placidness. I was alone among the yellowing alders and riverside birdsong. Large gravel bars extended to what felt like the horizon. It was here that I first cried about a rock.

The Chetco River is full of silicate treasures from the Yolla Bolly terrane, which was shoved onto the continent between the Jurassic and Cretaceous. A lot of it

The mist clears on a cold autumn day along the Chetco River.

A rainbow of silicate rocks from the Yolla Bolly terrane await you in the Chetco River.

comes in the form of big chunky jasper, minty green and rusty red, spiderwebbed with delicate white veins. Perhaps this stuff comes from the bountiful cherts of the Yolla Bolly, or perhaps it is hydrothermally altered argillite, a silicified mudstone. Hydrothermal activity is notorious for invading rocks and entombing them in silica. In the Yolla Bolly domain, it's likely both chert and argillite deposits are the source of these wildly colorful and silicified jaspers. We may never be able to document the full extent of what happened in those pressurized subduction trenches back in the Cretaceous, but we do know that they fabulously altered and deformed these old rocks in their journey onto the continent.

I fished a large chunk of minty-green jasper out of the river and noticed its white veins had margins of a candy-pink mineral along them. My heart fluttered a bit, but I dampened it quickly by reasoning it was merely a boundary of red jasper made pink by its faintness. Then everything changed. A few yards away, I spied more pink. Big pink. I lifted a cobble of white quartz from the frigid water. Half of the rock was consumed with baby-girl, Barbie-doll, cotton-candy pink. It was rho-

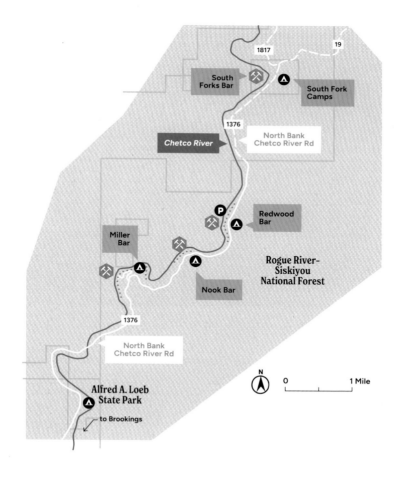

donite, my favorite mineral. Local rockhounds would be quite happy to find this material here, but they probably wouldn't cry. I did. Rhodonite is a material I use frequently in my lapidary craft, but I have always had to purchase it from miners. I had long given up on finding my own. Yet here I was, alone in an icy November river, holding a big chunk of it up to the sun. It was too much for my little rock-loving heart to bear.

This is why we rockhounds do what we do. It's all about the moment little kids squeal with delight when they split open a fossil, or a grown man laughs maniacally into the sky when he pulls a large crystal from a pit in the ground. It's me, crying alone in a mountain river, hugging a candy-pink rock. Will you have the same luck I had in the Chetco River? I don't know. But that's the joy of rockhounding. You've got to get out and try.

WHAT YOU'LL FIND: Jasper, argillite, white quartz, rhodonite, conglomerates, other metamorphic and plutonic rocks	**LIMIT:** Up to 10 pounds per person, per day
	LOCATION: 42.150444, –124.147250
GEOLOGIC AGE: Mesozoic era, Jurassic period	**VEHICLE:** Any, though some clearance and four-wheel drive are recommended to drive onto gravel bars
TOOLS: Wellies, waders, or water shoes; a hiking pole for balance	**SEASONS:** Summer and fall. Warning: Avoid the river in early spring. High runoff poses a danger to you, and you pose a danger to spring-spawning fish.
AGENCY: Rogue River-Siskiyou National Forest	

DIRECTIONS → Make your way to the intersection of the Oregon Coast Highway (US Highway 101) and Pacific Avenue in Brookings, Oregon. From here, drive south on US 101 for 0.7 mile. Turn left on North Bank Chetco River Road (Forest Road 1376) and drive north for 13.2 miles. Turn left at a sign for Redwood Bar. Drive downhill 500 feet on the access road to the large gravel bar. You may park here at the bottom of the road, or if you have good clearance and four-wheel drive, you may drive onto the gravel bar.

AT THE SITE → The gravels here are rich with large cobbles of silicate treasures. Getting close to the water's edge to look at wet rocks will clue you in to the abundance around you. The epically large gravel bars of the Chetco River are filled with campers and RVs in the summer months. I recommend coming in fall to have the place to yourself. If you come during the busy time, consider exploring the gravel bars at Miller Bar and Nook Bar downstream and South Forks Bar upstream as well (see map).

29 Rough and Ready Creek

Rough and Ready Creek puts on display one of Earth's most spectacular outcroppings of rock from the mantle—that red-hot interior you always see in diagrams of a dissected planet. Drawings depicting Earth's interior are always glowing, and the intention is to convey its hotness. But what those drawings fail to do is to convey the mantle's solidness. Earth's mantle isn't an ocean of molten magma. It's solid and crystalline, composed of something called peridotite, a rock made up of the beautiful green mineral olivine. In areas of upwelling or decompression, or when hot seawater trapped in subducted ocean crust gets into it, the mantle can melt and invade the crust (it's where new crust comes from), but for the most part, the mantle rests as a giant mass of dark-green crystalline mush. The mush is under so much heat and pressure that it flows with plasticity.

The mountains surrounding Rough and Ready Creek are an expanse of peridotite mush that has been thrust to Earth's surface. In the river, the greenness of the peridotite cobbles are disguised under a coating of rusty limonite. These rocks carry a lot of iron in their crystal matrix, which behaves dramatically in the presence of water and air. If you were to chip away at a cobble, you'd reveal its dark-green crystalline interior. Since you asked, the variety of peridotite found in Rough and Ready Creek is called harzburgite. This is one of the few places on Earth's surface where it can be found. Sculptors love to work with this material in their studios, mostly for its intrigue and rarity.

The harzburgite is part of a larger feature in the Klamath Mountains called the Josephine ophiolite, a jewel in the crown of geological research. Ophiolites are uplifted swaths of rock from the ocean floor that contain neatly divided structural features. In them, geologists can see where mantle peridotite transitioned to basaltic crust, and where deep marine sediments ac-

An ocean of harzburgite, a variety of peridotite, dominates the floodplain of Rough and Ready Creek.

Though the darkest of greens on the inside, harzburgite is characterized by a tan, rusty rind.

cumulated on top of all of it. Ophiolites are remarkable cross sections of the mantle-crust boundary and look nothing like what we see in the bright and colorful diagrams of textbooks. Now forced up into mountains, these rocks are dark and crystalline, crumbing and rusting from their epic journey from seafloor to mountaintop. They're exquisitely special because almost every rock on Earth's crust is of the crust. It's a rare and humbling opportunity to be able to hold the pure stuff of the mantle in the palm of your hand.

WHAT YOU'LL FIND: Harzburgite (peridotite), serpentinite

GEOLOGIC AGE: Mesozoic era, Jurassic period

TOOLS: Wellies, waders, or water shoes; a hiking pole for balance

AGENCY: Bureau of Land Management, Medford District, Grants Pass Interagency Office

LIMIT: A reasonable amount of rocks may be taken for personal use only. A reasonable amount is often defined as up to 25 pounds per person, per day, with a maximum of 250 pounds per year. Do you need 25 pounds of rocks? Probably not. Collect lightly and with intention.

LOCATION: 42.093417, –123.683417

VEHICLE: Any

SEASONS: Summer and fall. Warning: Avoid the creek in winter and spring. High runoff poses a danger to you, and you pose a danger to spring-spawning fish.

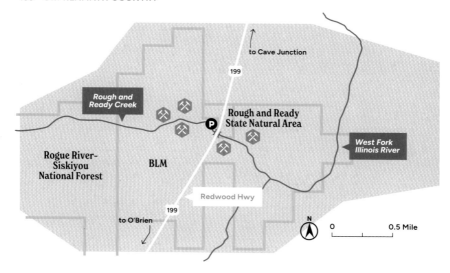

DIRECTIONS → Make your way to the intersection of Caves Highway (State Route 46) and Redwood Highway (US Highway 199) in Cave Junction, Oregon. From here, drive south on US 199 for 5.2 miles to a bridge that spans Rough and Ready Creek. Pull off the highway into a small gravel lot just before the bridge. Park here and explore the extensive gravel bars along the creek.

AT THE SITE → The cobbly floodplain of Rough and Ready Creek is extensive. Rusting cobbles of harzburgite dominate the landscape. This is an excellent location for sculptors to acquire large cobbles and small boulders of carving material. In addition, serpentinite can easily be found in small chunks among the ocean of harzburgite. It lacks the rusting rind, revealing patches of dark, gemmy green. Take caution using serpentinites for craft, as they contain chrysotile asbestos.

30 Josephine Creek

Walls of serpentinite rise from the ground around the confluence of Josephine Creek and the Illinois River. Here, gravels from the Josephine ophiolite pile up in colorful splendor. Dark, waxy serpentinite and rusty harzburgite dominate the creek bed. Beautiful greenstones, epidotes, shiny cherts, and other metamorphosed rocks mix themselves in. The Josephine ophiolite is an exceptional sequence of seafloor crust that carries its basement with it: rocks from the mantle. These are the harzburgites and serpentinites that rise in mountains above you.

Deep, deep underneath us, the mantle is a dark, crystalline mush made almost entirely of a material called peridotite, rich in the mineral olivine (or "peridot" in its gem form). Harzburgite is a variety of peridotite that remains very much unchanged from its mantle state of being. Serpentinite, however, is peridotite that has been extraordinarily changed by its proximity to water. Serpentinite is the stuff that was forced to have the crust as its unpleasant neighbor. The general theory is that seawater from above percolates down into faults and fractures between the crust and the mantle. The water gets hot. It dissolves a lot of minerals. It expands, but it has nowhere to go. So it invades the crystalline structure of the peridotites themselves. The metamorphosis is called serpentinization. The resulting serpentinized rocks are extremely sheared by their expansion and not nearly as dense as they were in their peridotite days.

There are also theories that serpentinization can occur if peridotites get caught up in subduction zones and burped up to the surface. What's so interesting about the Josephine ophiolite is that it is not considered to have been dragged down a subduction trench like all the other extraordinary terranes of the Klamath Mountains. Instead, it is theorized that between the extraordinary accretions of land during the Jurassic and Cretaceous, some rifting happened here and a small ocean was born. (That's how all oceans are born.) The small sea was fated for a short life, however. Accretion processes would kick back in, and another island arc riding in from the west would smash up against it, forcing portions of its seafloor up into high mountains between the gargantuan accreted terranes. The ophiolite is a memory of a small ocean that once lived here.

Mike Strickler, a geologist who has focused a great deal of interest on ophiolites, would want you to know that Josephine Creek was where gold was first discovered in Oregon. He would

Cobbles of rocks line the confluence of Josephine Creek with the Illinois River. You'd never suspect their extraordinary origins.

A cobble of severely deformed rock found in Josephine Creek is striped with white quartz and green epidote.

also want you to know that it is one of the few locations on Earth where an extremely rare variety of an iron-nickel mineral, aptly named josephinite, can be found. This is the stuff of meteorites and Earth's inner core. Strickler tells me that josephinite is only found in ophiolite deposits, and its origin is a subject of intense debate. This region of Oregon easily has the state's most fascinating rocks. If you're as curious about them as I am, I highly recommend reading Strickler's delightfully approachable work, "A Layperson's Guide to the Josephine Ophiolite" (see Appendix 3: Resources).

WHAT YOU'LL FIND: Peridotite, harzburgite, greenstone, epidote, schist, chert	**LIMIT:** Up to 10 pounds per person, per day
GEOLOGIC AGE: Mesozoic era, Jurassic to Cretaceous periods	**LOCATION:** 42.243306, -123.684583
	VEHICLE: Any
TOOLS: Wellies, waders, or water shoes; a hiking pole for balance	**SEASONS:** Summer and fall. Warning: Avoid the river in early spring. High runoff poses a danger to you, and you pose a danger to spring-spawning fish.
AGENCY: Rogue River–Siskiyou National Forest	

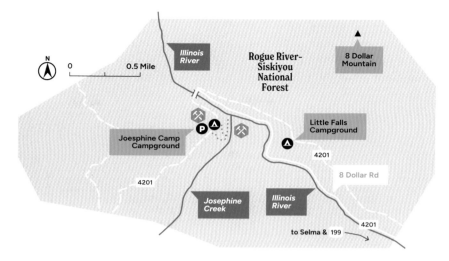

DIRECTIONS → Make your way to the intersection of US Highway 199 (Redwood Highway) and Deer Creek Road in Selma, Oregon. From here, drive south on US 199 for 3.7 miles. Turn right onto 8 Dollar Road (Forest Road 4201) and drive for 3.2 miles to Josephine Camp Campground. (After 2.8 miles 8 Dollar Road will traverse a bridge and backtrack along the opposite bank.) Josephine Camp is very small, with just a few roadside parking spots. Park here and follow one of the several paths leading downhill from the campground to the confluence of Josephine Creek and the Illinois River.

AT THE SITE → A lovely gravel bar gathers where Josephine Creek dumps out into the Illinois River. Beautiful greenstone, epidote, chert, and schist are common here, though the dominant rock is serpentinite. Large outcrops of serpentinite flank the banks of Josephine Creek. It is a dark, waxy rock that crumbles easily. Though it may be tempting, avoid breaking any of this material up with tools, since it may contain chrysotile asbestos. Serpentinite is safe to touch and look at. However, its dust is hazardous in the lungs. The greenstones, epidote, and cherts are the rocks of interest here for pebble puppies and lapidary artists.

WASHINGTON AND OREGON
High Lava Plateaus

Imagine cracks opening up in the earth, releasing a flood of lava so voluminous it spreads over hundreds of square miles in a matter of days. It may seem far-fetched, but 16.7 million years ago, the earth opened up and poured itself out, just like that. These flood basalts didn't erupt from a typical volcano but rather from dozens of fissures in the ground near present-day Walla Walla, Washington, and Monument, Enterprise, and Frenchglen, Oregon. Geologists refer to the features underneath the fissures as feeder dikes. These dikes are linked to the Yellowstone hotspot, which sat under southeastern Oregon at the time. Over the course of 10 million years, these lava floods raged and froze, layer by layer, into an ocean of basalt.

Basalt is not richly known for yielding treasures, but it is not entirely devoid of them either. In some areas of the Columbia Basin, rockhounds can find interesting agates, jaspers, and wood petrified in between the pulses of lava. The best places to search are among the barren slopes and dramatic canyons of this rugged landscape.

Opposite: Petrified wood found in a deposit of sediments sandwiched between lava flows at Saddle Mountain

Rockhounding along the John Day River on a chilly autumn day. Spectacular cliffs of flood basalts rise in the background.

31 Cottonwood Canyon (Oregon)

In Cottonwood Canyon, the John Day River carves a stunning path through epic layers of Columbia River flood basalts. These dark lava rocks flowed here during a period of extraordinary volcanism that began between 17 and 16 million years ago. The cause is known to have been an intense plume of energy in the mantle called a hotspot. As our continent drifted over the hotspot, it wreaked incredible havoc at the surface. The lavas that erupted covered much of Oregon and Washington within a few million years. Huge lava flows like these are known around the globe as large igneous provinces, and they've happened before—most notably 65 million years ago in India, 183 million years ago when southern Africa and Antarctica broke apart, and 252 million years ago in Siberia. Some of you reading this may feel a shiver hearing those dates. They go hand in hand with Earth's largest mass extinctions.

Researchers have shown that it's not the lava that's responsible for global collapse. It's the incredible amount of greenhouse gases that are released alongside them. They tip the delicate balance of gas exchange in the atmosphere and oceans, igniting a cascading series of not-so-friendly consequences. The Columbia River flood basalts were not as consequential as their predecessors, but they are still shown to have shaped a climate change event that coincided with large migrations and noticeable extinctions in the fossil record.

A handful of treasures: agates, jaspers, and volcanic sandstones that traveled from farther upriver

But wait, what about meteors? Isn't that what everyone talks about with mass extinctions? Trying to make sense of the relationship between known impact events, the eruption of huge lava floods, and mass extinctions is a lot like going out on a Friday night looking for trouble. You'll find it, and the details thereafter will be hazy. There is a possibility that meteor impacts may initiate hotspots in the mantle, but the trouble is that these hotspots persist long after their inception, muddying any proof. Geologists debate the origin of mantle hotspots with vigor and passion, and the meteor impact theory really brings out the fisticuffs. The hotspot that caused the immense Columbia River Basalts around 16 million years back was born off the proto–Pacific Northwest coast, possibly around 56 million years ago, or perhaps even before that. Here in Cottonwood Canyon, one thing is for certain: in extraordinary circumstances, the surface of the earth is capable of tearing open and pouring herself out.

WHAT YOU'LL FIND: Agate, jasper, possibly petrified wood, a few far-traveled granite-like rocks

GEOLOGIC AGE: Cenozoic era, Miocene epoch, plus older rocks from upriver

TOOLS: A hiking pole for balance; swim gear and water shoes for the river

AGENCY: Oregon State Parks, Bureau of Land Management—Prineville District Office

LIMITS: Oregon State Parks suggest hobby collecting at reasonable amounts. This area is a checkerboard of state and BLM land, formally overseen by Cottonwood Canyon State Park. The BLM allows a reasonable amount of collecting for personal use only. A reasonable amount is often defined as up to 25 pounds per person, per day, with a maximum of 250 pounds per year. Due to the joint oversight in this area, collect as lightly as possible.

LOCATION: 45.476972, –120.472111

VEHICLE: Any

SEASONS: Summer and fall. Warning: Avoid the river in winter and spring. High runoff poses a danger to you, and you pose a danger to spring-spawning fish.

DIRECTIONS → Make your way to the intersection of Clark Street and Old Wasco–Heppner Highway in the small town of Wasco, Oregon. From here, drive south on Clark Street a block and a half, and fork left onto State Route 206. Drive south on SR 206 for 14.8 miles. Turn right at the entrance of Cottonwood Canyon State Park. Drive 0.1 mile on the entrance road, then turn right into the parking area for the Hard Stone trailhead. Park here and follow the trail to access gravel bars along the river.

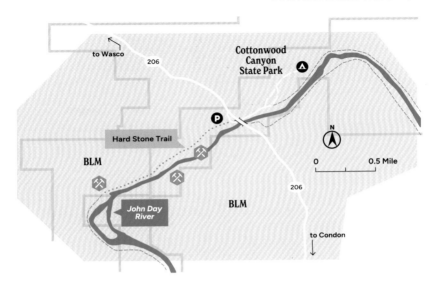

AT THE SITE → The Hard Stone trailhead is an old road that runs along the river. The first mile of trail that leads upriver from the trailhead is on Oregon State Park land, and for another half mile thereafter on BLM land. The large gravel bars are visible from the trail. Several side paths lead down to the water's edge. Agates, jaspers, some petrified wood, and a few granite-like rocks from very far upriver show up in the gravel bars, which are dominated by basalt. In summer when vegetation is dense, some bushwacking may be required to get to the water's edge.

③² Starvation Lane (Oregon)

Large meanders cut a steep canyon over 800 feet deep through the Columbia River flood basalts that comprise the expansive, quiet plateaus of north-central Oregon. The John Day River, the party responsible for such magnificent erosion, drags rocks from almost 300 miles away toward its merger with the mighty Columbia River. In the canyon that Starvation Lane drops into, gravel bars pile up with cobbles of local flood basalt, clear agates, red and yellow jasper, petrified wood, and even granite-like rocks from the river's mountainous headwaters. Highly silicified materials like agate, jasper, and petrified wood are resistant to erosion and pop out of the gravels in lumpy, irregular shapes. On sunny days, the translucent agates glow like gems in a treasure chest.

High above the canyon, broad swaths of sedimentary rocks cap the flood basalts. These sediments, known as the Alkali Canyon Formation, were laid down after the raging flows of lavas ceased. When ditches are cut into the sediments for infrastructure projects, paleontologists descend on them to search for fossils—signs that life came back after the catastrophic lava flows. In trenches cut in Alkali Canyon sediments, they have found fossil horses, ancestral coyotes, and ground sloths. In swampy sediments, they have found portions of tortoises and skeletons of ancestral beavers, evidence of a vibrant ecosystem that appeared after the lava flows ceased. "Life," explains Jeff Goldblum's iconic character in *Jurassic Park*, "finds a way." When hunting through the gravel bars in the canyon below, imagine the bones of these creatures lying 800 feet above, peacefully resting under the expansive wheat fields of the lava plateau.

Down here in the river canyon, any rare fossils that have eroded from the top are unlikely to survive the incredible tumble down cliff faces and the grinding rush of the John Day. The river is the domain of hardy rocks like agate and jasper. I tell you about the fossils because I want you to feel the passage of time in the depth of the canyon. Down here we stand in an era when molten rock invaded

Agates, jaspers, and occasional petrified wood can be found among the gravel.

The John Day River winds through the scenic canyon.

and destroyed everything in its path. The towering slopes and cliffs are composed of dozens of such floods that started over 16 million years ago and persisted for 10 million years. Geologists break the flows up into the Grande Ronde, Wanapum, and Saddle Mountain flows. Atop them, far out of our view, are the sediments that would follow, accumulating in a healing world. The fossils found within them are the remains of intrepid species that would find a way to begin again.

WHAT YOU'LL FIND: Agate, jasper, possibly petrified wood, a few far-traveled granite-like rocks

GEOLOGIC AGE: Cenozoic era, Miocene to Pliocene epochs, plus older rocks from upriver

TOOLS: A hiking pole for balance; swim gear and water shoes for the river

AGENCY: Oregon State Parks, Bureau of Land Management—Prineville District Office

LIMITS: Oregon State Parks suggest hobby collecting at reasonable amounts. This area is a checkerboard of state and BLM land, formerly overseen by Cottonwood Canyon State Park. The BLM allows a reasonable amount of collecting for personal use only. A reasonable amount is often defined as up to 25 pounds per person, per day, with a maximum of 250 pounds per year. Due to the joint oversight in this area, collect as lightly as possible.

LOCATION: 45.506222, –120.362361

VEHICLE: Any; good tires are recommended for lengthy dirt road travel

SEASONS: Summer and fall. Warning: Avoid the river in winter and spring. High runoff poses a danger to you, and you pose a danger to spring-spawning fish.

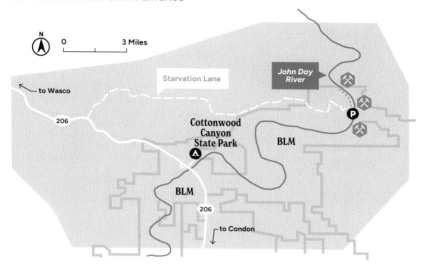

DIRECTIONS → *Do not ask Google for directions to Starvation Lane.* Make your way to the intersection of Clark Street and Old Wasco–Heppner Highway in the small town of Wasco, Oregon. From here, drive south on Clark Street a block and a half, and fork left onto State Route 206. Drive south on SR 206 for 10.9 miles. Turn left onto Starvation Lane and follow it for 11.1 miles. This road snakes along the plateau and then switchbacks down to the river.

This is a popular takeout for boaters, so make sure to park away from the boat ramp so trailers can get in and out. Follow the trail from the parking area that runs downstream along the river for 0.2 mile to the first large gravel bar.

AT THE SITE → Plenty of folks come down here to fly-fish, so try to give them space. The river runs broad with shallow rapids, and enormous amounts of gravel are exposed on both sides. Agates and jaspers are common. Granite-like rocks that have traveled a great distance from the mountainous headwaters of the John Day in eastern Oregon can occasionally be found.

33 Selah Butte (Washington)

Glorious views await you atop Selah Butte, Washington, and if you come in May and June, a super bloom of wildflowers awaits you too. Selah Butte was once a lowland area where catastrophic flood basalts pooled in deep sheets over 16 million years ago. These lavas traveled from fissures that opened up in the earth almost 200 miles away, near present-day Walla Walla, Washington, and Enterprise, Oregon. The flows blanketed the landscape, one after another. In the Yakima River Canyon below Selah Butte, each lava flood can be distinguished from another in distinct layers of columnar basalt—the rock that lava floods leave in their wake.

Periods of quiet intervened during the lava floods' reign of terror. On the highest crest of Selah Butte, a significant layer of sedimentary rock caps the basalts. Erosion is always happening, and when nothing exciting tries to get in its way, large volumes of sediments can accumulate in basins as the eons pass. And that's exactly what happened here. Hardy pebbles of agate, jasper, and breccias that were

An explosion of wildflowers bloom atop Selah Butte in May.

A small agate nodule found nestled beside a stubby hedgehog cactus

dragged into this once-upon-a-time valley now freckle the steep slopes among Selah Butte's sagebrush.

On a planetary scale, the Pacific Northwest is subject to compression in some directions and extension in others. These unbalanced forces are causing our whole region to rotate, but the process doesn't happen neatly. Sometime after the deposition of Selah Butte's sedimentary rocks, compressional forces squeezed and uplifted this part of Washington, forcing its valleys up into long, parallel ridges. Geologists call this topographical feature the Yakima Fold Belt. The meandering path of the Yakima River through the canyon below is evidence that it once ran through a low basin and continued to doggedly cut its path as the landscape rose around it. Today, pebbles from the ancestral river now crumble from the high hill of Selah Butte. The agate and jasper up here aren't plentiful, but you'll be certain to find a few pieces, especially the farther you walk. The real joy of coming up here is for the views of the Yakima Fold Belt and the snowcapped volcanoes of the Cascade Range, the source of the Yakima Canyon's icy waters.

WHAT YOU'LL FIND: Agate, jasper, possibly petrified wood	**LIMITS:** A reasonable amount of rocks may be taken for personal use only. A reasonable amount is often defined as up to 25 pounds per person, per day, with a maximum of 250 pounds per year. Do you need 25 pounds of rocks? Probably not. Collect lightly and with intention.
GEOLOGIC AGE: Cenozoic era, Miocene to Pliocene epochs	
TOOLS: Geology pick or small garden trowel	
AGENCY: Bureau of Land Management— Spokane District Office	**LOCATION:** 46.73253, −120.43395
	VEHICLE: Some clearance and four-wheel drive recommended
	SEASONS: Spring, summer, fall

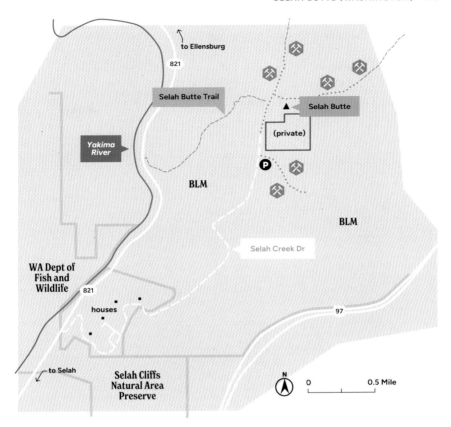

DIRECTIONS → Make your way to the town of Selah, Washington. In the center of town, find
the intersection of Wenas Avenue (State Route 823) and Naches Avenue. From this
intersection drive north on SR 823 for 3.2 miles. Turn left onto SR 821 and drive north for
2.2 miles. Turn right onto Selah Creek Drive (a gravel road) and follow it uphill for 3 miles.
(The first mile snakes up among a handful of hillside homes and then transitions into
a rough, steeper road after the last house.) At the 3-mile mark, an old, overgrown road
peels off to the right. Park here.

AT THE SITE → The old and overgrown roads that fork off to the north and south of the parking area tend to reveal the most material. The longer you stroll along them, the more
material you will find. Keep your distance from the radio towers themselves, which are
surrounded by a small parcel of private property.

In the diggings atop Saddle Mountain, large specimens can be obtained deeper in the pits, and smaller specimens are scattered among the tailings.

34 Saddle Mountain (Washington)

We might be standing on south-central Washington now, but let's travel back 15 million years to the middle of the Miocene epoch. We're standing in a temperate forest that grows in shallow soil atop deep layers of flood basalts. Ancestors of modern spruce, fir, oak, maple, sycamore, and beech trees grow here. Ancestral squirrels leap among the branches. Leaves tremble in the breeze. On the western horizon, the ice-capped volcanoes of the Cascades rise into the sky. A plume of smoke bursts from one peak and grows rapidly. The skies grow dark.

Whether the forest died that day or over months is uncertain, but what geologists do know is that hundreds of trees fell here and were petrified amid the volcanic ash. More lava floods from fissures to the east would soon blanket the area, encasing the fallen forest layer like an Oreo. Unusual tectonic forces would eventually uplift this area into a folded ridge now known as Saddle Mountain, part of the larger Yakima Fold Belt, causing the top of the basalt Oreo to erode away, exposing this fine layer of cream—the ash beds filled with petrified logs.

Rockhounds have been digging up petrified wood here for decades, and the area is still highly productive. You'll find—and probably leave with—several specimens. Some of the material is opalized and brittle, and some of it is nicely agatized and good for lapidary work. A great deal of material can be found by walking among the pits, but large pieces require digging. Remember: All digging tools have an on-off switch. They work well when your safety glasses are on, and they work terribly when your safety glasses are off.

WHAT YOU'LL FIND: Agatized and opalized petrified wood	**LIMITS:** The Petrified Wood Act states that people may collect up to 25 pounds per person, per day, with a maximum of 250 pounds per year. All holes must be backfilled
GEOLOGIC AGE: Cenozoic era, Miocene epoch	
TOOLS: Shovel, geology pick, chisels, and pry bar; safety glasses and gloves	**LOCATION:** 46.80767, –119.89023
	VEHICLE: High clearance and four-wheel drive required
AGENCY: Bureau of Land Management—Spokane District Office	
	SEASONS: Spring, summer, fall

DIRECTIONS → Find your way to the intersection of State Route 243 and Road 24 SW in Mattawa, Washington. Drive east on Road 24 SW for 2 miles. Turn left onto Road R SW and drive north through an agricultural area for 1 mile. At the 1-mile mark, the road turns to dirt and a fence splits the road in two. Continue straight, staying to the left side of the fence, and drive uphill for another 2 miles to a large parking area and BLM sign. The roads worsen from here, so be sure to have your all-wheel drive/four-wheel drive on. From the

Much of the petrified wood at Saddle Mountain is coated in caliche, calcite that slowly precipitates over time.

BLM sign, continue driving uphill for another 2 miles to an intersection. Turn right and follow the rough road uphill for another 0.8 mile. It will dump you out on the top of Saddle Mountain. Turn right and drive another 0.1 mile to reach the first of the diggings.

AT THE SITE → The digging area atop Saddle Mountain is expansive. These directions take you to the first set of pits in the main digging area, where both opalized and agatized wood are found. Park here and hike the area on foot to explore pits left by previous diggers. The tailings around the pits will reveal different types of petrified wood. If you find a hole that yields petrified wood that is particularly interesting to you, get out your shovel. Though few people take the time to do the right thing, BLM requires all diggers to fill in their holes before leaving. Do the right thing.

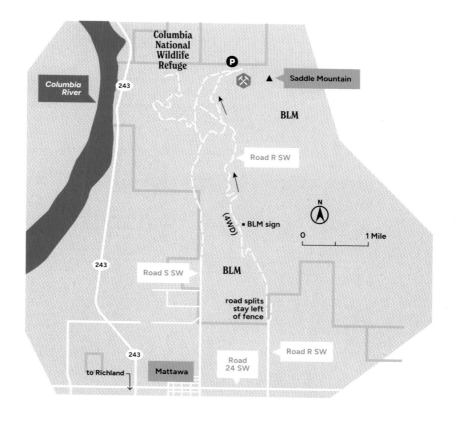

Petrified Wood:
The Stone of Transformation

FOR PETRIFIED WOOD enthusiasts, the big question isn't just how a tree can turn to stone—it's how can it turn to stone and still look exactly like a tree? Even down to the cellular structure, petrified wood can retain the finest of details though none of the wood remains. This phenomenon has fueled the quest for answers for generations of enthusiasts.

In the world of rockhounds, there's a variety of terminology used to refer to wood turned to stone. You'll hear terms like *petri-* *fied, opalized, agatized, silicified, mummi-* *fied,* and *fossilized. Petrified* and *fossilized* generally mean that minerals have replaced the original wood and turned it to stone. *Opalized, agatized,* and *silicified* all refer to silica being the mineral in question. *Mum-* *mified* usually hints at partial mineralization, meaning much of the original wood is still wood. Just very, very old.

In the Pacific Northwest, most petrified wood has been silicified and is closely associated with volcanic eruptions of the

Various specimens of agatized and opalized wood from Saddle Mountain

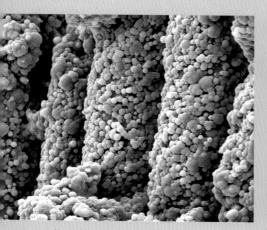

A scanning electron microscope (SEM) image of opal, a hydrated variety of silica. Notice the spherical structure. (Image by George Mustoe)

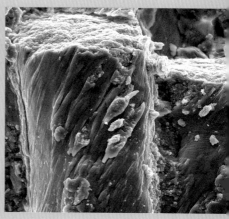

A SEM image of chalcedony, a fibrous variety of silica. Notice its dense, fibrous nature. (Image by George Mustoe)

past. Trees on the slopes of volcanoes are buried in explosions and mudslides. Lava flows through stands of trees, leaving perfect casts of each tree in its wake. Forests in the valleys below are buried in volcanic ash. Logs fall into lakes and bogs, eventually buried in sediments. Ultimately, if the tree is buried in sediments composed of volcanic ash, it's likely to petrify. But why? It's all about chemistry.

Volcanic ash is rich in a form of silica that dissolves in groundwater. Think of this ashy groundwater as a silica tea. When this tea invades a buried tree, it petrifies it. But how? The silica tea and the wood have different pHs. Remember pH? On each extreme of the pH scale, a substance is an acid or a base. When substances with different pHs interact, a chemical reaction occurs. Ions (parts of molecules) swap

around until the reaction stabilizes. It's worth understanding because this type of chemical interaction is what petrifies, or silicifies, wood.

Even if a tree is dead, its lignin (the woody material) still sucks up water, a feat of mother nature's passive engineering. When buried, a tree can still pull in a fantastic amount of groundwater. The lignin of the buried tree is more acidic than the silica tea it sucks up. When the lignin and the tea interface, a gradient in pH develops and a chemical reaction occurs. Silica swaps places with ions in the wood instantaneously, perfectly preserving the structure of the tree. This results in the stunning preservation of woody structures. But the process of silicification doesn't end here. Silica precipitates in wood in a few different forms, and over long periods of time, those forms can change.

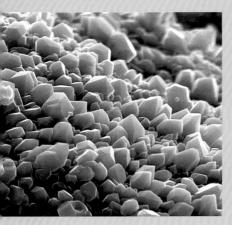

An SEM image of quartz crystals, a macrocrystalline variety of silica. Notice its geometric structure. (Image by George Mustoe)

What does that mean? Silica has several morphologies, meaning it can precipitate with different crystalline structures. Think of these structures like flavors. The first flavor of silica to precipitate in wood is opal. Opal is a hydrous form of silica, meaning some of that groundwater is still mixed into its chemical makeup. Researchers refer to opal as hydrous and amorphous, meaning it has a chaotic structure (or no real structure at all). Because of this, opal is unstable, fragile, and waxy looking. These qualities are what makes opal challenging for jewelers to work with. Over time (a lot of time), opal sheds its hydrous molecules—a process called devitrification—and transitions to a stronger flavor: chalcedony (pronounced *kal-sid-nee*). Chalcedony is known to rockhounds as agate and jasper. It's much more stable and well structured

than opal. Lapidaries love to work with it because of its hardness. In addition to opal and chalcedony, a third silica flavor can form: quartz. You know this mineral well. It makes a real show, from tiny carpets of sparkles that rockhounds call druzy to big pockets of crystal points. Quartz crystals tend to form in voids (empty spaces) in petrified wood after the tree has already been silicified.

In the Pacific Northwest, specimens of petrified wood often consist of all three silica flavors—mostly opal and chalcedony with a little quartz showing up in pockets or voids. In other rockhounding guides, you'll hear rockhounds discuss wood as opalized or agatized, and now you know what that means: wood that is composed of opal, or wood that is composed of agate/chalcedony. In truth, petrified wood is usually composed of a mix. Occasionally you'll hear talk of limb casts (see Congleton Hollow, Site 43). In some volcanic events, logs are incinerated as hot ash or lava flows around them and only their casts remain. Sometimes silica can entirely fill the voids left by small tree limbs, leaving a solid agate replica behind.

In the Pacific Northwest, petrified wood research is preeminently led by George Mustoe, a retired geologist from Western Washington University. His fascinating and easy-to-read research papers are freely available on the internet and contain a multitude of gorgeous images of petrified wood from our region. In your quest to better understand the fossilization of wood, make sure to look him up (see Appendix 3: Resources).

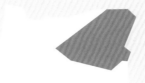

OREGON
Blue Mountains Province

Oregon's Blue Mountains are not a distinct range but rather a large geographic region of uplifted land that swoops from the state's northeast corner to its center. Its forested ranges—the Wallowas, the Strawberries, the Ochocos, the Greenhorns, and the namesake Blues—reveal Paleozoic and Mesozoic accreted terranes that have emerged from a deep blanket of much newer volcanic deposits, such as flood basalts from the Yellowstone hotspot and ash beds from the Clarno volcanoes and early Cascades.

Rockhounds search the old terranes for fossils, limestone, marbles, cherts, and colorful greenstones. Prospectors have long searched for gold, silver, and copper among the Greenhorn Mountains, where rock has melted and left granites rich with metallic veins. The younger Cenozoic volcanic rocks from the Clarno volcanoes, the Crooked River Caldera, and the early Cascades provide copious agates, jaspers, thundereggs, petrified wood, and leaf fossils. The best areas to search for rock material in this region are along mountain slopes, badlands, dry washes, and rivers.

Opposite: Cobbles abound in the deep side canyon cut by McGraw Creek.

㉟ Grande Ronde River

Not everyone loves porphyry, but everyone loves scenic river canyons. This stretch of the Grande Ronde River is one of the most charming and peaceful in all the state. It drains the high ranges of the Wallowa Mountains and eventually dumps out into the Snake River where Oregon, Washington, and Idaho meet.

The majority of rocks tumbling into the Grande Ronde hail from the deep layers of flood basalts that pulsed over this region for millions of years. The lava floods started between 17 and 16 million years ago when a plume of powerful melting energy from a hotspot in the mantle wreaked chaos on the crust. Three famous lava flooding events are recorded in the canyon walls here: the namesake Grande Ronde, the Wanapum, and the Saddle Mountain flows. Though the geologic story is fascinating, basalt remains unromantic for most rockhounds. (Unless you're me. I love it.) But alongside it, a much older basaltic rock shows up in the river. This stone, characterized by large, white, geometric crystals, is called porphyry (pronounced: *porf-er-ee*), and it really grabs your attention.

These porphyritic rocks likely tumble from old metavolcanic terranes along the base of the Wallowas. If you hike up into the Eagle Cap Wilderness south of Wallowa Lake, you will be met with dramatic outcrops of such porphyries along the steep trails. This material is found on the margins of ancient basalts that have been metamorphosed into greenstone. In porphyries, the large, white crystals are known as phenocrysts. The dark material that surrounds them is the groundmass. It is also crystalline, but the crystals are so fine, they cannot be individuated by the naked eye. The porphyry found in the Grande Ronde takes a nice polish, and the contrast between the black and white crystals makes an awesome lapidary material.

In the background, geologists are coughing and ahem-ing. They would want you to know that porphyry is a description of a texture, not a specific rock, and that many types of igneous rocks can technically be porphyry. For many centuries in Europe, several varieties of porphyritic stone have been used in sculpture, and each material fights for the grand title of porphyry. "What is in

Epic cliffs of flood basalts lord over the gravels of the Grande Ronde River.

A beautiful cobble of porphyry

my opinion important to understand," writes Siim Sepp of Sandatlas.org, "and what is agreed upon by all is that porphyritic rocks are always igneous rocks and they contain crystals that are noticeably larger than the crystals surrounding them." The porphyry in the Grande Ronde has been through some metamorphosis in its tectonic journey, but ultimately it was once just a humble basalt, just like the younger flood basalts that make up the towering canyon walls along the river.

WHAT YOU'LL FIND: Porphyry, basalt

GEOLOGIC AGE: Paleozoic to Mesozoic eras (porphyry); Cenozoic era, Miocene epoch (flood basalts)

TOOLS: Water shoes, wellies, or waders; a hiking pole for balance

AGENCY: Bureau of Land Management—Vale District Office

LIMIT: A reasonable amount of rocks may be taken for personal use only. A reasonable amount is often defined as up to 25 pounds per person, per day, with a maximum of 250 pounds per year. Do you need 25 pounds of rocks? Probably not. Collect lightly and with intention.

LOCATION: 45.898694, –117.473611

VEHICLE: Any

SEASONS: Summer and fall. Warning: Avoid the river in winter and spring. High runoff poses a danger to you, and you pose a danger to spring-spawning fish.

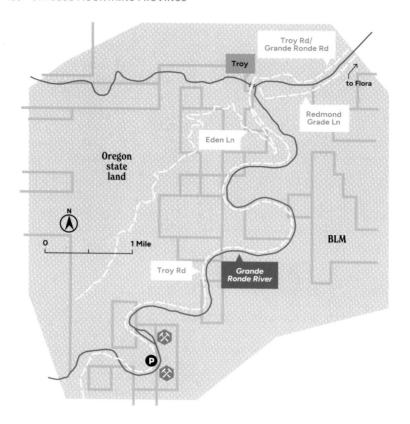

DIRECTIONS → Make your way to the intersection of North Street and River Street in the bustling town of Enterprise, Oregon. Drive west on West North Street for one block and turn right (north) on Northwest First Street (State Route 3). Drive north on SR 3 for 33.6 miles. Turn left (west) onto Flora Lane and drive for 3.2 miles. (Flora Lane zigzags through an agricultural area and passes through the historic town of Flora.) Turn left (west) onto Lost Prairie Road and drive 2.8 miles. (All turns will be marked with signs pointing to Troy.) Turn left onto Redmond Grade Lane, a scenic, switchbacking dirt road, and drive for 7.6 miles to where it bottoms out at the Grande Ronde River. Cross the bridge and turn left onto Troy River Road (Grande Ronde Road). Drive 1.5 miles, passing through the small riverside community of Troy, and cross the bridge. Drive 0.2 mile to a fork. Stay to the left to continue on Troy Road, which follows the river, and drive another 6.3 miles to a BLM parking area along a bend.

AT THE SITE → This BLM day-use area sits on a broad bend in the river, and gravels armor its flank. Search the gravel bar or within the river for cobbles of porphyry. Water shoes or waders can be helpful in this calm and shallow stretch of river. Porphyry is black with large white crystals scattered within it. It makes an excellent lapidary material.

36 Hurricane Creek

Hurricane Creek drains the mighty Wallowas. These stunning, glacially carved mountains are composed of some of the state's oldest rocks. Along the northeastern flank of the range, the remnants of an ancient island arc crop out at the base of the mountain. Some 295 million years ago, these rocks were part of an oceanic chain of volcanoes surrounded by sandy beaches and limestone reefs. Through slow tectonic forces, this island chain collided with North America, becoming one of many accreted terranes that compose the bedrock of present-day Oregon. In the Wallowas, the remnants of the terrane's volcanic rocks show up as veined, teal greenstone and dark, freckled porphyry. Its limestone reefs have been recrystallized into marble that looks soft, velvety, and gray. These rock materials resulted from the metamorphic pressures of being forced into a subduction trench and attached to the continent.

Accretion is not a cold-fusion process though. As these bits of ocean crust and island chains were glued to the continent, the forces of collision caused melting to occur deeper within the crust. These melts produced plutons in the crust, and the highest peaks of the Wallowas are large, exposed swaths of plutonic rocks. Though the terrane was born in the Permian, as much as 295 million years ago, its collision with North America wasn't complete until the Cretaceous period, about

Searching Hurricane Creek for cobbles suitable for carving

Light-gray marble is easy to find. It looks almost velvety compared to the hard granites and greenstones.

130 million years ago. The granites, tonalites, and granodiorites that make up the plutonic rocks in the Wallowas are barely half the age of the old terrane. It can be hard to wrap your head around these numbers.

In the Permian, when these island chains and seafloor sediments were deposited, the age of dinosaurs had yet to begin. Reptiles were still new on land and waddled low, with wide, gator-like stances. Primitive mammal-like creatures scurried about them. Almost none of these creatures would survive Earth's largest extinction, which dealt its final blow around 252 million years ago. This event, known as the Great Dying, brought the Paleozoic era to an end. But extinctions open new windows for life to fill the mournful, empty niches, and thus a new great era was born—the Mesozoic. By the Cretaceous (the third and final chapter of the Mesozoic), when the rocks of the Wallowas were accreting onto North America, whole dynasties of towering dinosaur families had come and gone. Bees would soon arrive on the scene, heralding a global explosion of flowers. Small mammals still scurried about, waiting in the evolutionary wings. The world did not yet know that another catastrophic extinction, which would wipe out the dinosaurs, was on the way. But the rocks that built the Wallowas would see all of it—and survive.

WHAT YOU'LL FIND: Marble, greenstone, granite	**LIMIT:** Up to 10 pounds per person, per day
GEOLOGIC AGE: Paleozoic and Mesozoic eras	**LOCATION:** 45.311750, -117.306556
TOOLS: Wellies, water shoes, or waders; a hiking pole for balance	**VEHICLE:** Any
	SEASONS: Summer and fall. Warning: Avoid the river in winter and spring. High runoff poses a danger to you, and you pose a danger to spring-spawning fish.
AGENCY: US Forest Service, Wallowa-Whitman National Forest. A Northwest Forest Pass is required (see Appendix 3: Resources).	

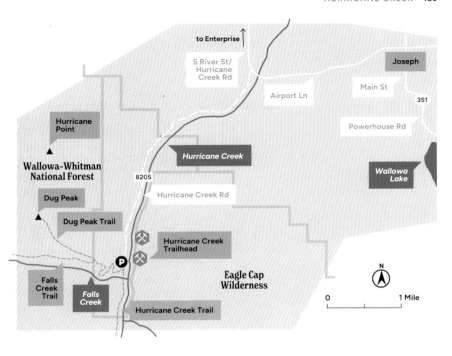

DIRECTIONS → Make your way to the intersection of North Street and River Street in the bustling town of Enterprise, Oregon. Drive south on River Street for 0.4 mile. Turn right at the curve to stay on South River Street (Hurricane Creek Road) for 5.1 miles to a junction. At the junction stay straight to continue on Hurricane Creek Road/FR 8205 for another 3.7 miles to a scenic pullout along the creek. Park here and explore the river rocks.

AT THE SITE → The boundary for the Eagle Cap Wilderness begins on the opposite (east) side of the creek. No collecting is allowed within national forest wilderness boundaries. In the creek, a walking stick may be helpful for balance. Explore the creek bed for cobbles of marble and greenstone. Both are wonderful materials for carving and sculpture. The marble tends to come in tones of grays, with a soft, velvety texture. The greenstone is exactly that, a green stone. Often it has veins of white mineralization running through it. If you are a sculptor, remember that the limit is 10 pounds per person, per day. So, think small sculptures.

A narrow trail along the dammed Snake River leads to McGraw Creek.

McGraw Creek

The story of Oregon from its very beginning can be told in the mile-deep gorge of Hells Canyon. Here, the Snake River carves its way through almost 300 million years of geologic history. Along the river's edge, the rocks of Oregon's earliest accreted terranes reveal themselves. At their birth, the oldest rocks here were the volcanic lavas of an island arc in a proto-Pacific ocean, surrounded by shallow reefs and seafloor muds. During this time, North America was part of Pangea, one of Earth's supercontinents. The world was on the cusp of its most profound mass extinction, which would wipe out almost all life on the planet. The causes of such a catastrophe, which crescendoed around 252 million years ago, are hotly debated. Most researchers point to epic flood volcanism poisoning the atmosphere with carbon dioxide. Others argue that the coalescing of the supercontinent Pangea killed global oceanic circulation, yet others insist that a large meteor (much like the one that would hit Earth 187 million years later) was the coup de grâce. Of all the theories, lava flooding and the coalescing of Pangea were the most likely culprits of the Great Dying of 252 million years ago.

Over the eons, the ancient rocks here have been compressed and deformed in their tectonic convergence with our continent. Some of them hail from the Paleozoic, the time before the Great Dying, and some came shortly after, forming in a slowly healing world. Today ancient volcanic material crops out along the Snake River as a beautiful porphyry (a dark stone freckled with white crystals) and greenstone (a dark-teal stone rich with veins of chartreuse epidote and white quartz). The shallow reefs and seafloor muds that traveled with them now tumble down creeks as velvety marbles and crimson jaspers, the products of squeezing and baking. The jaspers are bright red to deep purple, and the marbles are velvety and gray. Some of the marbles are less altered, resembling their original limestone selves and are rich in shell fossils.

"We call the ancient world into existence when we gather a stone," says geologist Ellis Morris Bishop. The rocks found in the creeks along Hells Canyon hold evidence of a world radically different from our own. But not every rock found here hails from the ancient terranes.

High above the canyon wall lies an imperious cap of flood basalts, much like the kind that tormented the Paleozoic world. However, these carpeted the landscape less than 17 million years ago—practically yesterday! The flood basalts were born here long after Oregon came into existence, thanks to a plume of energy coming from Earth's mantle. They are part of the Columbia River flood basalts that

Fossiliferous gray limestone, teal greenstone, green epidote, and red cinder are common in the creek bed.

blanketed much of the Pacific Northwest landscape in violent pulses for several million years. Today they tumble down the creeks in dark, blackish chunks, with airy nuggets of scoria and red cinder mixed in.

Though many creeks drain into this stretch of the Snake River, McGraw Creek is the one that catches our eye. It cuts a steep, dramatic canyon through the flood basalts, greenstones, and marbles, and dumps its contents out in a parade of cobbles. The sheer amount of material exported downstream by this creek is awe-inspiring and provides a full day's worth of exploring. You must hike 1.6 miles to reach the mouth of McGraw Creek from the Copper Creek Campground, as there's no access by road. The scenic trail that meanders along the bank of the Snake River is a worthwhile journey through a canyon of time.

WHAT YOU'LL FIND: Marble, fossiliferous limestone, jasper, epidote, greenstone, porphyry

GEOLOGIC AGE: Paleozoic, Mesozoic, and Cenozoic eras

TOOLS: A backpack, water, and hiking pole are recommended

AGENCY: Bureau of Land Management—Vale District Office

LIMIT: A reasonable amount of rocks may be taken for personal use only. A reasonable amount is often defined as up to 25 pounds per person, per day, with a maximum of 250 pounds per year. Do you need 25 pounds of rocks? Probably not. Collect lightly and with intention.

LOCATIONS:
Parking: 45.079806, -116.786889
McGraw Creek: 45.101250, -116.781472

VEHICLE: Any

SEASONS: Any. Warning: Avoid the area in wet weather. Canyons are treacherous in rainstorms.

DIRECTIONS → Make your way to the intersection of Record Street and South Main Street in the small town of Halfway, Oregon. Drive east for 0.9 mile on East Record Street (Pine Creek Highway). Turn left onto State Route 86 East and drive 16.1 miles to the town of Oxbow, Oregon. In Oxbow, bear slightly left to turn onto Homestead Road, which skirts the west bank of the Snake River. Homestead Road is intermittently paved and well maintained the whole way. Drive 6.7 miles and continue straight onto Homestead Road (also called Ballard Creek Road). Drive 2.4 miles to the road's end at the BLM Copper Creek Campground. Park at the trailhead at the north end of the campground. Hike the trail that leads north from the campground for 1.6 miles to the confluence of McGraw Creek with the Snake River.

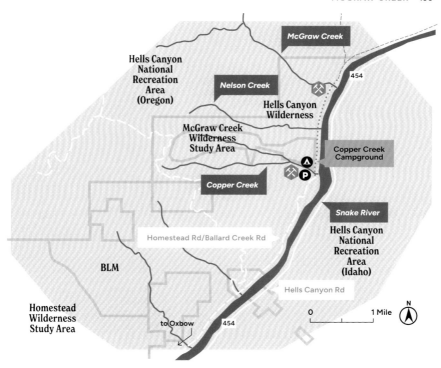

AT THE SITE → You'll know you're in the right place upon reaching McGraw Creek. It's a wide, often dry, riverbed of cobbles that dumps into the Snake River. Gray marble and limestone filled with marine fossils are found here. Colorful maroon jasper, chartreuse epidote, and bright-teal greenstone are common too. The hiking trail continues northward from McGraw Creek into the Hells Canyon National Recreation Area (NRA), which is managed by the US Forest Service (USFS). The boundary line between BLM land and USFS land is 0.6 mile north of McGraw Creek. If you continue hiking, know that rock collecting is not allowed once you cross into the Hells Canyon NRA.

If you don't want to make the 1.6 mile trek (one way) out to McGraw Creek from the BLM campground, do not despair. At the trailhead parking area, Copper Creek drains into the Snake River. There are plentiful rocks here: jasper, epidote, greenstone, porphyry, but no marble or limestone. Copper Creek is a smaller area to collect in but still worth your time.

38 Fossil

Crisp leaves drift on an eddy of damp, autumn wind. They lilt and fall, landing on the surface of a quiet forest lake. Elms, birches, maples, poplars, hickories, and oaks line the shore. Among them metasequoias rise like giants. As each season comes and goes, pulses of leaf litter and metasequoia needles sink to the bottom of the lake. Volcanoes of the early Cascade Range erupt in the distance, spreading ash into the sky, which falls like snow over the forest. Over the next 32 million years, Earth will change, the lake will disappear, and its ashy, leafy sediments will become solid rock. Humans will eventually show up and cut away at the rock to level an athletic field for a small high school in present-day Fossil, Oregon.

Today, the ancient lake fossils found here are known as the Bridge Creek Flora. They are beautifully preserved in a process paleobotanists call distillation. Over the eons, much of the easily degradable organic material that makes up a plant's cells breaks down, leaving behind a delicate film of carbon that outlines the leaf's shape, veins, and cell structures. Think of it as a leaf's skeleton being left behind. By cracking open the rock, you can reveal numerous leaf fossils that have not seen the light of day in 32 million years. Most fossil material here is fragmental,

Digging in the ancient lake sediments behind Wheeler High School (Photo by Nat West)

Fossils of needles of the ancient behemoth Metasequoia are abundant. (Photo by Nat West)

but sometimes whole leaf fossils can be found. Fronds of metasequoia needles are abundant. Very rarely flower, fish, and insect fossils are uncovered.

To get the most out of your visit, be sure to stop by the Oregon Paleo Lands Center (OPLC) while in town. This wonderful museum is open seasonally and is rich with information about the fossils behind the high school. The institute is a few blocks from the high school at 333 West 4th Street, Fossil, Oregon, 97830. Always call ahead of time to find out hours of service (see Appendix 3: Resources).

WHAT YOU'LL FIND: Plant fossils in lacustrine sediments	**AGENCY:** Local ownership. Fee required. Individuals: $5; family of four: $15; each additional child: $3; groups of 20 or less: $25.
GEOLOGIC AGE: Cenozoic era, Oligocene epoch, approximately 32 million years old	**LIMIT:** Collect within reason
TOOLS: A hammer and a flat chisel (or a paint scraper with a blunt handle); safety glasses and gloves	**LOCATION:** Wheeler High School, 600 E. B St., Fossil, OR 97830
	VEHICLE: Any
	SEASONS: Spring, summer, fall during OPLC's operating hours

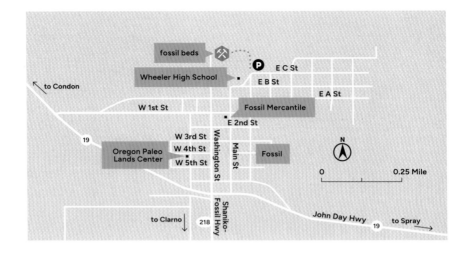

DIRECTIONS → Make your way to the intersection of Highway 19 and Highway 218/Washington Street in Fossil, Oregon. From the intersection, drive north on Washington Street for three blocks. Turn left onto West 4th Street and drive one block to its intersection with Adams Street, where you will see the Oregon Paleo Lands Center on the opposite corner. There is plenty of parking available in front of the center.

From here, volunteers at the Paleo Lands Center will direct you to the fossil beds behind the high school. Do not visit the fossil beds without first paying at the Paleo Lands Center.

AT THE SITE → The fossil quarry is a small, exposed ledge on the backside of the athletic field behind Wheeler High School. Search through the scattered rock for fossil imprints or use tools to split the rocks open along their bedding planes. Finding a complete leaf fossil may take some time, but you'll start seeing fragments right away. Tap a small hammer or flat chisel along the rock's bedding planes (layers) to get a nice split.

③⑨ Horseheaven

On the north side of the Ochoco Range, the remnants of extinct Clarno volcanoes emerge from the earth. Here sits Horseheaven. At this remote location, treasures of volcanic origin litter the hillsides. Sparkling druzy agates, white jaspers, and petrified wood emerge from the slopes. Though the Clarno volcanoes themselves are long gone, their lavas and ashes make up the bedrock of this crumpled and uplifted swath of Earth.

During the time of the Clarno eruptions, Earth was much hotter. Subtropical forests grew here, and strange mammals that have long been extinct roamed among them. The end of the Clarno volcanoes coincided with a decline in global temperatures, and a cooling period replaced these subtropical forests with the more temperate ones that we live among today.

During the days of Clarno volcanism, hydrothermal fluids rich in metals circulated among the volcanoes. In the 1930s, cinnabar—an ore of mercury—was discovered in an enriched deposit of volcanic rock at Horseheaven. Claims were staked, bought, and sold until they came into the hands of Sun Oil Company (known today as Sunoco), which operated here during the Second World War. The mines produced thousands of flasks of mercury, but dangerous fires and repeated tunnel collapses plagued the project, which shuttered in the 1950s. The land was eventually sold to local ranchers who are now held with the unfortunate responsibility of its cleanup. Plenty of litigation has ensued, but the Oregon Department of Environmental Quality has its eyes set on an eventual remediation of the site.

Luckily for us, the BLM land to the east of the Horseheaven site has been untouched by mining. The surface remains a safe place in which to search for agates, jaspers, and petrified wood. The area is scattered with these materials, but they

The stunning view of the ancient Clarno Volcanics from Horseheaven

Agate, some covered in druzy, petrified wood, and white jasper are common.

are widely dispersed, so plan to do a lot of exploring on foot. Occasionally, stumps of petrified logs emerge from the ground. To me, though now stone, a stump still rooted is still living its life. Neither the volcano, nor faulting, nor time has been able to remove this triumphant being from its home. So neither should we. These stumps are often surrounded with stony wood fragments that litter the ground. As a memento, take from those instead, and let the stumps continue onward through time with their triumphant legacy.

WHAT YOU'LL FIND: Agate, jasper, and petrified wood	**LIMITS:** A reasonable amount of rocks may be taken for personal use only. A reasonable amount is often defined as up to 25 pounds per person, per day, with a maximum of 250 pounds per year. Do you need 25 pounds of rocks? Probably not. Collect lightly and with intention.
GEOLOGIC AGE: Cenozoic era, Eocene epoch	
TOOLS: A geology pick or small trowel to tip specimens out of the dirt	
AGENCY: Bureau of Land Management—Prineville District Office	**LOCATION:** 44.723472, –120.501861
	VEHICLE: High clearance and four-wheel drive recommended
	SEASONS: Spring, summer, fall

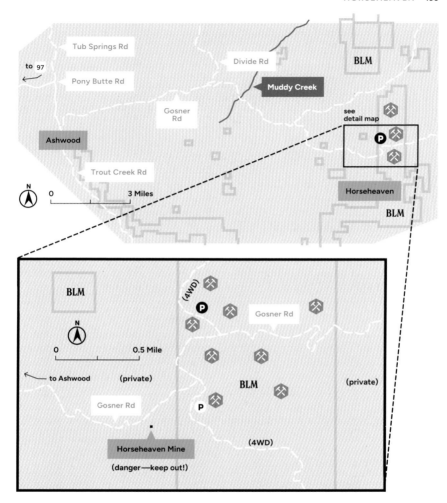

DIRECTIONS → *Do not attempt travel to Horseheaven during spring thaws or during any wet weather. The soft dirt roads will be impassable.* Make your way to the intersection of Trout Creek Road and Gosner Road in the hamlet of Ashwood, Oregon. Turn right (east) onto Gosner Road (which quickly veers north to exit town) and drive for 6.5 miles to a fork. Divide Road will be on the left, and Gosner Road will dip downhill straight ahead. Reset your odometer and stay straight to continue on Gosner Road for another 10.2 miles to the BLM parcel at Horseheaven. Notes for this section of the road: At 6.9 miles you will ford Muddy Creek (it's shallow), which flows year-round. At 9.4 miles you'll pass the Horseheaven mercury mine, which is on private property. *Do not trespass.* At 9.5 miles you'll cross a cattle grate that takes you onto BLM land. There are two good places to safely park and explore. At 9.6 miles there is a dirt track on the right, and at 10.2 miles (the stopping point) there is a dirt track on the left. Choose either to park at and begin your explorations. Please note that the dirt tracks that diverge from Gosner Road are in serious disrepair. Use them as places to pull over and hike, rather than to drive on.

AT THE SITE →   This parcel of public land overseen by the BLM is only a mile wide east to west. However, it runs for several miles north to south. Take great care to stay within its boundaries. The abandoned Horseheaven mercury mine sits on private property to the west of the collection area. *Do not trespass under any circumstances.* Stay on the public land and explore the hillsides for agates, jasper, and petrified wood. The views from the many buttes up here are stunning.

④⓪ Burnt Ranch

On geological maps of Oregon, the Clarno and John Day Formations are always intertwined. Geologists have long lumped them into a singular unit, even though each formation represents two entirely different volcanic systems from two entirely different worlds.

Between 53 to 50 million years back, an arc of volcanoes known as the Clarnos began erupting here. Stunning cliffs of their andesite lavas lord over the John Day River across from the Burnt Ranch Campground. During the days of Clarno eruptions, a mess of small oceanic plates was slipping beneath the North American continent. As these ocean plates sank into the mantle below, their water content boiled, rising into the crust above and sending molten material to the surface of the continent through volcanoes. During this time, an epoch known as the Eocene, the world was hot, humid, and entirely tropical. There were palm trees in Alaska, and large mammals from the Asian continent made warm, happy migrations into North America, radiating in an explosion of diversity. A period of tectonic stagnation followed, and the Clarnos went quiet. Perhaps the subduction zone offshore got jammed up. (Note to nerds: consult research on a terrane called Siletzia.) About 10 million years of quiet passed, and the basins around the Clarnos filled in with clay-rich soils and the remnants of plants and animals, which became fossils. Outcrops of rich, red badlands around the Burnt Ranch area are remnants of such ecosystems, known as paleosols.

Opposite: The collecting area nests within the striking topography of the ancient Clarno Volcanics.

Teal volcanic breccia from the infamous Clarno eruptions is exposed in the gullies above the river.

Then, offshore, about 10 million years later, the subduction trench got moving again and a new string of volcanoes was born, albeit much farther to the west. These were the baby Cascades, and as they erupted, huge plumes of ash drifted east and fell atop the old Clarno lavas and soils. These ash beds, and the new soils that would form among them, are known as the John Day Formation. Much like the Clarno Formation, the John Day is famous for its colorful paleosols and fossils too. However, in the 10 million years between them, Earth experienced a dramatic change in climate, ending the Eocene hothouse and dawning a new icehouse epoch: the Oligocene. The floral and faunal differences found between the Clarno and John Day Formations reveal such dramatic global changes.

Here near the Burnt Ranch Campground, along the scenic John Day River, we likely find ourselves within the final days of the Clarno volcanoes, before the early Cascades. Amid the old paleosols, walls of colorful volcanic breccias from ancient eruptions crop out in the gulches. Teal jasper, clear agates, and calcite crystals erode from these rocks. Each of these treasures hails from a hothouse world, when there was no ice at the poles. In the 50 million years that has elapsed since their creation, the world has seen a dramatic shift to a cooler, icier world. With great hope and swift action, humanity may be able to prevent itself from returning to the hot, hot world of the Clarnos.

WHAT YOU'LL FIND: Calcite, agate, jasper	**LIMITS:** A reasonable amount of rocks may be taken for personal use only. A reasonable amount is often defined as up to 25 pounds per person, per day, with a maximum of 250 pounds per year. Do you need 25 pounds of rocks? Probably not. Collect lightly and with intention.
GEOLOGIC AGE: Cenozoic era, Eocene to Oligocene epochs	
TOOLS: A geology pick or small trowel to tip specimens out of the dirt	
AGENCY: Bureau of Land Management— Prineville District Office	**LOCATION:** 44.739363, –120.354586
	VEHICLE: High clearance and four-wheel drive recommended
	SEASONS: Spring, summer, fall

DIRECTIONS → Make your way to the town of Mitchell, Oregon. At the general store on the corner of South Nelson Avenue and Main Street, drive west on Main Street for 0.2 mile. Turn left onto Ochoco Highway (US Highway 26) and drive for 3.6 miles. Turn right (north) onto Bridge Creek Road (also called Burnt Ranch Road) and drive for 5.6 miles. The entrance for the Painted Hills Unit of the John Day Fossil Beds National Monument is on your left. The pavement ends here. Continue straight onto Bridge Creek Road for another 8.8 miles to a kiosk on the right (north) side of the road. Park here and explore the gullies and dry washes along the slopes on foot.

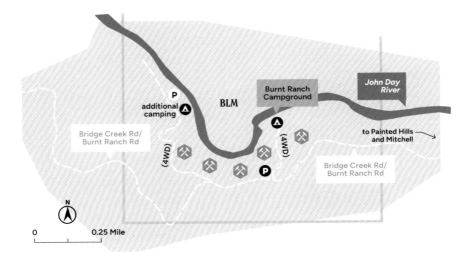

Drivers with a high clearance or four-wheel-drive vehicle may take the dirt track that dips 0.2 mile down to the camping area from the kiosk. Alternatively, you may continue driving west on Burnt Ranch Road for another 0.2 mile to another dirt track that dips down on the right. Drive 0.4 mile on this rough track to another camping area. You may explore the hillsides from here as well.

AT THE SITE →   The steep hillsides around the Burnt Ranch Campground are scattered with interesting material. Small cubes of white calcite, veins of clear agate, and dark-teal jasper-like material erode from the ground. The dry washes and gullies are the best places to search for interesting material that has been washed from the dirt during storm events. Because of the area's steepness and brushiness, this is not a good location to take youngsters to.

From Burnt Ranch Road, the access roads down to each of the two camping areas require high clearance and four-wheel drive. Folks without a rugged vehicle should park at the kiosk and travel on foot if they want to get down to the river.

41 Deb's Spot

The pickup truck barreled through the bumpy desert, swerving to avoid a large rock protruding from the old road. We hit it anyway, and the vehicle lurched over it like a bucking bronco. Deb was driving, which was never a good thing. Our companion Susie groaned in the rear seat. "I think I'm going to be sick." *Oh dear*, I

A worked mound of ash-flow tuff from ancient eruptions of the Crooked River Caldera. The active Cascade volcanoes rise in the distance.

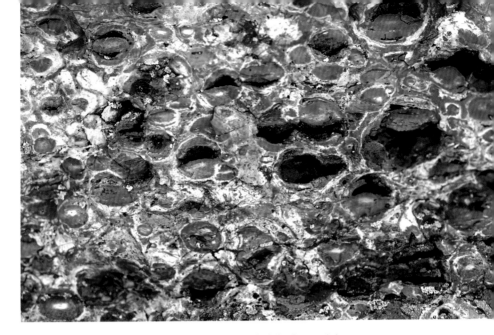

Ash-flow tuff riddled with pockets of minerals such as opal, chalcedony, and clays

thought. *Yee haw*, Deb smiled. An outcrop of strange, reddish rock came into view, and she slammed on the brakes. A cloud of dust rose around us. "Here we go!" Deb exclaimed. I jumped from the truck to let Susie out, who was definitely going to hurl. Poor Susie.

Deb trudged to the outcrop and inspected it through her thick, fishbowl glasses. Deb always wore casino T-shirts tucked into dungarees with a big old belt, and today was no different. She pointed out a boulder larger than a microwave—a rock she'd set her heart on the last time she'd been here—and insisted we try to lift it into the back of the truck. I inspected the unusual rock. It was rusty red and filled with open pockets shaped like frog eyes that were filled with strange minerals, lumpy and botryoidal (pronounced: *buh-troy-dal*). Deb called it "lilypad jasper" and knew nothing more about it. One day I would learn that this outcrop was a deposit of ash-flow tuff—fine, glassy volcanic ash that blanketed the landscape when the nearby Crooked River Caldera imploded some 29 million years ago. Glassy rock is chemically unstable, and over time it devitrifies, meaning its glassy stuff organizes into opal, agate, and clay. These were the minerals that now filled the lumpy, weathered vesicles.

A whole decade would pass before I returned to this outcrop, a very different person. When I first joined my local rock club on a whim, Susie and Deb took me under their wings. They taught me how to find rocks and make beautiful things from them. Little did they know that they were swiftly transforming my life. They wrapped me in a chrysalis, and I emerged a full-fledged rockhound. When the coronavirus pandemic swept through the Northwest, it took Deb from us, leaving a very big hole in my heart. No more of Deb's selfies from casinos or conspiracy theories would fill up my phone. No more talk of Deb's prize hoard of Oregon's ugliest rock (Biggs jasper), the value of which she single-handedly inflated by trying to buy every last speck of it.

In my research travels for this book, I drove past Deb's spot many times. Because it is so close to the highway, I hadn't considered including it. However, there are only so many times you can drive past pretty rocks and keep going. It would be a shame not to revisit. As I pulled up to the rusty outcrop of the ash-flow tuff, I noticed a familiar boulder sitting askew in the dirt. A decade ago, the three of us tried to lift it into Deb's truck and failed. It was too heavy to take. I could see her there suddenly, clear as day in her fishbowl glasses and dungarees, smiling. I touched the rock and smiled. Yee haw, Deb.

WHAT YOU'LL FIND: Deb's "lilypad jasper"—ash-flow tuff	**AGENCY:** US Forest Service—Ochoco National Forest and Crooked River National Grassland
GEOLOGIC AGE: Cenozoic era, Oligocene epoch	**LIMIT:** Up to 10 pounds per person, per day (Don't be like Deb, who broke the rules.)
TOOLS: Geology pick, small sledgehammer, point chisel, or pry bar (all optional); safety glasses and gloves	**LOCATION:** 44.468233, –121.194725
	VEHICLE: Any
	SEASONS: Spring, summer, fall

DIRECTIONS → Make your way to the intersection of US Highway 26 and US 97 in Madras, Oregon (the intersection in the north part of town, at the Sonic Drive-In and McDonald's). Drive south on US 97 for 12.8 miles to its intersection with Southwest Monroe Lane. Turn left (east) onto Southwest Monroe Lane (a gravel road) and drive 0.1 mile. Look for faint tire tracks leading into the grass on the left (north) side of the road. Park here and hike up the dirt tracks for 0.4 mile to the outcrop of rusty red rock protruding from the low hilltop. If you have a vehicle with good clearance, you may drive up these tracks, but note that the area is seasonally closed to vehicles December 1 to March 31 to protect wildlife habitat. It's a nice walk. Leave the car behind.

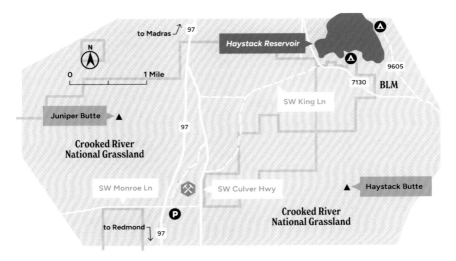

AT THE SITE → This is a small outcrop of ash-flow tuff from the Crooked River Caldera that exhibits desirable patterns for collectors. Some tuff material is a light purple with reddish stripes, and other material is rusty red and tan and dotted with vesicles in which botryoidal opal and agate form. Plenty of material has been broken up by previous miners if you just want to surface collect. Otherwise, bring tools to break fresh rock off of the outcrop. Remember that the collecting limit is up to 10 pounds per person, per day.

42 Eagle Rock Quarry

Around 29 million years ago, a volcanic eruption occurred that would go down in the history books. The power of the supervolcano that imploded here was so large that it would only be outranked by the likes of Yellowstone, Toba, and La Garita, the largest supervolcano systems known in Earth's history. Named for the river that runs through it, the remnants of this enormous explosion are known as the Crooked River Caldera. It's hard to imagine the central Oregon town of Prineville quaintly squared within its massive crater, but it is. Today, the rim of the caldera is not an obvious feature in the landscape. Some sections have eroded or been buried under younger lavas. Geologists have been able to map the caldera's original boundaries by tracing circular faults, called ring fractures, that mark the original zone of collapse.

Atop a forested butte southeast of Prineville is an outcrop of Crooked River Caldera ash-flow tuff that has been mined for agate and jasper. Ash-flow tuff is a rock formed from solidified glassy material that piles up after a caldera has imploded. Its glassiness is due to the extreme viscosity of blazing hot ash upon eruption. Under a microscope, geologists can see that tuffs are a smattering of obsidian

Old quarried walls of ash-flow tuff expose treasure along the steep mountainside.

A chunk of the ruddy tuff with spherules of white opal

and pumice fragments that have been fused together with bits of lava rock mixed in. Over time, the glassy volcanic material devitrifies. *Vitreous* means "glassy." To devitrify is to become un-glassy, and in this case the volcanic glass chemically weathers into simple crystalline forms, most notably silicates and clays. Silicates come in many varieties: opal, chalcedony (agate, jasper), and druzy quartz. At this quarry of ash-flow tuff, all of these materials can be found scattering the ground.

The forces that initiated the powerful Crooked River Caldera eruption are no longer potent in this part of Oregon, and its origins are still the subject of much speculation. Could it be related to the Yellowstone hotspot as Oregon passed over it? Or perhaps it is the result of subduction stalling and starting, some sort of linked trouble with the ancestral Cascades? What is known about it so far comes from clues left behind by the rocks it erupted, like the ash-flow tuff sitting high on this butte. Time and rocks would bury the rest of its story. "Eventually, all things merge into one," wrote Norman Maclean, "and a river runs through it."

WHAT YOU'LL FIND: Agate, jasper, tuff	**LIMIT:** A reasonable amount of rocks may be taken for personal use only. A reasonable amount is often defined as up to 25 pounds per person, per day, with a maximum of 250 pounds per year. Do you need 25 pounds of rocks? Probably not. Collect lightly and with intention.
GEOLOGIC AGE: Cenozoic era, Oligocene epoch	
TOOLS: Geology pick, small sledge and chisel, shovel (all optional); safety glasses and gloves; hiking poles may be helpful	
	LOCATION: 44.185293, –120.668947
AGENCY: Bureau of Land Management— Prineville District Office	**VEHICLE:** High clearance and four-wheel drive required
	SEASONS: Summer and fall. Dirt roads up to the quarry are closed Dec 1–Mar 31.

DIRECTIONS → Make your way to the intersection of Northeast 3rd Street (US Highway 26) and Northeast Combs Flat Road (State Route 380) in Prineville, Oregon. Drive south on SR 380 (Paulina Highway) for 14.5 miles to an unmarked dirt road on the right. It will be just after an enormous pillar of volcanic rock known as Eagle Rock. Turn right onto the dirt road and turn left at the fork that presents itself immediately. High clearance and four-wheel drive are required from this point on. Drive uphill for 0.9 mile and stay to the right as the road forks. A hundred yards after the fork is a gate, which might be closed. You

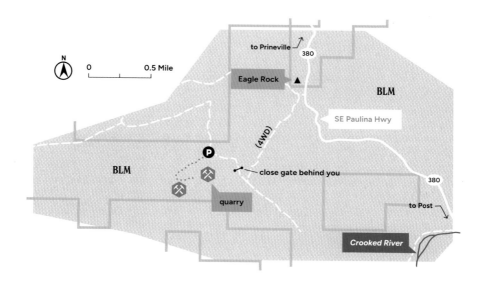

may open it to pass through but you *must* close it behind you! Drive another 0.4 mile to another fork and turn left. Though the road continues uphill here, it is entirely unpassable. Park here and hike the remainder of the steep road for 0.4 mile to the quarry at the top of the mountain.

AT THE SITE →   The hike up to the quarry is steep. Hiking poles will be helpful. The old road leads right up to the quarry. Inspect the tailing piles for interesting rock material when you reach the diggings. You'll find ash-flow tuff filled with pockets of minerals, as well as seams of agate. You may bring tools to break larger material apart, but they are not required. Always wear safety glasses when breaking rocks apart.

43 Congleton Hollow

The South Fork Crooked River carves its way through the juniper- and sage-mottled hillsides of the geographic center of Oregon. It's a quiet place filled with birdsong along the river. Layers of flood basalts and rhyolite lavas cap the hills, forming flat-topped buttes. These materials blanketed Oregon starting between 17 and 16 million years ago, in an era of violent hotspot volcanism. However, the rocks underlying

A small petrified twig coated in botryoidal (grape-like) agate

these buttes come from their own equally chaotic era, albeit much older. Faulting from tectonics and erosion from the Crooked River have cut down into these old layers, exposing swaths of the treasure-filled Clarno Formation.

The rocks in the basin of Congleton Hollow are old volcanic mudflows and lava deposits from the Clarno volcanoes, which erupted from 52 to 40 million years ago. Mudflows, or lahars, occur when volcanoes erupt through their own snow-caps or enter adjacent rivers, sending a cascade of smoldering rocks and water swiftly downslope and downstream. The mudflows would converge on forests and rivers, becoming ever more dangerous. In the rocks of Congleton Hollow, you can witness the ancient calamity that swept through here millions of years ago. Palisades of these ancient mudflows rise from the slopes, revealing a deluge of rock and debris.

Rockhounds come to Congleton Hollow seeking a specific kind of trace fossil that erodes from the ancient Clarno deposits: limb casts. These rocks were fragments of tree branches incinerated in hot ash, leaving a perfect cast of their shape behind. The casts formed as silica-rich fluids filled the voids left by the tree fragments and solidified, filling them with pure agate. These limb casts were swept up and dispersed in the mudflows that followed. Today, rockhounds dig among the dry, forested slopes in attempts to unearth them. Limb casts aren't the only treasures out here. Small agates, wee chunks of common opal, and beautiful altered andesite lavas (teal and green) are scattered among the hillsides that cascade down toward the peaceful Crooked River.

WHAT YOU'LL FIND: Limb casts, agate, jasper, common opal, lava rock

GEOLOGIC AGE: Cenozoic era; Eocene to Miocene epochs

TOOLS: Backpack, water, geology pick, and small shovel

AGENCY: Bureau of Land Management—Prineville District Office

LIMIT: A reasonable amount of rocks may be taken for personal use only. A reasonable amount is often defined as up to 25 pounds per person, per day, with a maximum of 250 pounds per year. These limits are inspired by the Petrified Wood Act, which sets strict limits of the same amounts for fossil wood specifically. Remember to collect lightly and with intention.

LOCATIONS:
Site A: 44.058051, –120.013754
Site B: 44.050908, –120.018107

VEHICLE: High clearance and all-wheel drive/four-wheel drive recommended

SEASONS: Summer and fall

Lava from the old Clarno volcanoes rises above Congleton Hollow.

DIRECTIONS → **Site A:** Make your way to the Post General Store at 28550 Southeast Paulina Highway in Post, Oregon. This is the only roadside business in this quiet ranching hamlet. Drive east on Paulina Highway (State Route 380) for 26.5 miles. Turn right (south) onto Congleton Hollow Road (unmarked dirt road) and drive for 3.9 miles to a faint dirt track on your left. Turn here and drive 0.3 mile and park. Explore the steep slope alongside the creek.

Site B: Backtrack 0.3 mile out to Congleton Hollow Road and turn left (south). Drive 0.3 mile to a fork and go left (uphill). Drive another 0.3 mile to a turnoff on the left. (I know, it's a lot of 0.3s.) Park here and explore the hills for rocks.

AT THE SITE → Congleton Hollow is a large area, and turning up cool material requires covering a lot of ground. Plan to spend a day or two hiking the hillsides. There's plenty of dispersed camping here both in the woods and along the South Fork Crooked River. There is a Tetris-shaped parcel of private land within Congleton Hollow that is fenced and gated (see map). Do not trespass.

Site A takes you to a steep slope where previous rockhounds have done a lot of digging for limb casts. The lava here has been altered to a beautiful deep green. Site B takes you to another jumping-off point in which to hike the broad hills that dip toward the Crooked River below. Bring a backpack, plenty of water, and your hiking poles. The key to success in Congleton Hollow is time. Limb casts are not richly abundant at the

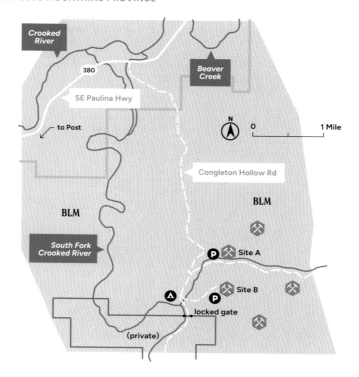

surface. However, you're likely to have some luck if you commit to covering a lot of ground. Remember that the tops of the buttes around Congleton Hollow are made of younger lavas that don't yield limb casts. Stay on the slopes to find the treasure.

44 Smoky Butte

So many geologic stories converge on Smoky Butte, it feels as if the Cenozoic Volcanism World Championships have landed here. In the lineup are the old Clarno volcanoes with their altered andesite lavas and colorful badlands. Above them rests the John Day Formation, ashy deposits from the dawn of the early Cascades. Among the John Day Formation are large deposits of caldera-spewn tuffs from massive eruptions associated with the mysterious Crooked River Caldera. To top it off, swaths of Columbia River flood basalt and tuffs of the Rattlesnake Volcanics cap the flat buttes that flank the collecting area. Geologists would tell you that these layers lie "unconformably" atop one another, meaning that the progression between their layers does not smoothly follow the rolled-out red carpet of time. Instead, large segments of time between each layer have gone entirely missing. These are known as unconformities. There are notable age differences between each layer, suggesting that periods of erosion likely occurred between each eruptive event. Or perhaps nothing much happened at all.

Smoky Butte is rich with colorful fragments of altered lavas from the various volcanic formations. I have found red, yellow, and teal jaspers and even bright-blue fragments of altered volcanic claystones, which are brittle and crumbly. Petrified wood and white agates filled with pockets of small quartz crystals are found on Smoky Butte too. All of these materials likely hail from the time of transition between the Clarno and John Day Formations. Toward the end of their volcanic life, the tectonic forces that gave the Clarnos their power shifted, and they went forever quiet. A new volcanic arc emerged farther west—the infant Cascades. The ashes they spewed would go on to become the John Day Formation. The parking area suggested for this location sits solidly on the transition zone between the two formations. When you first emerge from your vehicle, know that you will be standing on the boundary of change in an ancient world.

Colorful jaspers, agates, quartz, and petrified wood can be found along the slopes.

Wildflowers bloom along the slopes of the old volcanic rocks. Smoky Butte rises in the distance.

At Smoky Butte, interesting material tends to show up in patches, so be prepared to cover a lot of ground. New material makes its way to the surface as seasons pass. Unlike rivers, which renew themselves perennially, the hillsides here reveal material at a much slower pace. By taking rocks, you are intercepting them in their geological journey, removing them forever from the landscape, their home. Knowing this, it is essential to collect with intention; otherwise, the area is vulnerable to getting cleared out. Just because something is colorful, or pretty, doesn't mean you should take it.. Ask yourself what you intend to do with the material you take. If it's destined to live the rest of its life in a bucket in your garage, leave it. It is better to let these lovely rocks sleep their eternal life under the stars at Smoky Butte.

WHAT YOU'LL FIND: Colorful ash-flow tuffs, agate, jasper, quartz crystals, petrified wood

GEOLOGIC AGE: Cenozoic era; Eocene, Oligocene, and Miocene epochs

TOOLS: Geology pick or small trowel for tipping specimens out of the dirt

AGENCY: Bureau of Land Management— Prineville District Office

LIMITS: A reasonable amount of rocks may be taken for personal use only. A reasonable amount is often defined as up to 25 pounds per person, per day, with a maximum of 250 pounds per year. Do you need 25 pounds of rocks? Probably not. Collect lightly and with intention.

LOCATIONS:
Site A: 43.893323, –120.329793
Site B: 43.899778, –120.317417

VEHICLE: Some clearance recommended

SEASONS: Summer and fall

DIRECTIONS → Make your way to the old townsite of Brothers, Oregon. There are no services here, so make sure to fuel up beforehand. At the intersection of Camp Creek Road and Central Oregon Highway (US Highway 20), drive east on US 20 for 9.8 miles. Turn left (north) onto Van Lake Road, a well-maintained gravel road. Take Van Lake Road for 13 miles and look for a dirt track that peels off to the left (west), and turn here. Take this dirt track uphill for about 900 feet and park in an open area. This is Site A.

To get to Site B, drive another 0.6 mile north on Van Lake Road to another dirt track on the left. This track requires high clearance. Drive on it for up to a mile to get into rockhounding territory less frequented by others.

AT THE SITE → Hike west and north from either parking area. Colorful, weathering lavas are scattered across the hillsides as well as chunks of agate and quartz that had formed in vesicles and veins within the old ash flows. Some petrified wood shows up here as well. Smoky Butte is a popular rockhounding area, so be selective with what you take. The farther you hike, the more material you will find. A large parcel of private property abuts the BLM land about half a mile to the south of Site A. The collecting area is a Tetris game of public land surrounded by private ranches, so pay attention to signs and fences.

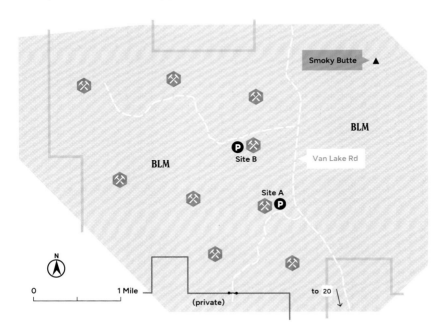

OREGON

Owyhee Uplands

The Owyhee Uplands are high lava plateaus of flood basalt and rhyo-lite from the era of hotspot volcanism that began between 17 and 16 million years ago and buried the landscape in lava and ash over a few million years. The Owyhee River, which flows northward toward the Snake River, carves a deep canyon through these volcanic rocks. Side canyons in Owyhee territory are known as gulches, and they are rich in agates, jasper, and petrified wood. Included in this section are locations within the Strawberry Volcanics farther to the west, which erupted in unison with the extraordinary Owyhee calderas and flood basalts.

Warm Springs Reservoir, a dammed section of the Malheur River, nests placidly among the ancient Strawberry Volcanics.

45 Warm Springs Reservoir

Just over 16 million years ago, a geological phenomenon occurred at such a massive scale that it would come to dominate the stories geologists tell about the Pacific Northwest today. It's theorized that a large plume of material from the mantle (far below Earth's brittle crust) upwelled to Earth's surface, initiating widespread volcanism that would bury much of Oregon, Washington, and parts of Idaho and Nevada in lava and ash. Fissures opened up in the earth above this plume—or hotspot—and poured out dark, basaltic floods. Massive calderas imploded, ejecting thousands of cubic kilometers of sticky rhyolite and volcanic ash into the sky. Andesite lavas, which fall chemically between basalt and rhyolite, erupted from tall, conical volcanoes in pyroclastic flows. In between, floods of red, molten basalt blanketed the valleys.

The majority of volcanism here occurred from 16 to 14 million years ago and drifted onward. It continues today, albeit no longer in southeastern Oregon. Geologists theorize that the hotspot is stationary in the mantle but the crust above it drifts as tectonic plates shift around. A path of volcanism neatly traces the direction of continental drift from its origins off the coast of Oregon (look up the origin of Siletzia), across the state, into Idaho, and onward into Wyoming. Today the hotspot sits under Yellowstone National Park and is responsible for the otherworldly boiling springs and legitimately explosive fears.

Back here, in quiet Oregon country, the hills surrounding Warm Springs Reservoir exhibit just how much stuff hotspot volcanoes can erupt. The peaks and buttes are composed of basalt, andesite, and rhyolite from several eruptions through volcanic vents that geologists have named the Strawberry Volcanics. Ashy sediments that piled up around the historic Strawberries yield crystal-pocketed agates, red jaspers, and petrified wood. All of these materials litter the hillsides and washes in a several-mile radius around the reservoir. Most visitors are here in search of agates, but for me it's the petrified wood that truly dazzles the imagination.

Treasures like this botryoidal agate are often tucked away in the fine soil that covers the low slopes around the reservoir.

It captures a singular moment when forces from inside Earth would rise to decimate the living. These fragments of wood carry within them the memory of a single catastrophic day, millions of years in the past.

WHAT YOU'LL FIND: Agate, jasper, petrified wood	**LIMIT:** A reasonable amount of rocks may be taken for personal use only. A reasonable amount is often defined as up to 25 pounds per person, per day, with a maximum of 250 pounds per year. Do you need 25 pounds of rocks? Probably not. Collect lightly and with intention.
GEOLOGIC AGE: Cenozoic era, Miocene epoch	
TOOLS: Small shovel or geology pick for tipping stones out of the dirt	
AGENCY: Bureau of Land Management— Burns District Office	**LOCATIONS:** **Site A:** 43.638806, –118.275806 **Site B:** 43.604000, –118.277139
	VEHICLE: Some clearance and four-wheel drive recommended
	SEASONS: Spring, summer, fall. Warning: Avoid the area in wet weather when the long dirt roads turn to mud.

DIRECTIONS → **Site A:** Make your way to the intersection of Monroe Street and Broadway Avenue in the bustling town of Burns, Oregon. From the intersection, drive north on North Broadway Avenue (US Highway 20 East) for 39.4 miles. Turn right (south) onto Warm Springs Road, which is gravel. Drive 12.8 miles to where a large wash crosses the road. Find a safe place to pull over here and begin your search along the drainage.

Site B: From Site A, continue driving south down Warm Springs Road for 3 miles and look for a dirt track heading uphill on your right. Turn right here and drive up this road for 0.3 mile. From this point, start to look for a reasonable place to pull over and begin your search.

AT THE SITE → Both locations offer a good place to pull over and explore the gullies and hillsides for material. Please note that the shores of the reservoir itself are overseen by the Bureau of Reclamation, which does not permit rockhounding. However, the dry land surrounding the reservoir is BLM land, and material in the dry washes and hillsides is plentiful.

Site A has a wonderful wash to search through in dry weather. Agate, jasper, and red ash-flow tuff show up here in great quantity. Search both up-creek and down-creek, but keep away from the reservoir waterline when collecting.

Site B is a wonderful place to find agates and petrified wood. Material is scattered along the hillsides here. Use a small shovel or geology pick to tip buried specimens out of the dirt.

46 Lars's Stock Pond

For many rockhounds, petrified wood has a lure. It draws us in, tangling us in a mystical conundrum. How can something living be so thoroughly turned to stone? Perhaps the petrifying gaze of the Gorgon Medusa is not myth, but truth. To hold such petrified remains is to open a portal and grasp the once-living tree itself, to feel its rough bark and hear its canopy of birdsong. "I think that, somewhere deep down inside, we are all animists," says my friend Martin Holden. "We know in our hearts that everything is alive and has some kind of spirit. Petrified wood reinforces the idea that a rock can be a living thing, and that a living thing can be a rock, that energy and matter can pass back and forth across the veil."

Through petrified wood, we time travel. Here, at a small livestock pond along a juniper-forested slope, fragments of ancient branches and logs have been unearthed, revealing a forest buried during the chaotic eruptions of the Strawberry Volcanics millions of years ago. Though the Strawberries erupted over a period of several million years (starting about 16 million years back) the wood here was likely buried in a single eruption. The fallen trees were invaded by the ash that buried them, and cell by cell, silica replaced life, and life became stone. Millions of years would pass before they would be exhumed.

I came to know this peaceful spot through the guidebooks of Lars Johnson. The stock pond doesn't have a name on any maps, so I've named it after him. The petrified wood here is plentiful and well-preserved. It's a quiet place to immerse yourself in the perpetual cycles of nature, to walk among the junipers and pick up the crystalline bones of trees from another time. The abundance of wood may tempt you to collect with abandon, so you must ask yourself how you intend to do right by each rock. After all, you are removing it from its resting place. Will you display it, gift it, or make something from it? Or will it languish in a bucket in

Juniper grow among the low hills scattered with petrified trees from millions of years in the past.

The dirt is rich with petrified wood. Despite the abundance, collect with intention.

your garage? (A tragic fate to bestow upon anything.) The petrified woods found here were once stately trees—deciduous hardwoods that dropped seeds and nuts around their flanks. Their leaves faded in cooling autumns and leafed out in the epiphanies of spring . . . until the volcanoes. Toppled, their tissue was replaced by stone, "particle by particle / carried across space and time," writes poet Helen Shewolfe Tseng, "tumbling from the wounds / until massive shards resurface / fossilized / into a jewel / that is also a clock / that is also an archive / that is also a grave."

WHAT YOU'LL FIND: Petrified wood	**LIMITS:** 25 pounds of petrified wood per person, per day, with a maximum of 250 pounds per year
GEOLOGIC AGE: Cenozoic era, Miocene epoch	
TOOLS: Small shovel or rock pick to tip specimens out of the dirt	**LOCATION:** 43.599890, –118.151570
	VEHICLE: Any
AGENCY: Bureau of Land Management—Vale District Office	**SEASONS:** Spring, summer, fall

DIRECTIONS → Make your way to the Oasis Cafe & Motel at 5838 US Highway 20 in Juntura, Oregon. From the café, drive northwest on US 20 West for 0.2 mile. Turn left onto Hildah Road and drive a few hundred feet. Turn right onto Juntura-Riverside Road, which is gravel, and drive 12.6 miles to a small stock pond on the west side of the road. Pull over safely and park.

AT THE SITE → Construction to trench a livestock pond here has unearthed a great quantity of petrified wood. You can use a small shovel or rock pick to tip buried specimens out of the dirt surrounding the manmade pond. Material will be very easy to find. Give cattle space if they have congregated in the area. Consider hiking the larger area around the stock pond in search of wood. And of course, collect with intention.

㊼ Beulah Reservoir

Low cliffs of blinding-white rock crop out along the edge of a quiet reservoir. This body of water, known as Beulah Reservoir, is a dammed section of the North Fork Malheur River, which snakes through the remnants of the Strawberry

Volcanics. The volcanic rocks emplaced here erupted from the earth beginning 16 million years ago. In the few million years of eruptions that followed, extensive lakes filled the basins below. Perhaps lava flows had blocked existing rivers, backing them up, or perhaps it was the work of beavers that engineered the extensive freshwater environment. (Beaver fossils are well documented near Beulah.) Either way, evidence of a large regional lake system remains behind in broad deposits of bright-white diatomaceous earth—the remnants of diatoms.

Diatoms are photosynthetic plankton that bloom in freshwater lakes. They build their shells from silica that is dissolved in the lake water, much of it derived from volcanic ash. Over the years, populations of diatoms bloom and die off, and their silica skeletons sink to the bottom of the lake. Seasonal

Beulah Reservoir, a dammed section of the Malheur River, nests among the ancient Strawberry Volcanics. Low cliffs of fossil-rich diatomite appear in the foreground.

pulses of leaves and debris join them. Over the years, the layers build up, and over millennia, they become stone. Here on the edge of Beulah Reservoir, one such outcrop of diatomaceous earth, known as diatomite, holds abundant fossils of leaves and woody debris. The stone is powdery, soft, and easy to split open. Some leaves have left behind a fine, dark skeleton of carbon within the rock, and others have left only a ghostly white imprint. When you split a layer of rock apart and reveal a leaf, you are looking at a leaf that has not seen the light of the sun since it dropped into a quiet lake millions of years ago.

The ecosystem that once surrounded the shores of these ancient lakes was likely similar to that of present-day central California, with its spindly live oaks, grassy savannas, and riparian shrubs. Large mammals grazed on abundant grasses, which were a relatively new type of plant to appear on Earth. (One might ponder if mammals and grasses coevolved, much like the flowers with the bees.) In the 1950s and '60s paleontologist J. Arnold Shotwell found fossil flamingos not far from Beulah Reservoir. Other paleontologists have come to study fish fossils, attempting to map not the evolution of fish but the evolution of ancient

A carbon distillation of a fossil leaf in diatomite

rivers. These fossils are found in sedimentary layers near Beulah Reservoir, but not necessarily in the diatomite itself—that is the domain of the sunken leaves. The diatomite, now a rock, is also a fossil, constructed of millions of microscopic skeletons of glassy plankton that sank to the bottom of this lake millions of years ago. It's all quite astonishing to think about when you hold it in your hand.

WHAT YOU'LL FIND: Diatomite with fossil leaves, leaf impressions, sticks, and possibly insects and fish	**LIMITS:** No set limits. The Vale Oregon Irrigation District asks that you collect within reason.
GEOLOGIC AGE: Cenozoic era, Pliocene epoch	**LOCATION:** 43.91182, –118.15853
TOOLS: Hammer, flat chisel, or paint scraper; safety glasses and gloves	**VEHICLE:** Any
AGENCY: Bureau of Reclamation. Rockhounding is traditionally not allowed on Bureau of Reclamation land. However, the dam's operator, Vale Oregon Irrigation District, allows visitors to the site. Visitors must keep away from the dam itself.	**SEASONS:** Spring, summer, fall

DIRECTIONS → Make your way to the Oasis Cafe & Motel at 5838 US Highway 20 in Juntura, Oregon. From the café, drive northwest on US 20 West for 0.2 mile. Turn right onto Hildah Road and drive 0.2 mile. Continue straight onto Beulah Road and drive for 14.3 miles to the Agency Valley Dam. At the dam, turn left onto Agency Mountain Road (unmarked) and drive 0.4 mile to a pull-off on the right. Park here and take the established footpath down to the reservoir.

AT THE SITE → Beulah Reservoir is a dammed section of the North Fork Malheur River. The reservoir that exists here today is manmade and is not the source of the sedimentary rocks along its shores. A low cliff of diatomite (ancient lakebed sediments) is exposed along the reservoir here. It is very close to the Agency Valley Dam, and its operator, Vale Oregon Irrigation District, allows visitors to the fossil site, which is on Bureau of Reclamation land. Visitors are required to stay away from the dam itself and practice good rockhounding etiquette: do not damage the cliff, work with material already on the ground, and fill any holes if you dig for any reason.

In the diatomaceous rocks along the cliff, leaf and stick fossils are abundant. Every chunk of white rock contains fossil material. Work through loose rock material that has already fallen from the cliff. You can use a hammer, flat chisel, or paint scraper to split the rock along its bedding planes. Or you can just pick fossils up off the ground. No tools required. Most fossils are imprints, ghostly white outlines of leaves within the rock, and some are distilled, leaving a black carbon skeleton of their former selves.

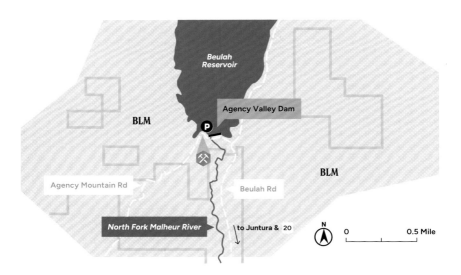

48 Cottonwood Creek

This is where Owyhee country really begins. In an ocean of sage-frosted buttes, a wide, braiding creek drains several million years of rocks from the massive calderas that began imploding here around 15 million years ago. During that time the crust was overriding the tempestuous Yellowstone hotspot in the mantle below. Cottonwood Creek, which drains the resulting caldera rocks, has the bones of a powerful river, but its water comes only in pulses of melting snow and heavy rains. For the remainder of the year, smaller currents meander through the much larger creek bed carved out by great floods. The result is a river of rocks all beautifully exposed.

The majority of rocks here are black basalts and dark-gray lavas of the calc-alkaline variety. These calc-alkaline rocks would have been basalt, too, had it not been for some stalling in the magma chamber that allowed time for calcium, magnesium, and alkali metals (think lithium) to concentrate before the big explosion. Rhyolite, the most "stalled" of all the lavas, caps many of the buttes surrounding the basin. Rhyolite lavas are so enriched in silica (from a lot of melting and then melting some more) that their eruptions lead to massive, gas-rich, explosive eruptions rather than crimson lava flows. The rhyolite rocks in Cottonwood Creek tend to be a purplish brown with wavy banding. Red and yellow jaspers and the equally colorful ash-fall deposits that they hail from stand out among the darker river rocks.

Perhaps the most eye-catching of all these materials is the chalky, white diatomite and the white opal that forms among it. The diatomite is composed of the microscopic skeletons of diatoms, a type of plankton that compose their bodies from silica (specifically opal!). These tiny plankton sank in great numbers to the bottom of ancient lakes that filled the caldera basins after the eruptions went quiet.

Cottonwood Creek runs year-round, flowing tumultuously in winter and spring and driest in summer.

White opal, red and yellow jasper, and dark petrified wood are common in the creek bed.

It's hard to imagine the tempests that have decimated this landscape over the millennia. Some of the Owyhees' caldera eruptions left behind craters the size of metropolises. That these happened several times over the course of a few million years speaks to the power of the molten energy that once sat underneath the crust in this now tenderly peaceful place. Be glad to be here now, rather than then.

WHAT YOU'LL FIND: Jasper, tuff, opal

GEOLOGIC AGE: Cenozoic era, Miocene to Pliocene epochs

TOOLS: A garden claw or trowel, and wellies or water shoes if water is present

AGENCY: Bureau of Land Management—Vale District Office

LIMITS: A reasonable amount of rocks may be taken for personal use only. A reasonable amount is often defined as up to 25 pounds per person, per day, with a maximum of 250 pounds per year. Do you need 25 pounds of rocks? Probably not. Collect lightly and with intention.

LOCATIONS:
Site A: 43.739194, –117.673667
Site B: 43.711083, –117.703111

VEHICLE: Any vehicle can make it to Site A. High clearance and four-wheel drive are required to get to Site B when the creek runs deep in winter and spring.

SEASONS: Any, though creek crossings should be expected during wet seasons.

DIRECTIONS → Make your way to Lewin City Park in the town of Vale, Oregon. Lewin is a small triangular park on the corner of Clark Street and Washington Street West. From the park, drive west on Washington Street West (Central Oregon Highway, US Highway 20) for 21.6 miles. Turn left (south) onto Crowley Road, which is a graded dirt road. Drive 9.4 miles to where Cottonwood Creek crosses Crowley Road. Pull over here and explore the river gravels. Any car can make the journey to this first location, Site A. Anticipate muddy spots along the way during the wet season.

To get to Site B, you may need high clearance and four-wheel drive to continue onward if there is water crossing the road. *Always walk the span of water-covered road on foot to test depth before driving across.* After crossing Cottonwood Creek, continue driving another 2.7 miles. Pull over into a broad parking area under a large tree on the right to access the creek gravels. The tree is a notable feature in the otherwise tree-less landscape. Take care not to block tire tracks leading right into the creek. Here, an almost invisible backcountry route fords the enormous gravel beds and leads deeper into desert country.

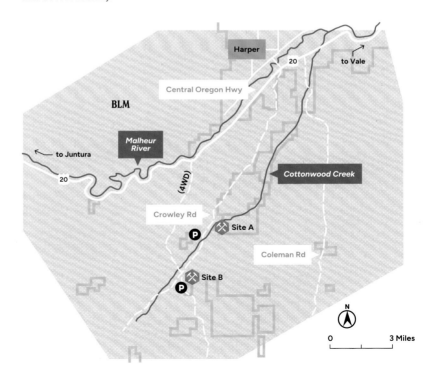

AT THE SITE → Both Sites A and B provide access to the brilliant expanse of rocks lining the bed of Cottonwood Creek. Red and yellow jaspers as well as the colorful volcanic tuffs they hail from stand out among the darker rocks. Small chunks of white opal and the chalky white diatomite from which the opal is derived are easy to spot as well. There is a possibility of agate and petrified wood too.

⓪ Sand Hollow

Behold the humble snail. And at Sand Hollow, behold multitudinous fossils of tiny freshwater snails from a long-gone Pliocene lake. After the era of caldera eruptions migrated onward, large fluvial lake systems filled in the scars left by volcanism. Over the millennia, populations of tiny clams and snails bloomed and died off, leaving behind deep layers of shell matter on the lake bottom. Most geologists consider these sediments and their fossils to be the remnants of ancient Lake Idaho, which lasted possibly from 12 million to 2 million years ago, filling in after the extraordinary caldera eruptions went quiet.

The hills surrounding Sand Hollow are composed of ancient lakebed sediments: diatomite, mudstone, and limestone.

The local stratigraphy (layers of sediments) reveals evidence of a mostly shallow lake system that persisted for millions of years. While large swaths of diatomite crop out west of Sand Hollow, this site and its sister sediments that sprawl eastward are composed mostly of fine siltstone and limestone. Occasionally, some of the limestone is fossiliferous—filled with shells. Most of the shell material is crushed and makes up the main substrate of the rock itself, but complete fossils of tiny clams and snails can be seen within. The shells are delicate, a feature typical of freshwater molluscs. Unlike seawater, freshwater rarely reaches the enrichment levels of the elements required to build heavy, wave-proof shells. But that's okay because in the gentler lakes, these small molluscs could get by with paper-thin shells. And in the Pliocene lake of Sand Hollow, they flourished.

In the court of the molluscs, clams are on the bivalve bench and snails are on the gastropod bench. Both groups hail from the Paleozoic, surviving untold ex-

Only some of the limestone at Sand Hollow is fossiliferous. Search as close to the given coordinates as you can.

tinctions and planetary change. A 2022 study published in *Nature* looked at the evolutionary pressures on freshwater gastropods over "deep time" and found that their evolution was not driven by breeding and natural selection, as Darwin once posited, but by distinct and immediate geological events that isolated or altogether destroyed populations. The findings contradict long-held views about what drives the evolution of species and what ingredients form the recipe for diversification. Who knew that the humble freshwater snail could upend the canon of Darwin?

It makes you wonder about the diminutive snail fossils in Sand Hollow. What can they tell us about the recovery of the Owyhee world post-caldera-volcanism? What kind of ecosystems surrounded this ancient lake? What water sources flowed into them? Were the snails of these Pliocene lakes unique, endemic species found only in this place? And when the lake system eventually disappeared, did these snail species vanish with it? These are the questions that drive intrepid researchers to look for answers.

WHAT YOU'LL FIND: Freshwater shell fossils in limestone	**LIMITS:** A reasonable amount of rocks may be taken for personal use only. A reasonable amount is often defined as up to 25 pounds per person, per day, with a maximum of 250 pounds per year. Do you need 25 pounds of rocks? Probably not. Collect lightly and with intention.
GEOLOGIC AGE: Cenozoic era, Miocene to Pliocene epochs	
TOOLS: A rock hammer or claw to tip specimens out of the ground; a hand lens to inspect small fossil shells	
	LOCATION: 43.880306, –117.442361
AGENCY: Bureau of Land Management—Vale District Office	**VEHICLE:** High clearance and 4WD required
	SEASONS: Any

DIRECTIONS → Make your way to Lewin City Park in the town of Vale, Oregon. Lewin is a small triangular park on the corner of Clark Street and Washington Street West. From the park, drive west on Washington Street West (Central Oregon Highway, US Highway 20) for 12.5 miles. Just after cresting the summit of Vine Hill, turn left (south) onto an unmarked and well-graded dirt road (which leads to a small mine). Drive for 0.5 mile and turn left onto a dirt track. *High clearance is required from this point on. Do not drive if wet. If in a low-clearance vehicle, you may pull over here and hike the remaining distance.* Follow the jeep track for 0.3 mile to a T-junction. Turn right (uphill) and drive another 0.2 mile to the fossiliferous outcrop. Find a safe place to pull off. *Do not block road access for others.*

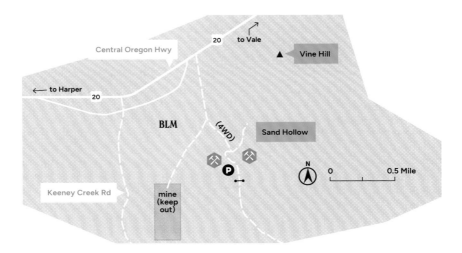

AT THE SITE → The ground here is made of eroding blocks of fossiliferous lake-bed sediments. The fossil shells are quite small, so some examination with a hand lens is recommended. The shells are fragile and rarely erode out of the rock singularly. You are most likely to find intact shells embedded in chunks of rock. A hammer won't do much here beside crush specimens. Gently collect from the surface and consider taking only a shelf specimen or two.

⑤⓪ Sagebrush Gulch

Sagebrush Gulch drains a layer cake of Owyhee geology and dumps it out into a quiet basin terraced with dusty badlands. Treasures from the days of tempestuous volcanism are washed down the gulch in seasonal storms and gather at its terminus. Around 15 million years ago, the Yellowstone hotspot was positioned underneath this part of Oregon. It caused the ground to implode—several times—releasing extraordinary volumes of rhyolite lava and volcanic ash. Intermittently, flood basalts were unleashed, too, and in the in-between times, sediments stacked up as each layer of volcanic stuff faulted and eroded. A variety of silicate treasures that are born in volcanic rocks and sediments show up along the slopes and dry riverbed of Sagebrush Gulch: common opal, agate, and jasper, to name a few. Many of the jaspers are colorful reds, greens, and teals. In rare instances, fossilized mammal bones and fragments of lacustrine deposits filled with freshwater shells turn up here too. (Remember: fossil bones must always be left in place.)

The agates found in Sagebrush Gulch tend to be the main draw, crumbling from seams within the volcanogenic sediments (sediments derived from volcanic rocks). The agate seams crop out intermittently for almost four miles up the gulch. Outcrops at some of the higher elevations have been staked with mining claims. The lower section of the gulch is free of claims, and material is easily found here. The agates are beautifully clear and feature opaque plumes, which look feathery or almost plant-like. It's likely these agates formed when a silica-rich solution invaded cracks or seams in the volcanogenic rock and solidified over time. During solidification, elements that had dissolved within the silica-rich fluids slowly precipitated out, branching like plants, building plumes. Think of the plumes as mineral gardens. As the plume minerals branch out of solution, they leave a silica solution behind, which hardens into a clear agate around them.

Sagebrush Gulch terminates in a basin of unconsolidated sediments, mostly clays from ancient basins and lakes. The roads through the area are soft, deep, and dusty—and completely impassable when wet. Backcountry driving experience and a high-clearance vehicle with four-wheel drive are required to visit this location.

Low hills guard the mouth of Sagebrush Gulch.

Colorful jasper and translucent plume agate are common here.

WHAT YOU'LL FIND: Agate and jasper	**LOCATION:** 43.795000, –117.381083
GEOLOGIC AGE: Cenozoic era, Miocene epoch	**VEHICLE:** High clearance and four-wheel drive/all-wheel drive required. Rock Canyon Road is deeply rutted and made of soft sediments.
TOOLS: Small shovel or geology pick for tipping specimens out of the dirt	
AGENCY: Bureau of Land Management—Vale District Office	**SEASONS:** Spring, summer, fall. Warning: Avoid the area in wet weather. Gulches are treacherous in rainstorms.
LIMITS: A reasonable amount of rocks may be taken for personal use only. A reasonable amount is often defined as up to 25 pounds per person, per day, with a maximum of 250 pounds per year. Do you need 25 pounds of rocks? Probably not. Collect lightly and with intention.	

DIRECTIONS → *Warning: do not drive Rock Canyon Road when wet.* Make your way to Lewin City Park in the town of Vale, Oregon. Lewin is a small triangular park on the corner of Clark Street and Washington Street West. From the park, drive west on Washington Street West (Central Oregon Highway, US Highway 20) for 7.6 miles. Turn left onto 4th Boulevard South (Bishop Road) and drive for 1.2 miles. Take a sharp right (it's almost invisible) onto Rock Canyon Road. From here you will need high clearance and four-wheel drive. Drive 0.4 mile and follow Rock Canyon Road as it makes a sharp left-hand hook to the south. Drive another 9.8 miles on Rock Canyon Road and look out for a large clearing on your left. Pull into this open, flat area and park. This is the mouth of Sagebrush Gulch.

AT THE SITE → From the flat parking area, hike into Sagebrush Gulch. Explore the wash and the low slopes around it for plume agate and colorful jasper. You may find petrified wood and fossil shells in lacustrine sediments, but these are not as common. Bring plenty of water if you plan to hike far. A geology pick can help tip stubborn rocks out of the dirt.

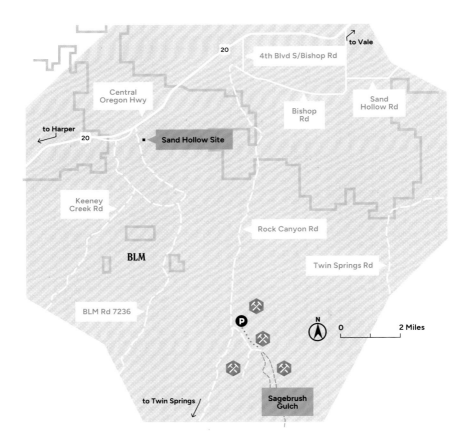

51 Haystack Rock

The picturesque butte of Haystack Rock nests deep in a gulch on the west side of the Owyhee River. Flood basalts, ash-flow tuffs, and sedimentary rocks from the days of caldera volcanism coalesce in this picturesque canyon. The Owyhee region is part of a historic feature geologists call the Oregon-Idaho graben, a large, down-faulted valley that evolved during the era of chaotic explosions 15 million years ago. A great deal of sediments derived from lavas filled this valley as volcanic activity began to quiet down. The sedimentary rocks seen in the basin around Haystack Rock are composed of this infill. Swaths of blinding-white tephra (sediments made of pumice and ash) crumble from the hillsides, and other sediments crop out among them. Dark basalt caps many of the buttes, giving them their distinct flat-top appearance.

A great deal of beautiful silicate treasure gathers around the flanks of Haystack Rock too. The large wash that runs through the gulch brings loads of material from the Owyhee uplands into the small basin around the butte. Red, green, and teal jasper are very common. A yellow-and-red wonderstone is also found here. Wonderstone is a jasper with wavy or bird's-eye patterning running throughout; various stages of oxidized iron within the stones are the likely culprit of the colors. All of these silicate rocks derive from the volcanic ash ejected from the immense caldera systems of the past. Agates and jaspers aren't born in eruptions, though. They come into existence after the fact. These rocks form as glassy volcanic ash devitrifies into simple minerals like opal, chalcedony, and clay.

If a geologist were to examine thin sections of agate or jasper microscopically, they would see cryptocrystalline silica, and probably note it in their lab report as chalcedony (pronounced: *cal-sid-nee*). It's a lot of words, but they're all the same thing. Cryptocrystalline silica is known formally as chalcedony and commonly as agate and jasper. In the field, if a specimen is translucent, rockhounds call it agate, and if it is opaque, they call it jasper. Microscopically, it's all the same. The inclusion of elements like iron and fine clay minerals impart color in the stones. Opal is common down by Haystack Rock too. It's not the precious, optical stuff of dreams, but rather solid in color and somewhat crumbly. The presence of water within its silica fabric makes it a less hardy sister to chalcedony.

In the creation story of opal, agate, and jasper, groundwater often assists in their deposition. As groundwaters invade volcanic rocks and ash layers, they carry dissolved silica away, depositing it in vesicles, cracks, and seams. This is the after-the-fact stuff. These pretty rocks precipitate in voids slowly over time. When the

Red and green jasper, as well as wonderstone, litter the washes and hillsides.

host rock around them erodes away, these sturdy silicate materials are released into the wild. They tumble down gulches and gather at the flanks of lonesome desert buttes.

WHAT YOU'LL FIND: Agate, jasper, opal, possibly petrified wood	**LIMITS:** A reasonable amount of rocks may be taken for personal use only. A reasonable amount is often defined as up to 25 pounds per person, per day, with a maximum of 250 pounds per year. Do you need 25 pounds of rocks? Probably not. Collect lightly and with intention.
GEOLOGIC AGE: Cenozoic era, Miocene epoch	
TOOLS: Small shovel or geology pick; backpack and a lot of water	
AGENCY: Bureau of Land Management—Vale District Office	**LOCATION:** 43.713444, –117.253083
	VEHICLE: High clearance and four-wheel drive required
	SEASONS: Spring, summer, fall. Warning: Avoid the area in wet weather. Gulches are treacherous in rainstorms.

DIRECTIONS → *Backcountry driving experience is required.* Make your way to the gas station at 2499 Succor Creek Highway in Owyhee, Oregon. It sits at the corner of Owyhee Avenue and the Succor Creek Highway (State Route 201). From the gas station, head west on Owyhee Avenue for 6 miles. Turn left onto Mitchell Butte Road (which eventually turns to dirt) and drive 5.5 miles to a fork. Stay left to continue on Mitchell Butte Road. Drive for 2.4 miles and stay straight (downhill) to continue onto Haystack Rock Road. Drive 1 mile to a cattle guard and turn left onto a dirt track after crossing it. Take this dirt track for 0.6 mile and park along the wash.

AT THE SITE → The broad wash that runs along Haystack Rock is filled with jasper and wonderstone. Common opal can also be found here. Lithics, or debris from toolmaking, are common in the area. (See the "Lithics: Identifying Archaeological Material" sidebar in the Basin and Range Province section for information on how to avoid collecting archaeological material.) The gulch is large, so once parked, plan to make a day of it. Bring a backpack and plenty of water, and hike the wash and hillsides for treasure.

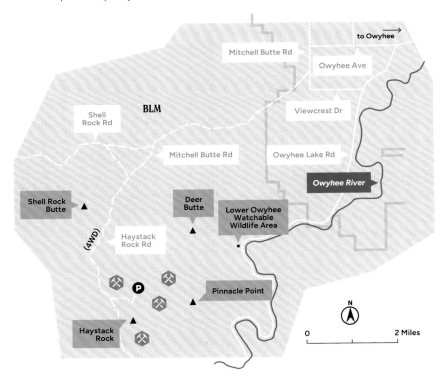

52 Twin Springs and Grassy Mountain

Grassy Mountain rises from the Owyhee landscape like a fortress. On its southern rim, spire-like hoodoos and cascading badlands inspire awe. The slopes of Grassy Mountain yield large logs of petrified wood, some of it nicely preserved and some of it chalky and crumbling. It's a full day of hiking, but deeply enriching, to explore the flanks of this mountain. Around every bend it seems another ancient tree is eroding from the earth. In the basin below Grassy Mountain's southern flanks, striking swaths of cross-bedded sandstone crop out. These sedimentary

Preparing to hike around Grassy Mountain on a hot summer day

rocks filled the ancestral basin after caldera volcanism quieted about 14 million years ago.

The north side of Grassy Mountain slopes much more gently. The valley below the north side of the mountain is a site of hydrothermal enrichment. Hot fluids from deeper in the crust invaded the bedrock here sometime after volcanism ended and left behind veins of quartz and gold. This area is entirely under claim, with plans for Oregon's largest gold mine in the works. If the mine gets permitted, big changes are headed for this quiet corner of the Owyhees. Luckily for rockhounds, the southern, scenic flank of Grassy Mountain is safe from mining claims . . . for now.

Twin Springs Creek runs along the west flank of Grassy Mountain and drains southward into a deep, shadowy gulch, where it merges with Dry Creek. Copious agates, picture stones, and some petrified wood can be found by following the gulch to its depths. The agates here are white, lumpy nodules filled with small quartz crystals (like a geode) and pretty waterline banding. Waterline banding is a nonscientific term for a feature in agates where you can see visible layers of silica deposition one atop the other. Inside the white nodules, the agate is crystal clear.

An extremely rough road dips down into the gulch, which eventually leads into the remote Dry Creek area of the Owyhees. This is an excellent hike to take all the way down to the creek's confluence with the Owyhee River if you're up for an all-day adventure. The gulch that Twin Springs Creek dives into is steep and narrow, so take great care to avoid it during rainfall. Flash floods are inescapable in such a place.

WHAT YOU'LL FIND: Petrified wood, agate, picture stone

GEOLOGIC AGE: Cenozoic era, Miocene epoch

TOOLS: Small shovel, geology pick, backpack, and a lot of water

AGENCY: Bureau of Land Management—Vale District Office

LIMITS: A reasonable amount of rocks may be taken for personal use only. A reasonable amount is often defined as up to 25 pounds per person, per day, with a maximum of 250 pounds per year. Do you need 25 pounds of rocks? Probably not. Collect lightly and with intention.

LOCATIONS:
Site A, Grassy Mountain:
43.609887, −117.397393
Site B, Twin Springs Creek:
43.575944, −117.406694

VEHICLE: High clearance and four-wheel drive recommended

SEASONS: Spring, summer, fall. Warning: Avoid Site B in wet weather. Gulches are treacherous in rainstorms.

Petrified wood is abundant, albeit patchy, on the slopes. Prepare to explore.

DIRECTIONS → *Backcountry driving experience is required.* This region is a maze of roads so carry a road atlas and follow directions closely. Make your way to the gas station at 2499 Succor Creek Highway in Owyhee, Oregon. It sits at the corner of Owyhee Avenue and the Succor Creek Highway (State Route 201). From the gas station, head west on Owyhee Avenue for 6 miles. Turn left onto Mitchell Butte Road, which leads out of the agricultural area into the Owyhee wilderness, quickly turning to dirt. Drive 5.5 miles to a fork. Stay right to continue onto Shell Rock Road (unmarked). Drive another 0.3 mile and continue straight. Drive 0.9 mile and stay straight again. Drive 0.4 mile and stay straight again. (I include these details because the web of roads out here can get confusing.) Drive another 2 miles and stay left at the fork to continue onto Twin Springs Road. Drive 12.7 miles to the Twin Springs Campground, which is noticeable thanks to its tall stand of trees.

Site A, Grassy Mountain: From the Twin Springs Campground, drive south on Twin Springs Road (which becomes Dry Creek Road) for 1.2 miles. Turn left onto Oxbow Basin Road (an unmarked dirt track) that dips into a wash (often muddy) and heads east. Drive

0.6 mile and park safely off the road. From here, hike north up into the badlands of Grassy Mountain in search of petrified wood.

Site B, Twin Springs Creek: *Warning: Avoid the gulch in wet weather as it is subject to flash flooding.* From the Twin Springs Campground, drive south on Twin Springs Road (which becomes Dry Creek Road) for 2.6 miles. Find a safe place to pull over here and park. Hike down along the rough road into the gulch and follow it downstream.

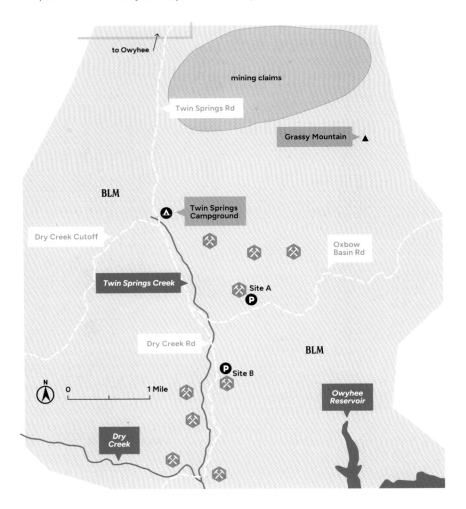

"Waterline" agate is common in the gulch.

AT THE SITE → **Site A, Grassy Mountain:** From the parking area along the broad meadow, hike north up into the badlands of Grassy Mountain in search of petrified wood. The wood starts to show up on the slopes, which are about a 0.4-mile hike from the road. Bring a backpack, plenty of water, and make a day of exploring the beautiful badlands that cascade from the prominent ridge of Grassy Mountain.

 Site B, Twin Springs Creek: The gulch drops into the Dry Creek Area of Critical Environmental Concern. Surface collecting within the ACEC is allowed. Digging is not. From the parking spot, hike down into the gulch along the rough road. If you have a high-clearance vehicle with four-wheel drive, you may continue farther down the road, but the gulch narrows and there are few places to park. The creek bed is filled with agates, picture stone, and some petrified wood. I would recommend taking at least a 1-mile hike down the gulch to find good material. Bring a backpack, plenty of water, and make a day of exploring the beautiful canyon below.

53 Three Fingers Gulch

In the Owyhee wilderness, side canyons that drain material down into the Owyhee River are known as gulches. These dramatic gulches drop down through mountains of lava and ash layers that blanketed the landscape between 16 and 15 million years ago. It's theorized (and agreed upon) that a plume of molten rock rising from the mantle—a hotspot—initiated an era of violent volcanism that consumed great portions of Oregon and Washington. Great floods of lava poured over the

Some nicely "landscaped" picture jasper from the abandoned diggings

A rockhound inspects picture jasper for quality in the depths of Three Fingers Gulch.

landscape, and here, in the southeast quadrant of Oregon, several massive calderas erupted, ejecting viscous lavas and hot, powdery ash into the skies. "Calderas do not build mountains up," writes geologist Ellen Morris Bishop in her magnum opus, *In Search of Ancient Oregon*. Instead, calderas "spread their eruptions far afield as a turbulent cloud of hot gas and ash that often moves 60–100 miles per hour." Little was spared in such cataclysms. Trees were buried and petrified, and over time silicate minerals coalesced in the deep, ashy deposits forming opals, agates, and jaspers.

The journey into Three Fingers Gulch is a long, rugged drive, dropping almost a thousand feet in elevation from plateau to canyon bottom. The final three miles of the journey meander through prime rockhounding territory, where the earth is composed of ash-fall tuffs from the ancient eruptions. (Tuff is a rock composed of hardened ash.) A great deal of green jasper, petrified wood, and picture jasper can be found. The picture jasper is the most sought-after material, found at the bottom stretch of the gulch in outcrops that are dominantly composed of palagonite. Palagonite is a type of basaltic tuff that has interacted with water. Normally these ingredients would create basalt. But if enough water is involved in its eruption, the molten rock can explode into glassy ash rather than red, hot lava.

The richness of iron within the palagonite tuff of Three Fingers Gulch shows its influence in the picture jasper that is found here. *Picture* refers to the landscape-like images created by iron banding in the jasper (Liesegang banding) that occurred during its formation. When cut perpendicularly, the banding often creates impressions of desert-like landscapes reminiscent of the surrounding gulches. Three Fingers Gulch has been one of several sources for Owyhee picture jasper for many decades. Near the bottom of the gulch, old tailing piles from some of the historic diggings are still filled with beautiful specimens. This portion of the Owyhees no longer has mining claims, and surface collecting for rock material is welcome.

WHAT YOU'LL FIND: Picture jasper, green jasper, petrified wood; some agate and common opal possible

GEOLOGIC AGE: Cenozoic era, Miocene epoch

TOOLS: Geology pick for tipping specimens out of the dirt

AGENCY: Bureau of Land Management—Vale District Office

LIMITS: A reasonable amount of rocks may be taken for personal use only. A reasonable amount is often defined as up to 25 pounds per person, per day, with a maximum of 250 pounds per year. Do you need 25 pounds of rocks? Probably not. Collect lightly and with intention. Three Fingers Gulch is within a wilderness study area. Surface collecting is allowed. Digging is not.

LOCATION: 43.389889, –117.281028

VEHICLE: High clearance and four-wheel drive required

SEASONS: Spring, summer, fall. Warning: Avoid the area in wet weather. Gulches are treacherous in rainstorms.

DIRECTIONS → *Backcountry driving experience is required.* Make your way to the gas station at 2499 Succor Creek Highway in Owyhee, Oregon. It sits at the corner of Owyhee Avenue and Succor Creek Highway (State Route 201). Make sure to gas up here. From the station, head south on SR 201 for 12.5 miles. Turn right onto Succor Creek Road (dirt) and drive south for 25.2 miles. Turn right onto Leslie Gulch Road. Drive for 3.3 miles to a dirt

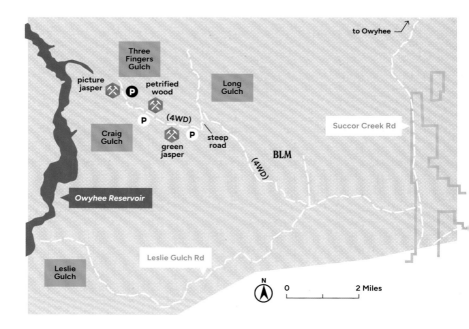

road on the right. Turn here. Drive 0.3 mile and take a slight left at the fork. Drive 4.6 miles and make a sharp left onto a dirt track that snakes downhill. (The road is steep through here; four-wheel drive required.) Drive 0.6 mile and stay right at a fork. Continue downhill for 3.2 miles to the road's end at an overlook for Three Fingers Gulch and Long Gulch. The last 3.2 miles of road has good rocks all along it, and recommendations of where to stop and park are marked on the map.

AT THE SITE → The gulch drops into a wilderness study area. Surface collecting is allowed. Digging is not. This is a long and rugged drive down into one of the Owyhees' most scenic gulches. Only experienced backcountry drivers should make the trip. Plan to spend at least one full day here. Even better, bring supplies and camp down here for a night or two. The final 3.2 miles of road drive through prime rockhounding territory, and I recommend stopping along the way to look for interesting material. Look for signs of old diggings at the 3-mile mark. Picture jasper is common where the directions terminate.

54 Birch Creek

Along a remote stretch of the Owyhee River, a side canyon leads into an unusual formation of rocks. Here, narrow hoodoos and ridges emerge from the talus slopes that gather under towering cliffs. They are composed of a tawny mudstone filled with veins of crystalline calcite. Clusters of milky white and clear honey crystals tumble from the cliffs and hoodoos into the wash below. Upon my first visit here, I was both surprised and thrilled to find an abundance of calcite in a place where I expected to be among cliffs of rhyolite lavas and ash-flow tuff. When you first

Searching for calcite crystals in the broad wash near Birch Creek

A chunk of white calcite crystals

arrive in the Birch Creek bottomlands, you are indeed met with canyon walls made only of those things. However, a short hike around a river bend yields an entirely different kind of rock—spires of mudstone veined with calcite. It wasn't until I looked at this place via satellite that its story began to unfold.

From the eagle's view, layers of soft sedimentary rock lie atop the explosive caldera deposits of rhyolite and tuff. These were likely lakes and basins that filled in as the calderas went quiet. The first thing I found here was not a calcite crystal but a fossil leaf. A clue! And a member of my rock club found a beautifully agatized snail. Both were embedded in the mudstone. Sometime after caldera volcanism ended, faulting and buckling down-dropped large swaths of the mudstones and a canyon formed along the fault. You'll see evidence of this here: tuffs and rhyolite are angularly shoved up against the mudstone outcrops near the mouth of the gulch.

It's not unusual for calcite to be found in old volcanic sediments, but that doesn't account for Birch Creek's extraordinary ridges made almost entirely of it. I took my curiosity to Tom Benson, an exploration geologist who researched Owyhee calderas before moving into lithium mining. He surmised that these mineralized ridges of calcite could be the product of hydrothermal fluids that invaded the rock post-eruption. It's possible that the hydrothermal system even made it to the surface at one point, with springs feeding a wetland system that infilled with sediments (the mudstone). Ultimately, what is evident is that at some point the calderas went quiet, their depressions filled in with sediments (and leaves and snails), and underneath it all, a beautiful and enigmatic amount of calcite took root. Faulting and erosion would one day bisect these deposits, revealing their crystalline calcite treasures.

WHAT YOU'LL FIND: Calcite crystals; possibly fossils	**LIMITS:** A reasonable amount of rocks may be taken for personal use only. A reasonable amount is often defined as up to 25 pounds per person, per day, with a maximum of 250 pounds per year. Do you need 25 pounds of rocks? Probably not. Collect lightly and with intention.
GEOLOGIC AGE: Cenozoic era, Miocene epoch	
TOOLS: Small shovel or geology pick for tipping specimens out of the dirt (no digging inside the wilderness study area boundary, see map)	
	LOCATION: 43.234472, -117.490306
AGENCY: Bureau of Land Management— Vale District Office	**VEHICLE:** High clearance and four-wheel drive required
	SEASONS: Access to Birch Creek is open Apr 15–Nov 30. Warning: Avoid the area in wet weather. Canyons are treacherous in rainstorms.

DIRECTIONS → *Backcountry driving experience is required. The descent into Birch Creek is steep and bouldery, and it features several creek crossings.* Make your way to Jordan Valley Post Office at 509 Yturri Boulevard in Jordan Valley, Oregon 97910. (There are two Jordan Valleys in Oregon, so getting to the right one matters.) From the post office in the correct Jordan Valley, turn left (west) onto Yturri Boulevard and immediately right onto Bassett Street (US Highway 95 North). Drive north for 8.1 miles and turn left (west) onto Jordan Craters Road (Curly Lodge Road), which is unmarked. From here, all roads

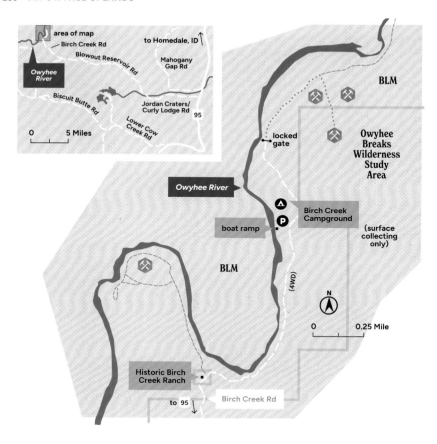

are gravel and dirt. Drive 11.3 miles on Jordan Craters Road to a fork and stay right for Blowout Reservoir Road. Drive 12.2 miles on Blowout Reservoir Road to another fork and stay right for Birch Creek Road. Descend on Birch Creek Road (steep and rocky) for 5.7 miles to the Historic Birch Creek Ranch (BLM rangers live here). The drive will be slow going. At the ranch, turn right and drive along the Owyhee River for 1.1 miles to the Birch Creek Takeout and Campground. Park here. From this point, it is a 1.2-mile hike to the calcite collecting area.

AT THE SITE → From the Birch Creek Takeout (a dirt boat ramp that leads into the river), walk 0.4 mile north to the north end of the campground (a former alfalfa field). You'll see an old road leading uphill to a locked gate (see map). Hike up to the gate and crawl through. You'll notice the gate is bolted to an outcrop of colorful gray and red breccia—debris deposited here by an explosive eruption. Follow the road for another 0.6 mile to a large wash on the right. Hike up the wash for 0.2 mile, and calcite clusters large and small will reveal themselves in the dirt. They erode from the monolithic hoodoos that crop out on the hills above the wash. At 0.2 mile up the wash, you'll also cross the boundary into the Owyhee Breaks Wilderness Study Area, which means no digging. Surface collecting only past this point.

The stretch of river along the campground is ideal for swimming in summer months. (And p.s., the gravel bars along the river are rich with jaspers the size of toasters.) Birch Creek is a wonderful place to camp for a few nights and explore. Upon leaving Birch Creek, make sure to stop at the Jordan Craters volcanic field on top of the plateau. The lava up there is brand-new, having erupted only 3,200 years ago.

OREGON
Basin and Range Province

The Basin and Range territory of southeast Oregon is blanketed in pulses of relatively young volcanic rock, with the oldest material dating back well into the age of mammals. The region's rocks look like a layer cake of all of the possible lavas that Earth can provide: dark flood basalts, gray andesites, wavy brown rhyolites, silvery ash-flow tuffs, glassy obsidians, and nearly weightless pumices. As these lavas erode, they reveal agates, jaspers, crystalline sunstones, and petrified wood. The earth is stretching out here—or spreading—causing the spectacular basin-and-range topography that gives the area its name. The surface of Earth is brittle, so as it spreads, it can't stretch. Instead it cracks. These cracks offset—one side slips down, forming a basin, and the other rises up as a spectacular range. The crack is a fault, and the steep side of the range is known to geologists as a fault scarp. Steens Mountain and Hart Mountain are two notable scarps among the hundreds that characterize the region.

Opposite: A large felspar crystal, or sunstone, from the public collection area in Rabbit Basin

55 Glass Buttes

Imagine a lava so thick, it cannot flow. This is the problem of high-silica volcanics. An image problem, you could say. When most people imagine volcanoes, they visualize a mountain, elegant and conical, with red, hot lava running down its flanks. These are the cover girls of volcanoes. The Mount Hoods and Rainiers. But that's not what happened at Glass Buttes. What happened here was messier. With high-silica volcanics you get powerful, ashy explosions that are incapable of building an elegant cone. These kinds of volcanoes explode goopy, sticky lavas and pumice bombs, and sometimes the stuff that comes to the surface freezes into a smooth, black glass: obsidian. The twin peaks at Glass Buttes are made of it.

Glass Buttes erupted some 5 million years ago. Geologists would want you to know that what happened at Glass Buttes wasn't purely high-silica volcanism—it was bimodal volcanism. Some eruptions yielded a familiar lava called basalt. Basalt is low in silica and high in iron and magnesium. It flows fast and smooth. But other eruptions here yielded a lava that was so rich in silica, it produced glass upon exploding. At Glass Buttes the obsidian is interfingered with layers of basalt. However, the sheer volume of obsidian makes it incredibly easy to find. The ground is made of it!

Humans have been collecting obsidian at Glass Buttes for thousands of years to make spear points and arrowheads. Archaeologists travel from all over to analyze obsidian from Glass Buttes in an attempt to trace its trading routes throughout the ancient world. Small differences in rare elements can make obsidian from Glass Buttes chemically distinct from, say, Yellowstone or the Mono-Inyo Craters obsidian. Archaeologists use these chemical

The slopes below Little Glass Butte are littered with obsidian.

Remember: Obsidian is glass. Collect with gloves!

footprints to identify the origins of obsidian points found as far away as the Great Lakes. These differences can also make obsidian from distinct eruptions within Glass Buttes easy to tell apart. Geologists use these clues within the glass to unlock the history of this unusual geologic site.

WHAT YOU'LL FIND: Obsidian	**LIMIT:** A reasonable amount of rocks may be taken for personal use only. A reasonable
GEOLOGIC AGE: Cenozoic era, Pliocene epoch	amount is often defined as up to 25 pounds per person, per day, with a maximum of 250
TOOLS: Trowel or shovel; gloves and safety glasses are essential	pounds per year. Do you need 25 pounds of rocks? Probably not. Collect lightly and with intention.
AGENCY: Bureau of Land Management— Prineville District Office	**LOCATION:** 43.535105, –119.977063
	VEHICLE: Some clearance and four-wheel drive recommended; good tires are essential
	SEASONS: Spring, summer, fall

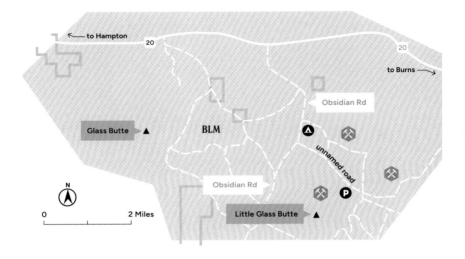

DIRECTIONS → Make your way to the townsite of Hampton, Oregon, on US Highway 20. From the café (the only business), drive east for 13.5 miles on US 20. Turn right (south) onto Obsidian Road just before milepost 77. (There is a large staging area for trailers here if you are exploring by ATV.) If you are exploring by car, drive south on Obsidian Road for 1.4 miles. Keep left and drive another 3.4 miles to get to the base of Little Glass Butte, which I consider a wonderful collecting area. You can park here and begin your search.

AT THE SITE → Obsidian Road runs between the twin buttes that make up the Glass Buttes. About a mile in, several dispersed campsites start to appear. In another mile of driving, you will start to get into the obsidian digging areas. The Glass Buttes collecting area is quite large and covered with a tangle of unmarked roads leading to various deposits. If it's your first time, I recommend starting at the base of Little Glass Butte, where the directions send you.

Some precautions: Obsidian is the sharpest material in the world, so make sure to have gloves and a trowel or shovel for pulling large pieces out of the soft earth. Don't ever hit obsidian with a hammer. It can also do a number on tires. Make sure to have a full-size spare. Additionally, there are a few mining claims at Glass Buttes. Make sure to stay outside their well-marked signs and posts.

Obsidian: The Psychic Mirror

NO GEOLOGIC MATERIAL may have a stronger grip on the mind of humanity than obsidian. This inky-black glass has been in use throughout the world for thousands of years as everyone's favorite dagger, arrowhead, and spear. No other stone material can yield a sharper edge. In Paleolithic times it was the hottest of commodities. A recent dive by archaeologist John O'Shea and his team in Michigan's Lake Huron turned up flakes of obsidian that came from Oregon over 9,000 years ago. In the 1500s, a magician in the court of Queen Elizabeth I acquired a black scrying mirror of polished obsidian. It was stolen from the Aztecs in Mexico by Cortezian raiders and shipped back to Europe with other geologic treasures. Surgeons today use finely engineered obsidian scalpels for their precision and finesse. Rockhounds in the Pacific Northwest have the great fortune of being near some of the finest obsidian in the world.

I've heard obsidian called a lot of things. Dreamers will tell you it's a psychic vacuum cleaner, a spiritual maid service, the black mirror. Rockhounds will tell you it's a tire-popper. Geologists will tell you it's a mineraloid or a volcanic glass. They'll get frustrated if you call it a rock. They would want you to know that obsidian is not a rock since it lacks the foundation that could lead to such a classification. Rocks are mixtures of minerals. Minerals are organized arrangements of elements in repeating, geometric patterns (crystals!). Obsidian, however, is chaos. Obsidian is amorphous, lacking dis-

tinct geometric arrangements of crystals. It's more like a felted wool, a cotton candy, a stretched piece of gum. Though obsidian is made of all the same elements other volcanic rocks are made of, it lacks the crystalline structure. This is because structure requires organizing—the ability of elements to move around. In order for crystals to arrange neatly, elements need to be able to join forces.

A scrying mirror from an Elizabethan court, circa the 1580s. The obsidian mirror, looted from Aztec peoples by Spanish colonizers, brought only bad luck with it. (Photo courtesy Wellcome Images)

Obsidian comes to the surface in volcanic eruptions that contain a lot of silica, which is a perfect recipe for creating sticky, viscous lavas. Both obsidian and pumice form from the most viscous parts of such lava flows. The only difference between the two is that pumice is filled with all the volatile gases trying to escape from the lava, and obsidian is depleted of them. When pumice and obsidian freeze, the sticky, slovenly stuff they're made of is unable to organize into crystals. Thus, both materials freeze into glassy, chaotic *stuff*. This is why geologists classify them as mineraloids or amorphous glass. These same qualities are what allow obsidian to fracture easily, yielding sharp edges that make fine arrowheads, spears, and scalpels.

In the Pacific Northwest, obsidian is more than just a black glass. You'll hear rockhounds discuss varieties like rainbow, mahogany, silver sheen, snowflake, and fire. Each of these varieties have beautiful colors or patterns. Despite what I've told you, during obsidian's freezing, some trace elements can indeed manage to organize into microscopic crystals. Amid the amorphous chaos, minerals like magnetite and feldspar can precipitate as nanocrystals in thin bands that cause colorful refractions when hit with visible light. Because the nanocrystal banding is planar, the obsidian has to be cut at the perfect angle to experience color and flash. If done correctly, the results are spectacular.

A large boulder in the Big Obsidian Flow at Newberry Craters

Oolitic agate is scattered along the top of a low bluff overlooking Harney and Mud Lakes.

56 Harney Lake

Above the broad playa of Harney Lake lies an outcrop of a very unusual agate. This material hails from lakebed sediments laid down by a freshwater system that existed as much as a few million years back. The playa of Harney Lake that exists here today is likely what remains of a much more ancient lake system. The agates eroding from these old lake sediments are freckled with oval-shaped specks called ooids. Ooids form in shallow freshwater lakes and salty seas that become highly saturated with calcium carbonate. The carbonate precipitates around sand and other specks and rolls into small oval-shaped bits by wave action. Over time, ooids can build up en masse, eventually forming a carbonate rock layer called oolite. (And, technically, if the individual ooids are larger than 2 millimeters, the rock is called pisolite.)

The oolite/pisolite outcrop on the edge of Harney Lake exhibits some unusual changes, however. Over time the material encasing the individual ooids has been

Chunks of oolitic agate large and small are common at the edge of the butte.

replaced by silica in the form of agate. The resulting stone found here is therefore an oolitic agate. This combination is quite rare, which makes this a special collecting site for rockhounds. The agate replacement is likely due to the fact that this lakebed was flush with volcanic ash and silica derived from the surrounding Rattlesnake Tuff, which erupted about 7 million years ago. As time and erosion marched onward, the ashes and lavas broke down, and rivers drained a great deal of silica-rich sediments into the ancient lake. Groundwater rich in silica likely replaced the sediments surrounding the oolite, forever turning it to stone.

WHAT YOU'LL FIND: Oolitic agate (okay, pisolitic agate for the purists)	**LIMIT:** A reasonable amount of rocks may be taken for personal use only. A reasonable amount is often defined as up to 25 pounds per person, per day, with a maximum of 250 pounds per year. Do you need 25 pounds of rocks? Probably not. Collect lightly and with intention.
GEOLOGIC AGE: Cenozoic era, Pliocene to Pleistocene epochs	
TOOLS: A small shovel or geology pick to tip specimens out of the dirt	
	LOCATION: 43.245071, -118.994648
AGENCY: Bureau of Land Management— Burns District Office	**VEHICLE:** Any
	SEASONS: Any

DIRECTIONS → Make your way to the intersection of East Monroe Street and South Broadway Avenue in the bustling town of Burns, Oregon. From the intersection drive east on East Monroe Street (State Route 78) for 1.7 miles. Monroe becomes Steens Highway (SR 78) just outside of town. Turn right (south) onto Frenchglen Highway (SR 205) and drive for 23.9 miles. Turn right onto South Harney Road (dirt) and drive 2.2 miles. The site of a former quarry will appear on your left. Turn left into the quarry and park at the south end of the lot. You will see a steep, washed-out road leading to the top of the bluff above the quarry. Hike this road for 0.3 mile to get to the top. The quarry is a small parcel of private property (see map), but the bluff above is on public land.

AT THE SITE → The top of the bluff above the old quarry is covered with oolitic agate. The material up here is plentiful. Bring a geology pick along to tip specimens out of the dirt. From the top of the bluff, you can hike due east up to 1.7 miles in search of interesting oolitic material. If you walk far enough, you may also start to find small fragments of petrified wood, larger concretions, and some agate and jasper.

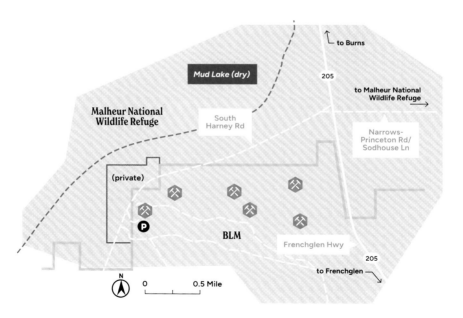

A rockhound strolls through the ocean of sagebrush in search of sunstones.

57 Rabbit Basin

You are hiking through a sloping, grassy plain on the flanks of a low-slung shield volcano. Golden grasses bend in the breeze, and large hulking mammals browse in the distance. Something about them is strange. Their silhouette matches no mammal you've seen before. That's because we're 16 million years in the past, when Oregon was undergoing some of its most epic geological changes. The ground rumbles. The herd of strange mammals startles. Suddenly, the slope splits violently open and a wall of red lava pours out from it. Within days it will cover dozens of square miles of landscape in a smoldering blanket.

This dramatic episode of lava flooding would be only one among hundreds more to pulse over the landscape. The rocks that resulted from these lava flows are called flood basalts, and they are a star player in the geologic history of the Pacific Northwest. During this time, a powerful plume of melting energy upwelled from the mantle. Incredible volumes of lava forced their way up through weaknesses and faults in the crust, erupting at the surface. The lava that hosts the famed Oregon sunstones traveled from fissures that opened up over a hundred miles north of Rabbit Basin and traveled here.

Often basaltic lavas cool into a dark, unremarkable stone. The crystals that make up the stone are so fine-grained that it is hard to differentiate them with the naked eye. But in some rare places, like Rabbit Basin, the basaltic lava is filled with unusually large, golden feldspar crystals. Rockhounds call them sunstones. As the remnants of this lava flow eroded over the millennia, the tough sunstones remained behind, blanketing the desert with their sparkle. Some sunstones are even found with inclusions of color: red iron, green chromite, or planes of shimmering copper. Such colorful sunstones are rarely found on the surface. They tend to hail from the bottom of the lava flow. Several mining operations have set themselves up on the periphery of the public collecting area, and for a not-so-small fee, you can pay to dig through rough lava excavated from the bottom of the flow that may yield the color-filled stones.

Small but mighty sunstones: felspar crystals that eroded from an ancient lava flood

WHAT YOU'LL FIND: Feldspar crystals known as sunstones	**LIMITS:** A reasonable amount of rocks may be taken for personal use only. A reasonable amount is often defined as up to 25 pounds per person, per day, with a maximum of 250 pounds per year.
GEOLOGIC AGE: Cenozoic era, Miocene epoch	
TOOLS: A tiny jar; some rockhounds bring shovels and screens for sifting	
	LOCATION: 42.7231, –119.8607
AGENCY: Bureau of Land Management—Lakeview District Office	**VEHICLE:** Any. Good tires and tire-changing equipment are required. The dirt roads are level but graded with sharp, angular gravel.
	SEASONS: Spring, summer, fall

DIRECTIONS → Make your way to the ranching hamlet of Plush, Oregon, which prides itself as "a small drinking town with a big cattle problem." From the Hart Mountain Store in Plush (the only business in town), take Hogback Road (County Road 3-10) north for 10 miles. (After 4 miles, Hogback Road turns to dirt.) Turn right onto County Highway 3-11 and drive for 0.5 mile. Turn left onto BLM Road 6155 and drive for 8.2 miles. At a junction,

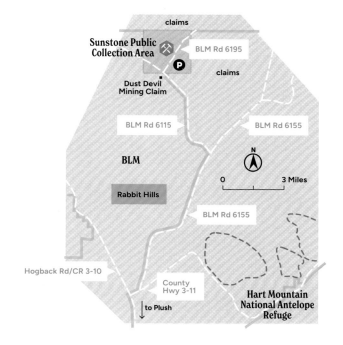

turn left onto BLM Road 6115 (yes, the road numbers are much too similar) and drive 5 miles to the entrance for the Sunstone Public Collection Area. You will see the Dust Devil Mine across from the public collecting area entrance. Turn right onto an unmarked dirt road (some maps may show it as BLM Road 6195) to enter the public area and drive 0.7 mile to the main parking area.

AT THE SITE → From the developed parking area, which has picnic shelters and vault toilets, you can walk or drive the maze of roads radiating throughout the collection area. Turn back often to orient yourself with where you parked. Clear, champagne-colored sunstones litter the ground, so you will have no trouble finding many, though expect them to be quite small. The farther you walk, the more you will find. Plan on spending the day in the area, and perhaps consider visiting one of the several fee mines nearby. Sunstones at the bottom of the old lava flow are known to have color and schiller (copper reflectance), so many people stake mining claims and dig to the bottom of the flow to get at the more valuable crystals. Be careful to stay outside of the mining claims that surround the edges of the public area.

58 Flook Lake

Atop the spectacular rim of Hart Mountain lies a shallow depression called Flook Lake. Only in stormy years does Flook contain any water. It is perennially empty, a common desert feature known as a dry lake bed. Fine clay sediments and evaporites (gypsum, halite) accumulate in the dry lake basin as rains evaporate, leaving behind a blindingly white hardpan surface. (Bring your sunglasses.) The bedrock surrounding Flook Lake is a layer of flood basalts, and underneath those lie fantastically deep and varied beds of rhyolite lavas and ash-flow tuffs—solidified volcanic ash. Obsidian litters the top of Hart Mountain as well. These geologies erode over time, and water carries bits of rock down to Flook Lake during heavy rains. Over time, the surface of the lake bed becomes rich in agates, jasper, obsidian,

A rockhound with her treasures during a dry season on Flook Lake

After wet winters Flook Lake grows green with life. Occasionally, the lake floods but rocks are still easy to find.

and welded tuff—a light-blue breccia. You'll know the blue stuff when you see it. Other rockhounds report finding fire agates, and I can confirm this myself, though only small cracked specimens have caught my eye. I have also found dark-purple fossil bone fragments up here, to my great surprise. These I photographed and left in place, as must be done with all vertebrate fossils.

Jewelry made by the author from blue welded tuff, and red and yellow jasper collected on Flook Lake.

The most important thing to know about Flook Lake is that the beautiful material that draws us here has drawn people for thousands of years. The area was an important source of stone material for tool making, and evidence of this is everywhere. Archaeological material is protected by federal law. Rockhounds are prohibited from collecting it, even small flakes and chips. Because the area is rich in lithics—stone tools and the debris from making them—rockhounds are required to be able to identify them if they want to rockhound here. When I take my rockhounding groups to Flook Lake, more than half of the materials participants pick up off the ground are archaeological flakes. At first they're sad when I explain it must be left in place, but as they get the hang of identifying the signs of tool making, the search stops being about *keeping* and starts being about *seeing*.

Consider rockhounding on Flook Lake an educational opportunity to become capable of identifying worked material. (See the "Lithics: Identifying Archaeological Material" sidebar in this section.) If you see something worked, pick it up, take a picture, and then put it back in place. There's no law against looking at it, but there are strict laws against taking it. If you're unsure if something has been worked, always leave it in place.

WHAT YOU'LL FIND: Agate, jasper, obsidian, petrified wood, welded tuff	**LIMITS:** Up to 7 pounds of rock and mineral material per person, per day. Rockhounds are required to leave archaeological material in place.
GEOLOGIC AGE: Cenozoic era, Miocene epoch	
TOOLS: A camera to take pictures of worked stone!	**LOCATION:** 42.5825, –119.53551
AGENCY: US Fish and Wildlife Service, Sheldon-Hart Mountain National Antelope Refuge Complex	**VEHICLE:** Some clearance recommended. Do not drive on the lake during wet weather. Vehicles must stay on established tracks.
	SEASONS: Any

DIRECTIONS → Make your way to the town of Plush, Oregon. From the Hart Mountain Store in Plush (the only business in town) take Hogback Road (County Road 3-10) north for 0.9 mile. Turn right onto Hart Mountain Road (CR 3-12) and drive for 23 miles to the Hart Mountain National Antelope Refuge headquarters on top of Hart Mountain. (The lower portion of Hart Mountain Road zigzags through agricultural fields and turns to dirt at 13.7 miles.) At the headquarters, turn left (east) on Frenchglen Road and drive for 7.5 miles. Look for a small sign marked Flook Lake Road and turn right. Drive straight for 1.1 miles to a parking area on the edge of Flook's dry lake bed. (On the way you'll pass two turnoffs for the Flook Lake Bypass Road.) There is a cleared area for parking vehicles here in the dry sage above the lake bed. Do not drive onto the lake bed itself.

AT THE SITE → The surface of the dry lake bed is scattered with agates, jaspers, obsidian, and occasional petrified wood. Walk far and you'll find beautiful material. In your search, you

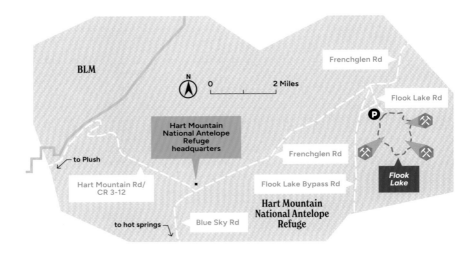

will absolutely pick up archaeological material. Make sure to read the primer on lithics identification (on the following pages) before you decide to keep anything. When in doubt, leave material in place. Most of the agate here is clear, white, or gray. The jasper is red and yellow. The welded tuff is a beautiful light blue. The obsidian is black, and the petrified wood looks just like wood. Fossil mammal bones tend to be dark purple. They must be left in place. Fire agate is red, crazed, and has some flash to it. It is quite rare.

Flakes of obsidian, agate, and jasper that have been knapped. Notice their thinness and fine edges.

Lithics: Identifying Archaeological Material

LITHICS ARE STONE TOOLS and the waste products of the tool-making process. Rocks rich in silica like agate, jasper, opal, chert, flint, quartzite, and obsidian are ideal materials to make stone tools from because they break in predictable ways in all directions. These materials were highly sought after during Paleolithic times for tool making and for trading to distant populations that lacked access to them, especially obsidian.

Thanks to its volcanic history, the Pacific Northwest is rich in silicate rocks. Rockhounds today are searching for the same material that early peoples were searching for too. Therefore, it's likely that many good rockhounding locations have some archaeological overlap. Does this cause problems? Yes. Are rockhounds unwittingly collecting archaeological material? All the time. But the problem can be remedied by learning to identify it and leaving it in place.

In 1979 the federal government passed the Archaeological Resources Protection Act (ARPA), which protects all artifacts on public land, even flakes. Lithics can be touched and photographed but must be left in place. A permit from the federal government is required to remove them. Even then, a stronger ethic should encourage all of us (including archaeologists) to just leave artifacts in place. Some rockhounds will tell you about the "Carter loophole," which many think allows the collection of arrowheads, but this is a misinterpretation of the law. Collection of arrowheads is expressly forbidden by ARPA. Rather, the language states that people cannot be prosecuted or fined for unwittingly having them. Legend has it that President Jimmy Carter, who signed the act into law, was an arrowhead collector and wanted to protect his hobby. Is this true? Who's to say.

The most important thing to know is that people who have knowingly collected arrowheads have indeed been prosecuted for violating other archaeological laws that coincide with arrowhead collecting, such as tampering with archaeological sites, theft of government property, and attempting to sell artifacts on the market. Taking artifacts knowingly is a bummer all around. Learning to identify lithics, or stone artifacts, is the best way for rockhounds to avoid trouble with the law and disappointing the pantheon of ancestors in the sky.

A Humbolt point found on the playa at Flook Lake. A scale card is a standard tool used by field archaeologists to catalogue lithics without having to remove them from the landscape.

The Basics of Identification

Lithics are ancient stone tools and their debitage—all the stone waste created in their fabrication. The most common lithics in the archaeological record are debitage, not tools. Finding finished tools is quite rare. Across the Pacific Northwest, archaeological "tool workshops" can be found almost anywhere there is a good source of agate, jasper, opal, or obsidian. Learning to see the signs of tool making is your goal. Flakes (the debitage) are usually the first clue.

In tool making, a person starts with a rough stone and strikes it, sending flakes of rock flying. A large amount of material is removed to make a fine tool, and flakes litter the ground. Striking a rock produces a conchoidal fracture, which looks like ripple marks along the surface of the rock. Archaeologists refer to these as percussive marks, and they are a telltale sign of tool making. Look for them. In addition to the percussive marks, blanks and flakes have fine edges that are quite sharp. Rockhounds are also likely to find cores and blanks. These are rocks that have been hit a few times to see if they were worthy of using. If not, they were tossed away. Cores still have evidence of the rock's "outer rind," or rough surface, and blanks are pieces that have been worked down to a usable size from which to fashion a final tool.

There are two excellent ways to train your eyes to see lithics:

A flake of obsidian showing percussive waves undulating outward from each strike.

- Look at images of worked stones on the internet. Look at a lot of them. Using the search term "lithic flake identification" will turn up the best results for images of debitage. It's more important to learn to identify debitage (flakes, cores, blanks). Anyone can identify a finished tool when found in the wild.

- Look up images using terms such as "percussion flaking," "pressure flaking," and "flint knapping." These will give you images of finished tools but rarely debitage.

- Acquire books about flint knapping that show the process. Bring the book with you on rockhounding trips.

If your eyes see images of worked stone enough, this will train them to spot lithics quickly in the landscape. The process is a lot like riding a bicycle. Once you feel familiar with the signs of workmanship, it becomes easy to identify artifact material. You'll start seeing it everywhere, and it will amaze you how often rockhounding sites and archaeological sites overlap.

Rifting in the Basin and Range Province has exposed rocks of an ancient terrane on the Pueblo Mountains' eastern face. Steep creeks drag interesting specimens to the valley below.

59 Pueblo Mountains

In southeast Oregon, exposures of ancient terranes are altogether uncommon. Baked and squeezed scraps of Paleozoic island chains and seafloors are the stuff of the Blue and Wallowa Mountains, of the North Cascades, but not the Steens or Pueblos. Yet here they are, on the southeastern face of the Pueblo Mountains, emerging from under the epic weight of Cenozoic flood basalts. There's likely 250 million years of time that passed between the birth of the ancient terrane and the basalts above them. They sandwich together in a great unconformity.

The ancient rocks found here were once Hawaii-like volcanoes and seafloor sediments that have been altered into colorful greenstone and shimmery phyllite, a rock similar to schist. Chunks of white quartz and chartreuse epidote litter the steep slopes where these metamorphosed rocks erode. This is the stuff of exotic terranes, rocks that come from somewhere else. In the few hundred million years of their existence, they have been dramatically altered. Small exposures of granite-like rocks crop out in the peaks of the Pueblos, evidence of the terrane stitching itself onto the continent sometime during the Mesozoic, perhaps around 130 million years ago.

"Remember about mountains," the great writer John McPhee said, "what they are made of is not what made them." The Pueblos, and their sister the Steens, were only very recently exhumed. Here, Earth is relaxing and extending, but its crust isn't stretchy—it's brittle. To accommodate the stretching, it snaps and cracks like a dried-out rubber band. These cracks become faults, and they tend to tilt and lean. Over time the faulting can cause enormous offset, in which one block of land rises (the Steens and Pueblos) and the other block sinks down (the valley below them). The process is known as rifting, or crustal extension,

A colorful array of rocks such as epidote, quartz, greenstone, phyllite, and agate can be found here.

and it is the defining story of the Basin and Range Province, of which the Pueblo Mountains are a part. Though the oldest rocks were forced here in the process of accretion, and the flood basalts capped them in dramatic volcanism eons later, it was the recent rifting phenomenon that exhumed them all.

The east face of the Steens and Pueblos are not mountains in the traditional sense, they are fault scarps. To this day, they are still rising, shedding rocks as they go. McPhee reminds us that behemoths like mountains and fault scarps "are not somehow created whole and subsequently worn away. They wear down as they come up." The faulting that has exposed the old terrane rocks of the Pueblos is like a peek behind a curtain of what may underlie much of the Pacific Northwest. Their exposure provides a small portal into a deeper past, a rare place in which to bask in the shimmering cobbles of a long-forgotten world.

WHAT YOU'LL FIND: Phyllite, epidote, white quartz, porphyry, and schist

GEOLOGIC AGE: Paleozoic, Mesozoic, and Cenozoic eras

TOOLS: A small shovel or geology pick for tipping specimens out of the dirt

AGENCY: Bureau of Land Management—Burns District Office

LIMITS: A reasonable amount of rocks may be taken for personal use only. A reasonable amount is often defined as up to 25 pounds per person, per day, with a maximum of 250 pounds per year. Do you need 25 pounds of rocks? Probably not. Collect lightly and with intention.

LOCATIONS:
Site A: 42.067972, -118.607528
Site B: 42.048694, -118.612028

VEHICLE: Any

SEASONS: Spring, summer, fall

DIRECTIONS → **Site A, Colony Creek:** Make your way to the Fields Station General Store at 22276 Fields Drive in the hamlet of Fields, Oregon. From the general store, turn right (south) onto Fields-Denio Road (State Route 205) and drive 15.6 miles. Look for a faint dirt track on the right that leads uphill along Colony Creek. Turn here and drive uphill for 0.3 mile. This road is steep and a bit rocky. Pull off and park in a grassy spot alongside the creek.

Site B, Van Horn Creek: To get to Van Horn Creek, skip the turn for Colony Creek. Continue south on SR 205 for another 1.4 miles. Van Horn Creek crosses underneath the highway here. Turn right onto a dirt track just after crossing over the creek's large culvert. Pull in a hundred feet or so and park under the powerline.

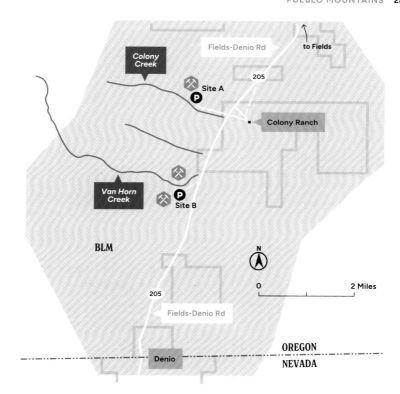

AT THE SITE → **Site A, Colony Creek:** This is a steep hike that ascends into the Pueblo Mountains. The hills parallel with the parking zone feature metavolcanic rocks like greenstone. Higher up on the slopes, metasedimentary rocks are exposed, dominantly phyllite, which is flaky, gray, and shiny. The phyllite is mixed with hydrothermal rocks like white quartz and epidote. For hikers, this is a wonderful starting point with beautiful views of the valley.

Site B, Van Horn Creek: This location has plentiful metamorphic material but on terrain that is much less steep than the Colony Creek site. Search the wash for interesting specimens of epidote, white quartz, schist, phyllite, greenstone, and porphyry.

⑥⓪ Chalk Canyon

You might be catching on by now that between 17 and 16 million years ago, things were getting pretty spicy in southeast Oregon. The continent was passing over a hotspot in the mantle, and a perfect storm of tectonic situations in the crust unleashed a brutal era of volcanism at the surface. Fissures opened up along the eastern margins of Oregon and Washington, pouring out lava floods that would make their way to the sea. In southeastern Oregon, massive calderas would implode, again and again, burying the landscape in smoldering ash. Streams of lava blocked rivers, damming numerous lakes in which diatoms bloomed. Diatoms are a type of plankton that use silica from ash to build their skeletons. With the seasons, diatom populations came and went in the dammed lakes. Their skeletal

Fossil collectors carefully removing layers of diatomite from an outcrop near the top of the hill

A ghostly imprint of a fossil broad leaf in diatomite

remains would sink to the bottom, becoming just silica once more. The Persian poet Rumi would have said that they died as a mineral.

The silica skeletons of diatoms joined sticks, leaves, and seeds at the bottom of the lakes. Over time the plant debris encased in the silica skeletons would become a rock called diatomite. Blindingly white, exposed layers of diatomite outcrop along the northern flanks of the Trout Creek Mountains today. The leaf fossils

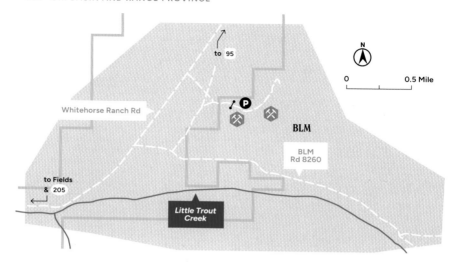

found within them are known as the Trout Creek flora and occur within the harmoniously named Trout Creek Formation. Few surveys of the flora—or plant life—have been conducted at this location, and most of what is known about this formation is inferred from plant fossils found in similar sedimentary formations of the Owyhee calderas where leaves of deciduous trees from ancestral maple, oak, elm, alder, and birch are common. The ecology of this region was likely a cool, temperate lowland, much wetter than the desert that surrounds it today.

The leaf fossils found within the diatomite at Chalk Canyon are practically ghosts. Few have left any sort of distilled carbon skeleton behind. However, the circular nature of life is wholly evident in these spectral specimens. Here, ancient plants derived from sunshine and minerals are enclosed in ancient plankton derived from sunshine and minerals. They were fed by minerals, died as minerals, and fossilized under their weight. As the diatomite of

A scanning electron microscope (SEM) image of diatomite. Broken tests of individual diatoms make up the rock. (Photo by David Siodłak)

today erodes, these minerals feed back into surface systems that nourish new life once more. All of it is fated to ride the wheel of time, just like Rumi surmised, some 750 years ago. We may die as a mineral and become a plant. We may die as a plant and become an animal. Some may die as an animal and become human. Rumi asked why should we fear? When were we less by dying?

WHAT YOU'LL FIND: Leaf fossils in diatomite	**LIMITS:** A reasonable amount of rocks may be taken for personal use only. A reasonable amount is often defined as up to 25 pounds per person, per day, with a maximum of 250 pounds per year. Do you need 25 pounds of rocks? Probably not. Collect lightly and with intention.
GEOLOGIC AGE: Cenozoic era, Miocene to Pliocene epochs	
TOOLS: Hammer, flat chisel, or paint scraper; safety glasses and gloves	
AGENCY: Bureau of Land Management— Burns District Office	**LOCATION:** 42.17861, –118.39483
	VEHICLE: Any
	SEASONS: Spring, summer, fall

DIRECTIONS → Make your way to the Fields Station General Store at 22276 Fields Drive in the small hamlet of Fields, Oregon. From the general store, turn right (south) onto Fields-Denio Road (State Route 205) and drive 8.2 miles. Turn left (east) onto Whitehorse Ranch Road and drive 15.4 miles to a faint dirt track on your right. Turn right and drive 0.3 mile to a T-junction. Turn left and drive 0.1 mile to a gate. Open it and drive through, closing it behind you. (In general, always leave gates the way you find them.) Drive another 300 feet and park. The low cliff of pure white rock ahead of you is the diatomaceous formation that holds the leaf fossils. Hike up to any of its exposures and get to work.

AT THE SITE → The low cliffs of diatomaceous sediment are somewhat steep. Scramble close to the top of the outcrop to get access to fresh, solid diatomite. Take great care as you explore around the outcrops for fossils. The diatomite can be easily split with a hammer and flat chisel or paint scraper. Hold the chisel to the rock along the bedding plane and tap it with the hammer. Most fossils here are ghostly imprints, so keep a sharp eye as you work through material. When you leave, remember to leave the cattle gate the way you found it, which is most likely closed.

Acknowledgments

This book is a distillation of all that I have learned in my first decade of rock-hounding. I stand on the shoulders of many people who paved the way. First, eternal gratitude goes to the Mount Hood Rock Club in Gresham, Oregon, and the Butte Mineral & Gem Club in Butte, Montana. These venerable clubs are responsible for my blossoming as a rockhound. Secondly, my appreciation goes to the hardy Washington and Oregon rockhounding guidebook writers who came before me: Garrett Romaine, James Mitchell, Lanny Reams, and Lars Johnson. My dream is that this guide is a worthy companion to the groundwork they have laid. I would be geologically lost without the phenomenal *Roadside Geology* guides for Washington and Oregon written by Marli B. Miller and Darrel S. Cowan, and I thank Marli for her attentive correspondence! In addition, the exceptional publications of geologists Ellen Morris Bishop and George Mustoe have equally enriched my understanding of Pacific Northwest geology.

I always owe gratitude to Martin Holden, stone philosopher and dear friend. My rockhounding world would be incomplete without the effervescent enthusiasm of Kirsten Southwell. Complete adoration goes to my dirt-road-partner-in-crime Dennis Kenney, and the easy-traveling Amelia Zimmerman. Thanks to flint knapper Zack Hansen for use of his lithic debris shown in the ID section. And endless appreciation goes to Jonette Swanson, who knows Pacific Northwest rockhounding better than anyone.

There are real-life angels in the rank and file of our public land agencies. Special thanks go to retired paleontologist Greg McDonald, wizard of the rule books at the Bureau of Land Management. I extend my thanks to Jason Center at the Washington State Department of Natural Resources, as well as Stephanie Earls, geologic librarian for the state of Washington, and Theresa Nation at the Washington Department of Fish & Wildlife, all who offered clarity on Washington State's conflicting rockhounding rules. I tip my hat to Oregon and Washington BLM geologists Greta Krost, Steve Flock, and Kevin Weldon, who helped me get to the bottom of murky details concerning salable vs. locatable aspects of mining law, as well as recreation planner Michael Anderson for his help with paleontology rules around the secretive Areas of Critical Environmental Concern that encircle Clarno, Mitchell, and Kimberly, Oregon.

I heartily thank everyone at Mountaineers Books for their support and labor making this book a reality. They are a wonderful crew, and I am humbled to work with them. And I would be remiss if I didn't thank geologist Dave Tucker for his fierce geo-editorial eye and geologist Richard Gaschnig for discussing the enigmatic terranes with me. And a big shout-out to everyone in the North America Research Group (NARG) who supplied me with awesome images of their Oregon Coast fossil finds.

My wife, the ever dreamy Lisa Ward, deserves my gratitude the most. I took a huge amount of time away from work that supported us to make this project come to life. She encouraged me unwaveringly, and I now know that I am truly the luckiest wife in the world. Everybody, go get yourself a Dreamy Lisa.

Appendix 1: Glossary

All definitions are sourced from a glossary of technical geological terms prepared by the National Park Service's Geologic Resources Inventory, except those definitions with asterisks, which are sourced from Mindat.org, the *Oxford English Dictionary*, the *Merriam-Webster Dictionary*, Wikipedia, and the Royal Geological Society of the United Kingdom.

accretion: The addition of island-arc or continental material to a continent via collision, welding, or suturing at a convergent plate boundary

agate: Agate is made of fibrous chalcedony, a variety of cryptocrystalline silica, sometimes with layers of quartzine, or macrocrystalline, fibers.*

amphibolite: A metamorphic rock consisting mostly of the minerals amphibole and plagioclase, with little or no quartz

amygdule: A gas cavity or vesicle in an igneous rock that has become filled with secondary minerals

andesite: A volcanic rock characteristically medium dark in color and containing approximately 50 to 60 percent silica and moderate amounts of iron and magnesium

aragonite: A carbonate (carbon + oxygen) mineral of calcium, $CaCO_3$; the second most abundant cave mineral after calcite, differing from calcite in its crystal structure

argillite: A weakly metamorphosed rock, derived from mudstone or shale, but more highly indurated; lacks the fissility of shale and the cleavage of slate

badlands: Eroded topography characterized by steep slopes and surfaces with little or no vegetative cover; composed of unconsolidated or poorly cemented clays or silts

basalt: A volcanic rock that is characteristically dark in color (gray to black), contains approximately 53 percent silica or less, and is rich in iron and magnesium

blank: An intentional fragment extracted from a "core" from which to furnish a stone tool

botryoidal: Minerals having a shape reminiscent of a cluster of grapes*

calcite: A carbonate mineral of calcium, $CaCO_3$; calcium carbonate. It is the most abundant cave mineral.

calcium carbonate: $CaCO_3$; a solid occurring in nature as primarily calcite and aragonite

caldera: A large, more-or-less circular, basin-shaped volcanic depression formed by collapse during an eruption

Cenozoic: The most recent geological era, or the system of rocks deposited during it*

chalcedony: A cryptocrystalline variety of quartz

chrysotile: A mineral consisting of a fibrous silky variety of serpentine and constituting a common form and principal source of asbestos*

cinder: A type of tephra that forms as blobs of magma splatter out of a volcanic vent or cinder cone*

cinnabar: A bright-red mineral consisting of mercury sulfide. It is the only important ore of mercury and is sometimes used as a pigment.*

clast: An individual constituent, grain, or fragment of a rock or unconsolidated deposit, produced by the mechanical or chemical disintegration of a larger rock mass

concretion: A hard, compact aggregate of mineral matter, rounded to irregularly shaped; composition generally differs from that of the rock in which it occurs

conglomerate: A coarse-grained, generally unsorted, sedimentary rock consisting of cemented, rounded clasts larger than 2 millimeters (0.08 inches) in diameter

core: A chunk of stone from which flakes are removed. The core itself can be shaped into a tool or used as a source of flakes to be formed into tools.*

Cretaceous: The era of time on Earth ranging from 145 million years ago to 66 million years ago

cryptocrystalline: Describes a rock texture in which individual crystals are too small to be recognized or distinguished with an ordinary microscope

debitage: Small pieces of stone debris that break off during the manufacturing of stone tools. These are usually considered waste and are a by-product of production.*

devitrification: Conversion of glass to crystalline material

diabase: An intrusive igneous rock consisting primarily of the minerals labradorite and pyroxene

diatom: A microscopic, single-celled alga that secretes walls of silica, called frustules; lives in freshwater or marine environments

diatomite: A light-colored, soft, silica-rich sedimentary rock consisting mostly of diatoms

dike: A narrow igneous intrusion that cuts across bedding planes or other geologic structures

diorite: A coarse-grained, intrusive igneous rock characteristically containing plagioclase as well as dark-colored amphibole (especially hornblende), pyroxene, and sometimes a small amount of quartz. Diorite grades into monzodiorite with the addition of alkali feldspar.

distillation: The process of decomposition whereby the original chitinous material of certain fossils has lost its nitrogen, oxygen, and hydrogen and is now represented by a film of carbonaceous material. Synonymous with carbonization.*

Eocene: The second epoch of the Tertiary period, between the Paleocene and Oligocene epochs

epidote: A characteristically green silicate (silicon + oxygen) mineral, commonly occurring as slender, grooved crystals in hand specimens

fault: A break in rock characterized by displacement of one side relative to the other

fault scarp: A steep cliff or topographic step resulting from displacement on a fault or as a result of slope movement or erosion. Synonymous with escarpment.

fossil: A remain, trace, or imprint of a plant or animal that has been preserved in Earth's crust since some past geologic time; loosely, any evidence of past life

Franciscan Complex: An assemblage of metamorphosed and deformed rocks, associated with an east-dipping subduction zone at the western coast of North America*

glendonite: A variety of calcite. Also a name for a calcite pseudomorph after ikaite. Originally reported from Glendon, New South Wales, Australia.*

gneiss: A foliated metamorphic rock with alternating bands of dark and light minerals. Varieties are distinguished by texture (e.g., augen gneiss), characteristic minerals (e.g., hornblende gneiss), or general composition (e.g., granite gneiss).

granite: A coarse-grained, intrusive igneous rock in which quartz constitutes 10 to 50 percent of the felsic (light-colored) components and the alkali feldspar/total feldspar ratio is generally restricted to the range of 65 to 90 percent; perhaps the best known of all igneous rocks

granodiorite: A coarse-grained intrusive igneous rock intermediate in composition between quartz diorite and quartz monzonite, containing quartz, plagioclase, and potassium feldspar as the felsic (light-colored) components, with biotite, hornblende, or, more rarely, pyroxene, as the mafic (dark-colored) components

graywacke: A dark gray, firmly indurated, coarse-grained sandstone that consists of poorly sorted angular to subangular grains of quartz and feldspar, with a variety of dark rock and mineral fragments embedded in a compact clayey matrix

greenstone: A general term for any compact, dark-green, altered, or metamorphosed basic igneous rock with a green color due to chlorite, actinolite, or epidote mineral content

groundmass: The finer grained and/or glassy material between the large crystals of an igneous rock; also, sometimes used for the matrix of a sedimentary rock

harzburgite: A peridotite composed chiefly of olivine and orthopyroxene

hotspot: A volcanic center, 100–200 kilometers (60–120 miles) across, persistent for at least a few tens of millions of years, with a surface expression, commonly at the center of a plate, that indicates a rising plume of hot mantle material

igneous: Describes a rock or mineral that solidified from molten or partly molten material; also, describes processes leading to, related to, or resulting from the formation of such rocks. One of the three main classes of rocks: igneous, metamorphic, and sedimentary.

intrusive: Pertaining to intrusion, both the process and the rock body

island arc: An offshore, generally curved belt of volcanoes above a subduction zone

jasper: A variety of chert associated with iron ores and containing iron-oxide impurities that give it various colors, especially red

josephinite: A natural alloy of iron and nickel*

Jurassic: The second period of the Mesozoic era, between the Triassic and Cretaceous periods*

lacustrine: Describes a process, feature, or organism pertaining to, produced by, or inhabiting a lake

lahar: A mixture of water and volcanic debris that moves rapidly down the slope of a volcano, characterized by a substantial component (>50 percent) of fine-grained material that acts as a matrix to give the deposit the strength it needs to carry the bigger clasts

lapilli: Pyroclastic materials ranging between 2 and 64 millimeters (0.08 and 2.5 inches) across with no characteristic shape; may be either solidified or still viscous upon landing. An individual fragment is called a lapillus.

liesegang banding: Colored bands of cement observed in sedimentary rocks that typically cut across bedding

limestone: A carbonate sedimentary rock consisting of more than 95 percent calcite and less than 5 percent dolomite

limonite: A general field term for any brown, amorphous, to cryptocrystalline naturally occurring coatings (such as ordinary rust), loose or dense earthy masses, and pseudomorphs after other iron minerals formed by oxidation of iron or iron-bearing minerals; may also be formed as an inorganic or biogenic precipitate in bogs, lakes, springs, or marine deposits. Synonymous with bog iron ore, brown iron ore, and brown hematite.

marble: A metamorphic rock formed from limestone—also fizzes with dilute acid*

mélange: Describes heterogeneous rock units that contain blocks, typically of hard or structurally competent lithologies, surrounded and supported by a fine-grained matrix of shale, slate, or serpentinite*

Mesozoic: The era between the Paleozoic and Cenozoic eras, comprising the Triassic, Jurassic, and Cretaceous periods*

metamorphism: The mineralogical, chemical, and structural changes of solid rocks, generally imposed at depth below the surface zones of weathering and cementation

metasedimentary: A metamorphic rock of sedimentary origin

mineral: A naturally occurring chemical compound (e.g., calcium carbonate), often with a regular crystal structure. The "building blocks" of rocks.*

mineraloid: A naturally occurring mineral-like substance that does not demonstrate crystallinity*

Miocene: The fourth epoch of the Tertiary period, between the Oligocene and Pliocene epochs*

mudstone: Hardened mud having the texture and composition of shale but lacking its fissility

nephrite jade: One of two mineral species called jade. Nephrite's chemical formula is $Ca_2(Mg,\dagger Fe)_5Si_8O_{22}(OH)_2$.

obsidian: A black or dark-colored volcanic glass, usually of rhyolite composition, characterized by conchoidal fracture

oceanic trench: A narrow, elongated depression, which may be thousands of kilometers long, of the deep seafloor associated with a subduction zone, oriented parallel to a volcanic arc and usually to the edge of the adjacent continent

Oligocene: The third epoch of the Tertiary period, between the Eocene and Miocene epochs

olivine: A silicate (silicon + oxygen) mineral of magnesium and iron, $(Mg,Fe)_2SiO_4$; commonly olive-green and an essential mineral in basalt, gabbro, and peridotite

oolite: A sedimentary rock, usually limestone, composed of ooids

opal: A hydrous silicate (silicon + oxygen) mineral or mineral gel, $SiO_2 + H_2O$, consisting of packed spheres of silica and varying amounts of water (as much as 20 percent but usually 3 to 9 percent)

ophiolite: An assemblage of ultramafic and mafic intrusive and extrusive igneous rock, probably representing oceanic crust

palagonite: An altered volcanic, specifically basaltic, glass that becomes pillow lava or occurs in amygdules

Paleocene: The earliest epoch of the Tertiary period, between the Cretaceous period and the Eocene epoch*

paleosol: A soil layer preserved in the geologic record

Paleozoic: The era between the Precambrian eon and the Mesozoic era*

percussive marks: A crescentic scar on a pebble caused by impact*

peridotite: A coarse-grained intrusive igneous rock composed primarily of olivine and other mafic minerals; commonly alters to serpentinite

Permian: The last period of the Paleozoic era, between the Carboniferous and Triassic periods

phenocryst: A coarse-grained crystal in a porphyritic igneous rock

phyllite: A metamorphic rock, intermediate between slate and mica schist, with minute crystals of graphite, sericite, or chlorite that impart schistosity (a silky sheen)

pisolite: A sedimentary rock, usually limestone, made up of pisoids (round or ellipsoidal accretionary bodies commonly composed of calcium carbonate) cemented together

placer: A concentrated deposit of minerals, usually heavy, such as gold, cassiterite, or rutile, in a beach or stream deposit

plate tectonics: A theory of global tectonics in which the lithosphere is divided into rigid plates that interact with one another at their boundaries, causing seismic and tectonic activity along these boundaries

Pleistocene: The first epoch of the Quaternary period, between the Pliocene and Holocene epochs

Pliocene: The last epoch of the Tertiary period, between the Miocene and Pleistocene epochs

pluton: A deep-seated igneous intrusion

porphyry: An igneous rock consisting of abundant coarse-grained crystals in a fine-grained groundmass

pseudomorph: A mineral whose outward crystal form resembles that of another mineral; described as being after the mineral whose outward form it has (e.g., quartz after fluorite)

pumice: A highly vesicular pyroclast with very low bulk density and thin vesicle walls

pyroclastic flow: A hot, typically >800°C (1,500°F), chaotic mixture of rock fragments, gas, and ash that travels rapidly (tens of meters per second) away from a volcanic vent or collapsing flow front

pyroxene: A group of silicate (silicon + oxygen) minerals composed of magnesium and iron with the general formula $(Mg,Fe)SiO_3$; characterized by short, stout crystals in hand specimens

quartz: Silicon dioxide, SiO_2, the only silicate (silicon + oxygen) mineral consisting entirely of silicon and oxygen; synonymous with crystalline silica

quartzite: Metamorphosed quartz sandstone; a medium-grained, nonfoliated metamorphic rock composed mostly of quartz

radiolarian: Any actinopod (protozoan) belonging to the subclass Radiolaria, characterized by a siliceous skeleton and a marine pelagic environment

rhodonite: A pale-red triclinic mineral that consists essentially of manganese silicate and is used as an ornamental stone*

rhyolite: A volcanic rock that is characteristically light in color, contains approximately 72 percent or more of silica, and is rich in potassium and sodium

rock: An aggregate of one or more minerals (e.g., granite), a body of undifferentiated mineral matter (e.g., obsidian), or a body of solid organic material (e.g., coal)

sandstone: Clastic sedimentary rock composed of predominantly sand-size grains

schist: A medium- to coarse-grained, strongly foliated, metamorphic rock with eminently visible mineral grains, particularly mica, which are arranged parallel, imparting a distinctive sheen, or schistosity, to the rock

scoria: A pyroclast that is irregular in form and generally very vesicular

sedimentary rock: A rock resulting from the consolidation of loose sediment that has accumulated in layers; it may be clastic, consisting of mechanically formed fragments of older rock; chemical, formed by precipitation from solution; or organic, consisting of the remains of plants and animals. One of the three main classes of rock: igneous, metamorphic, and sedimentary.

serpentine: A group of silicate (silicon + oxygen) minerals with the general formula $(Mg,Al,Fe,Mn,Ni,Zn)_{2-3}(Si,Al,Fe)_2O_5(OH)_4$, characterized by a greasy or silky luster, a slightly soapy feel, and conchoidal fracture

serpentinite: A nonfoliated, metamorphic rock characterized by mottled shades of green and a resemblance to the skin of a serpent; consists almost entirely of serpentine minerals

silica: Silicon dioxide, SiO_2, an essential constituent of many minerals, occurring as crystalline quartz, cryptocrystalline chalcedony, and amorphous opal

silicate: A mineral group composed of silicon (Si) and oxygen (O) plus an element or elements, for example, quartz, SiO_2; olivine, $(Mg,Fe)_2SiO_4$; and pyroxene, $(Mg,Fe)SiO_3$; as well as the amphiboles, micas, and feldspars

stitching pluton: An igneous intrusion that has intruded and obscured the contact of a terrane with adjacent rock

stratovolcano: A volcano that is constructed of alternating layers of lava and pyroclastic deposits, along with abundant dikes and sills. Viscous, high-silica lava may flow from fissures radiating from a central vent, from which pyroclastic material is ejected. Synonymous with composite volcano.

subduction: The process of one lithospheric plate descending beneath another

subduction zone: A long, narrow belt in which subduction takes place

tephra: A collective term used for all pyroclastic material, regardless of size, shape, or origin, ejected into the air during a volcanic eruption

terrane: A fault-bounded body of rock of regional extent, characterized by a geologic history different from that of contiguous terranes or bounding continents

tonalite: An intrusive igneous rock composed primarily of quartz and plagioclase with 10 percent or less alkali feldspar

trace fossil: A fossil of a footprint, trail, burrow, or other trace of an animal rather than of the animal itself

Triassic: The earliest period of the Mesozoic era, between the Permian and Jurassic periods

tuff: Consolidated or cemented volcanic ash and lapilli

unconformity: A substantial break or gap in the geologic record where a rock unit is overlain by another that is not next in stratigraphic succession, resulting from either a change that caused deposition to cease for a considerable span of time or erosion with loss of the previously formed record

vesicular: Describes the texture of a rock, especially lava, characterized by abundant vesicles formed as a result of the expansion of gases during the fluid stage of the lava

volcanic arc: A large-scale (hundreds of kilometers) generally curved belt of volcanoes above a subduction zone

volcanism: The processes by which magma and its associated gases rise into Earth's crust and are extruded onto the surface and into the atmosphere

volcanogenic: A large-scale (hundreds of kilometers) generally curved belt of volcanoes above a subduction zone

welded tuff: A glass-rich pyroclastic rock that has been indurated by the welding together of glass shards under the combined action of the heat retained by the particles, the weight of overlying material, and hot gases. Cinders and bombs may also be welded together to form solid outcrops of rock.

zeolite: A group of silicate (silicon + oxygen) minerals that commonly occur as well-formed crystals in the cavities of mafic igneous rocks, particularly basalt

zircon: A very durable silicate mineral (silicon + oxygen), $ZrSiO_4$. When cut and polished, the colorless variety provides exceptionally brilliant gemstones.

Appendix 2:
Geologic Time Scale

Eon	Era	Period	Epoch	MYA	Notable Events
Phanerozoic	Cenozoic	Quaternary	Holocene	0	Humans alter atmosphere, initiating global extinctions.
			Pleistocene	0.0117	Cordilleran ice sheet retreats approximately 11,700 years ago.
				0.3	Humans migrate into North America.
		Neogene	Pliocene	1.8	
				2.6	Cordilleran ice sheet grows, buries Washington.
			Miocene	5.3	Glass Buttes erupt in central Oregon.
				17	Hotspot volcanism ravages eastern Oregon and Washington: flood basalts, supervolcanoes.
		Paleogene	Oligocene	23.8	
				25.2	Crooked River Caldera erupts, likely source is Yellowstone hotspot.

Eon	Era	Period	Epoch	MYA	Notable Events
Phanerozoic	Cenozoic	Paleogene	Eocene	33.7	
				37	First eruptions of the Cascade volcanic arc.
				47	Tillamook Volcanics erupt.
				52	First eruptions of Washington's Sanpoil volcanoes.
			Paleocene	55.5	Siletzia is born: early evidence of Yellowstone hotspot. Clarno volcanism begins.
	Mesozoic	Cretaceous		65	Another famous extinction, loss of non-avian dinosaurs.
					Flowers and bees appear.
		Jurassic		145	Old island arcs begin accretion onto North America, becoming first lands of Oregon and Washington.
					First birds appear.
				175	Supercontinent Pangea begins to break apart, birth of Atlantic Ocean.
		Triassic		213	First true mammals appear.
	Paleozoic	Permian		248	Largest mass extinction on Earth; almost 90% of species are lost.
		Pennsylvanian		286	More island arcs that will become Oregon and Washington are born far out to sea.

Eon	Era	Period	Epoch	MYA	Notable Events
Phanerozoic	Paleozoic	Mississippian		325	
					Supercontinent Pangea begins to merge around 335 million years ago
		Devonian		360	
				370	Amphibians evolve, take to the land!
					Earliest rocks of Oregon and Washington are born as island arcs and coral reefs.
		Silurian		410	
		Ordovician		440	
		Cambrian		505	
Proterozoic				544	
Archean				4,000	
Pre-Archean				4,500	

Appendix 3: Resources

Land Managers

Bureau of Land Management
(Select offices related to sites in this guide)
. . . .

Burns District Office
28910 US Highway 20 West
Hines, OR 97738
(541) 573-4400
www.blm.gov/office/burns-district-office

Lakeview District Office
1301 S. G Street
Lakeview, OR 97630
(541) 947-2177
www.blm.gov/office/lakeview-district-office

Medford District Office
3040 Biddle Road
Medford, OR 97504
(541) 618-2200
www.blm.gov/office/medford-district-office

Prineville District Office
3050 NE 3rd Street
Prineville, OR 97754
(541) 416-6700
www.blm.gov/office/prineville-district-office

Spokane District Office
1103 N. Fancher Road
Spokane Valley, WA 99212
(509) 536-1200
www.blm.gov/office/spokane-district-office

Vale District Office
100 Oregon Street
Vale, OR 97918
(541) 473-3144
www.blm.gov/office/vale-district-office

US Forest Service
(Select offices related to sites in this guide)
. . . .

A Northwest Forest Pass is required in all Washington National Forests and in all Oregon National Forests except Malheur, Ochoco, and Rogue River–Siskiyou National Forests. Inquire with headquarters to find out where passes are available for purchase. Or visit www.discovernw.org to find a vendor near you.
. . . .

Crooked River National Grassland
274 SW 4th Street
Madras, OR 97741
(541) 416-6640
www.fs.usda.gov/ochoco

Gifford Pinchot National Forest Headquarters
987 McClellan Road
Vancouver, WA 98661
(360) 891-5000
www.fs.usda.gov/detail/giffordpinchot

Mount Baker–Snoqualmie
National Forest
1000 SE Everett Mall Way, Suite 410
Everett, WA 98208
(425) 783-6000
www.fs.usda.gov/mbs

Ochoco National Forest
3160 NE 3rd Street
Prineville, OR 97754
(541) 416-6500
www.fs.usda.gov/ochoco

Olympic National Forest
1835 Black Lake Boulevard SW
Olympia, WA 98512
(360) 956-2402
www.fs.usda.gov/olympic

Rogue River–Siskiyou National Forest
3040 Biddle Road
Medford, OR 97504
(541) 618-2200
www.fs.usda.gov/rogue-siskiyou

Wallowa-Whitman National Forest
1550 Dewey Avenue, Suite A
Baker City, OR 97814
(541) 523-6391
www.fs.usda.gov/wallowa-whitman

Oregon State Parks & Beaches

Oregon Parks and
Recreation Department
725 Summer Street NE, Suite C
Salem, OR 97301
503-986-0707
https://stateparks.oregon.gov

U.S. Fish & Wildlife Service

Sheldon-Hart Mountain National Wildlife
Refuge Complex
20995 Rabbit Hill Road
Lakeview, OR 97630-1818
(541) 947-3315
www.fws.gov/refuge/hart-mountain
-national-antelope

Washington Department of Natural Resources
(Select offices related to sites in this guide)

A Discover Pass is required at all recreation
sites managed by the State of Washington.
Visit www.discoverpass.wa.gov for purchasing
information.

Olympic Region
411 Tillicum Lane
Forks, WA 98331
(360) 374-2800
www.dnr.wa.gov/olympic

Internet-Based Maps

BLM NATIONAL DATA VIEWER MAP:
blm-egis.maps.arcgis.com/apps/webappviewer/index.html

BLM MINERAL & LAND RECORDS SYSTEM (MLRS) REAL-TIME MAP:
www.mlrs.blm.gov/s/research-map

WILDERNESS AREAS OF THE UNITED STATES:
www.arcgis.com/apps/webappviewer/index.html?id=a415bca07f0a4bee9f0e894b0db5c3b6

Mapping Apps

AVENZA APP: www.avenza.com/avenza-maps

BENCHMARK ATLASES AVAILABLE THROUGH THE AVENZA APP:
www.store.avenza.com/collections/benchmark-maps

CALTOPO AP: www.caltopo.com

ONX OFFROAD APP: www.onxmaps.com/offroad/app

GOOGLE MAPS APP (DOWNLOADING OFFLINE MAPS):
www.support.google.com/maps/answer/6291838

Paper Maps and Atlases

BENCHMARK MAPS: *Washington Road & Recreation Atlas,*
www.benchmarkmaps.com/product/washington-road-recreation-atlas

BENCHMARK MAPS: *Oregon Road & Recreation Atlas,*
www.benchmarkmaps.com/product/oregon-recreation-map

MOUNTAINEERS GREEN TRAILS MAP SERIES:
www.mountaineers.org/books/books/green-trails-maps

BLM AND USFS CENTRAL OREGON ROCKHOUNDING GUIDE:
www.fs.usda.gov/detail/deschutes/recreation/rocks-minerals/?cid=stelprdb5381929

HIGHLAND ROCK SHOP GLASS BUTTES MAP: www.oregondiscovery.com/glass-butte

Further Reading

Bishop, Ellen Morris. *Hiking Oregon's Geology*, 2nd ed. Mountaineers Books, 2004.

——. *In Search of Ancient Oregon: A Geological and Natural History*. Timber Press, 2006.

"Gold and Fish: Rules for Mineral Prospecting and Placer Mining." Washington Department of Fish & Wildlife, 2021, https://wdfw.wa.gov/publications/02150.

Judah, Hettie. *Lapidarium: The Secret Lives of Stones*. Penguin, 2022.

Luedtke, Barbara E. *An Archaeologist's Guide to Chert and Flint*. Cotsen Institute of Archaeology Press, 1992.

Miller, Marli B. *Roadside Geology of Oregon*, 2nd ed. Mountain Press, 2014.

Miller, Marli B., and Darrel S. Cowan. *Roadside Geology of Washington*. Mountain Press, 2017.

Moclock, Leslie, and Jacob Selander. *Rocks, Minerals & Geology of the Pacific Northwest*. Timber Press, 2021.

Moore, E. J. *Fossil Shells from Western Oregon: A Guide to Identification*. Chimtimini Press, 2000.

Mustoe, George E. "Geologic History of Eocene Stonerose Fossil Beds, Republic, Washington, USA." *Geosciences* 5, no. 3 (July 6, 2015): 243–63.

Mustoe, George E., and Thomas A. Dillhoff. "Mineralogy of Miocene Petrified Wood from Central Washington State, USA." *Minerals* 12, no. 2 (January 23, 2022).

Orr, E. L., and W. N. Orr. *Oregon Fossils*. Oregon State University Press, 2009.

Ream, Lanny R. *Nephrite Jade of Washington and Associated Gem Rocks*. Self-published, 2022.

Strickler, Michael. "A Layperson's Guide to the Josephine Ophiolite and Associated Volcanic Arc Materials." Uoregon.edu, n.d., homework.uoregon.edu/mstrick/GeoTours/Josephine%20ophiolite/JoOphiolite.html. Accessed January 29, 2024.

Tabor, Rowland, and Ralph Haugerud. *Geology of the North Cascades: A Mountain Mosaic*. Mountaineers Books, 2008.

Tucker, D. S. *Geology Underfoot in Western Washington*. Mountain Press, 2015.

Institutes
and Museums

Burke Museum
4303 Memorial Way NE
Seattle, WA 98195
(206) 543-7907
www.burkemuseum.org

Oregon Paleo Lands Institute Center
333 W. Fourth Street
Fossil, OR 97830
(541) 763-4480
www.oregonpaleolandscenter.com/

Rice Museum of Rocks & Minerals
26385 NW Groveland Drive
Hillsboro, OR 97124
(503) 647-2418
www.ricenorthwestmuseum.org

Stonerose Interpretive Center
& Eocene Fossil Site
15 N. Clark Avenue
Republic, WA 99166
(509) 775-2295
www.stonerosefossil.org

Thomas Condon Visitor Center—
John Day Fossil Beds
32651 State Route 19
Kimberly, OR 97848
(541) 987-2333
www.nps.gov/joda/planyourvisit/hours.htm

Rock and
Mineral Clubs

Oregon

Central Oregon Rock Collectors Club
Redmond, OR
www.corockcollectors.com

Clackamette Mineral & Gem Club
Oregon City, OR
www.clackamettegem.org

Columbia Gorge Rockhounds
Corbett, OR
www.columbiagorgerockhounds.com

Columbia Willamette Faceters Guild
Portland, OR
www.facetersguild.com

Far West Lapidary and Gem Society
North Bend, OR
*www.facebook.com/farwestlapidaryand
gemsoc*

Hatrockhounds Gem and Mineral Society
Hermiston, OR
www.hatrockhounds.org

Lower Umpqua Gem & Lapidary Society
Winchester, OR
*www.facebook.com/p/Lower-Umpqua-Gem
-Lapidary-Society-100064472451091*

Mount Hood Rock Club
Gresham, OR
www.mthoodrockclub.com

North America Research Group
Tualatin, OR
www.narg-online.com

Oregon Agate & Mineral Society Inc.
Portland, OR
www.oregonagate.org

Rock and Arrowhead Club of Klamath Falls
Klamath Falls , OR
www.klamathrockclub.org

Rogue Gem & Geology Club
Grants Pass, OR
www.roguegemandgeology.org

Springfield Thunderegg Rock Club
Springfield, OR
www.springfieldthundereggrockclub.org

Trails End Gem & Mineral Society
Astoria, OR
www.facebook.com/groups/1393653434011791

Tualatin Valley Gem Club
Forest Grove, OR
www.tvgc.org

Umpqua Gem & Mineral Club
Roseburg, OR
www.facebook.com/Umpquagem

Willamette Agate & Mineral Society, Inc.
Salem, OR
www.wamsi.net

Washington

Bellevue Rock Club
Bellevue, WA
www.bellevuerockclub.org

Clallam County Gem & Mineral Association
Sequim, WA
www.sequimrocks.org

East King County Rock Club
Kirkland, WA
www.eastkingco.org

Everett Rock and Gem Club
Everett, WA
www.everettrockclub.com

Hells Canyon Gem Club, Inc.
Clarkston, WA
www.hellscanyongemclub.com

Kitsap Mineral and Gem Society
Bremerton, WA
www.kmgsrockclub.com

Maplewood Rock & Gem Club
Edmonds, WA
www.maplewoodrockclub.com

Marcus Whitman Gem & Mineral Society
Walla Walla, WA
www.marcuswhitmangem.com

Marysville Rock & Gem Club
Marysville, WA
www.marysvillerockclub.com

Mount Baker Rock & Gem Club
Bellingham, WA
www.mtbakerrockclub.org

North Seattle Lapidary & Mineral Club
Seattle, WA
www.northseattlerockclub.org

Northwest Stone Sculptors Association
Seattle, WA
www.nwssa.org

Panorama Gem & Mineral Club
Colville, WA
www.panoramagem.com

Puyallup Valley Gem & Mineral Club
Puyallup, WA
www.puyallupvalleygemandmineralclub.com

Skagit Rock and Gem Club
Mount Vernon, WA
www.skagitrockandgem.com

Index

Index by Rock Type

Locations with the greatest abundance of materials are noted in bold.

Photo by Robbie Augspurger

About the Author

Alison Jean Cole is an author, artist, and outfitter guide based in Portland, Oregon. Her expertise is in locating rock and mineral materials to use in lapidary craft and sculpture, and she guides several rock-hounding tours throughout Oregon and Nevada each year. In Utah, she partners with the Bureau of Land Management and nonprofit Epicenter to run "the best geology fest in the West," Green River Rocks! Alison self-publishes *Thunderegg*, a zine focused on rock and mineral culture and is the author of *Beautiful Rocks and How to Find Them*.

YOU MIGHT ALSO LIKE